MW01002702

Salo Wittmayer Baron

MODERN JEWISH MASTERS SERIES
General Editor: Steven T. Katz

SALO WITTMAYER BARON

ARCHITECT OF JEWISH HISTORY

Robert Liberles

NEW YORK UNIVERSITY PRESS
New York *and* London

NEW YORK UNIVERSITY PRESS
New York and London

Library of Congress Cataloging-in-Publication Data
Liberles, Robert.
Salo Wittmayer Baron : architect of Jewish history / Robert
Liberles.
p.   cm. — (Modern Jewish masters series)
Includes bibliographical references and index.
ISBN 0-8147-5088-5
1. Baron, Salo Wittmayer, 1895–   . 2. Jewish historians—United
States—Biography. 3. Rabbis—United States—Biography. 4. Jews,
Polish—United States—Biography. 5. Jews—History—Study and
teaching (Higher)—United States. 6. Judaism—History—Study and
teaching (Higher)—United States. 7. Jews—Historiography.
8. Judaism—Historiography. I. Title. II. Series.
DS115.9.B37L53   1995
909'.04924'007202—dc20   94-23487
[B]   CIP

Manufactured in the United States of America

10   9   8   7   6   5   4   3   2   1

In Memory

of

HERMAN POLLACK

who was part of the story

DANIEL DUMAN

with whom this would have been a better book

and

FRANK TALMAGE

who didn't approve

CONTENTS

CONTENTS

CONTENTS

ACKNOWLEDGMENTS

The relevant divisions at Columbia University were extremely cooperative in providing materials and granting permission for their use and even for searching at times in dark file rooms and long-abandoned attics to find letters and records that pertained to my subject. I wish to express my appreciation to Corinne H. Rieder, secretary of the university; to Sarah Vos, clerk of Central Files; to the history department, which attempted—unfortunately unsuccessfully—to locate departmental records dating back to Baron's arrival at Columbia; to Hollee Haswell, curator of Columbiana; and to the librarians of the Rare Book and Manuscript Library.

Both the American Jewish Archives of Cincinnati's Hebrew Union College and the Jewish Theological Seminary made it possible for an Israeli scholar to undertake this study by facilitating the frequent trips required for research. My special thanks to Abraham Peck, administrative director of the American Jewish Archives, who supported this project from the outset. At the Jewish Theological Seminary, I was assisted in my work by Mayer Rabinowitz, director of the seminary's library; Jerry Schwarzbard, director of its rare book room; Roger Kohn, then seminary archivist; Julie Miller, archivist of the Ratner Center; and Jack Wertheimer, director of the Ratner Center.

The Conference for Jewish Social Studies extended its total cooperation: my appreciation to its president, Leon Feldman; to Tobey Gitelle, managing editor; and to Adele Maurer, its secretary at the time. At the Hebrew Union College-Jewish Institute of Religion in New York, I wish to thank Dean Norman Cohen for granting me access to institute records; to Philip Miller, librarian of HUC, New York, for his cooperation and his helpful suggestions; and Marlene Schiffman of the JIR Library for sharing her relevant materials with me. The late Nathan Kaganoff, librarian of the American Jewish Historical Society, searched conscientiously until he located the materials I required from the society's files.

Stanford University Special Collections adjusted work schedules and managed my heavy xerox demands, all with a smile. Most important, they made the Baron collection available to me promptly. My special gratitude to Margaret Kimball and her staff for their professional and courteous cooperation.

Of course, I am most grateful to the Baron family itself. Baron met with me on a number of occasions and allowed me free rule of the house in Canaan as I searched for materials. His daughters, Tobey Gitelle and Shoshanna Tancer, provided full cooperation with regard to interviews and access to materials.

ACKNOWLEDGMENTS

The following responded to my request for materials that appeared in the *New York Times Book Review:* Sam Hartstein, New York City; Rachel B. Heimovics, Longwood, Florida; Harold Jonas, Goshen, New York.

Finally, my gratitude to the family, friends, and former students who agreed to be interviewed and shared their recollections and impressions.

A bibliography of the material accumulated through these efforts can be found at the end of this work.

Carole Fink, Evyatar Friesel, and Lloyd Gartner gave of their valuable time to read versions of the manuscript and share their comments. I wish to thank them for their helpful suggestions.

A fellowship from the National Endowment for the Humanities provided me with a free year to pursue my work. Further support was provided by the Memorial Foundation for Jewish Culture, and by research grants from the American Jewish Archives and the Center for the Study of North American Jewry at Ben Gurion University.

Publication of this work was assisted by a generous grant from the Littauer Foundation.

My wife Adina and our children, Sarit-Chein, Ahuva, and Yedida, have borne with my many absences from home as this work unfolded. Their continued support made its completion possible, and they know how grateful I am.

This book is dedicated to the memory of three dear friends who each in their own way significantly affected my life. Each of them is sorely missed.

Beersheva, 1994

INTRODUCTION

Salo Baron, who died at the age of 94 in November 1989, was for six decades the finest symbol of the reciprocal confidence between Jewish studies and the American university.

At the time of Baron's move from Vienna to America during the 1920s, Jewish scholarship stood at a crossroads. Only a few Judaica scholars were natives. But even before the Nazi rise to power, both America and Palestine were beginning to enjoy the results of a migration of scholars like Yitzhak Baer and Gershom Scholem to Palestine and Baron and Jacob Mann to America. Meanwhile, a second fundamental change was taking place as several major universities established chairs in Jewish studies. Until that time, the few university professors of related subjects were generally scholars of Semitic languages. But in the mid-1920s Harry Wolfson was appointed to a chair in Jewish religious philosophy at Harvard, and a few years later, the Miller chair in Jewish history was established at Columbia.

When in 1928 Linda Miller, the widow of a Wall Street broker, decided to donate a chair in Judaica to Columbia in memory of her husband, neither donor nor university seemed to realize how difficult it would be to fill that chair. Columbia's president, Nicholas Butler, responded warmly to the idea of expanding its programs in the study of religion and appointed a select committee to pursue the search. But in 1928, there were few academically oriented scholars of Judaica anywhere in the world, and of these, most were still teaching in Europe. The committee was caught in a bind: rabbinic figures were not necessarily appropriate for a university position; older critical scholars were usually affiliated with a theological seminary of one of the religious movements and met with opposition from factions opposing too close an identification of that kind; younger scholars lacked sufficient accomplishments to match the rank and distinction that had been intended.

There were other problems. Columbia had a definite predilection for European-trained scholars, while the donor was hoping for a native English speaker who could better influence the student body.

After a two-year search and serious negotiations with German scholar Ismar Elbogen, Salo Baron, then teaching in New York at the Jewish Institute of Religion, was selected and assumed the position in the fall of 1930. Baron's European training helped him win out over several native American scholars. Besides, Baron had the advantage of having studied English in Vienna with an exchange student from Alabama. Thus he was authentic on both grounds—his scholarship and his diction.

Baron was not adamant about an appointment to the history department and, in fact, seemed rather cool toward the idea. He favored an affiliation with either the religion or Semitics departments, and preferred an independent status. For reasons not made clear in the documents, Baron obviously did not feel welcomed by the history department. Yet, on Nicholas Butler's insistence, Jewish studies at Columbia became enlodged in the Department of History, and Jewish studies in America turned a new corner with the recognition that Jews as a people had a history of their own. Nevertheless, it would be decades before many universities would concur—preferring, regardless of subject matter or the expertise of the incumbent professors, to plant Jewish positions elsewhere. Thus, until his retirement from Columbia in 1963, Baron remained the reigning and unchallenged symbol of the academic study of Jewish history.

Although I had studied briefly with Baron some twenty years before, my contact with him was primarily concentrated in the last two years of his life. Toward the end of the summer of 1987, I traveled from Boston to Tanglewood country and beyond, making my way to Canaan, Connecticut. Here I went to the legendary Baron residence, *Yifat Shalom*—which had graced the bottom of almost every preface of his writings that I had studied.[1] Somehow as a young graduate student I had been sure that a town named Canaan had to have been as much a product of Baron's achievement as the books themselves.

I arrived in the middle of a hot summer's day. Yet despite Baron's age of ninety-two and the effects of the heat, we talked for close to five hours that day. I didn't know if I would be able to see him again, so we covered oceans together: from Morningside Heights back to Vienna and to his native Galicia. The longer we talked, the more alert he became. At first, he complained about the heat. He was also concerned about something else that eluded me for a while. Over the previous few weeks he had given several lengthy interviews, and he was concerned about the possibility of giving different answers to similar questions. It was an expression of the strangeness for the historian to become the actual subject of scholarly inquiry. By the end of that session, Baron seemed much more relaxed. He told me my questions had been different, taking off into other directions than the previous interviewers. We both felt gratified.

Over the next two years, I saw Baron about six more times: twice in his New York apartment near the Columbia campus and the other times in Canaan. Still, it was the first meeting that was the most intense and, in my view, the most successful.

Baron was the third link in the chain of modern masters who wrote sweeping, multivolume sets of Jewish history from ancient to modern times. Others have attempted the task, but three climbed above their shoulders: Heinrich Graetz, Simon Dubnow, and Baron.

Graetz (1817–91), a child of Posen in eastern Prussia, spent most of his life no further west than Breslau and remained a champion of a traditional Judaism. Graetz wrote what was until recently the most successful *History of the Jews*.[2] His twentieth-century successors have severely criticized Graetz's selectivity of material, his emphasis on developments in Germany at the expense of East European Jewry, and his judgmental writing, especially concerning mystical thought and movements. But his lively style and coherent, largely chronological organization made him the most read, translated, and frequently cited Jewish historian through at least the middle of our century, until the mere pace and intensity of developments such as the Holocaust and the establishment of the State of Israel simply left him too far behind.[3]

Like many of Graetz's successors, Dubnow (1860–1941) recorded his gratitude both to Graetz's pioneering efforts and to the influence the earlier work had in stirring his Jewish consciousness. Neither Dubnow nor Baron could affect the public through the written word as Graetz had done. But Dubnow also anticipated many of Baron's critiques of Graetz, most especially the overemphasis on suffering and scholarship.[4]

Dubnow was Russian Jewry's answer to Graetz. Whereas Graetz ridiculed Hasidism, Dubnow made it the center of an early modern social revolution, and whereas Graetz glossed over the importance of East European Jewry or measured it primarily by Western standards of enlightenment, Dubnow made their history the nucleus of his research. Dubnow's monographs, his teaching, and his political involvement all endeared him to the hearts of the Jews of Eastern Europe.

But Dubnow came late to the writing of an encyclopedic history of the Jews. Although seventy years separated Graetz's first volume (1853) from Dubnow's (1925), the first edition of Baron's three-volume history appeared only eight years after Dubnow's set was completed. Dubnow's history, published in Berlin and completed in 1929, was written in German, then still the lingua franca of Jewish scholarship; but events rapidly created new centers of Jewish life and Jewish studies.[5] In short, the hegemony of Dubnow's history was short-lived.

Both Graetz and Dubnow were largely autodidacts in the discipline of history. Graetz received his doctorate relatively late in his development, and Dubnow didn't get that far. Thus, Baron was not only the first of the three to regularly teach Jewish history at a university, but also the first to be properly trained in a university setting.

Baron's own history of the Jews originated in a series of 1931 lectures at Columbia on the reciprocal relationship between Jewish society and religion. These lectures not only provided Baron with an introduction to the Columbia community, but also provided the opportunity for a first run on his own emerging version of a history of the Jews. Six years later, that history appeared as *A Social and Religious History of the Jews.*

Although usually identified today as Baron's classic but unfinished eighteen-volume work, which covers ancient and medieval Jewish history through 1650, the original 1937 edition had two volumes of text and a third for notes and bibliography and covered Jewish history through the time of publication.[6] Personally, I have remained partial toward the original edition, not just because it included the modern period, which is my own specialty, but because of its more concise presentation of the special Baronian approach; the expanded revised edition became so entangled and burdened with a multitude of detail that the line of interpretation often became blurred.

In a way, it was the chaos of Baron's history that made it special. The work was controversial primarily because of its topical arrangement—chronological order was a secondary priority. The index volume was not an accessory of convenience. Rather, it was the coordinating center of the entire work, directing readers to the scattered entries on a person, country, or subject being pursued. The topical arrangement—noted by all and criticized by some of the reviewers—represented an historiographic statement for Baron that major historical developments had to be understood in their broad social context and as such, they unfolded only gradually.

The difficulties faced by Baron in the publication of his *History* reveal the reluctance of even a university press to undertake publication of a masterpiece in Judaica, although it must be recalled that we are talking about the 1930s. Eventually, however, as Jewish studies was integrated into the university world, university publishing had to follow suit. In turn, the effort was rewarded by commercial success as well. When the second printing sold out, Baron and Columbia's press decided on an expanded, new edition, to which Baron devoted most of the last four decades of his life.

Thus the first edition dates from the 1930s, while the revised work was written from the late 1940s through the 1980s. Ostensibly, this should provide an interesting opportunity to test the effects of the Holocaust on the writing of one of the great twentieth-century masters of Jewish historiography. But Baron repeatedly claimed—with some justification—that few of his fundamental tenets had changed over time, regardless of what events intervened.

INTRODUCTION

Indeed, one of the interesting questions about twentieth-century Jewish historical writing is to determine what the effects of the Holocaust have been on this genre of literature. Two recurring themes stand out as examples of what might be called post-Holocaust revisionism. Yet, each already appears in Baron's writings of the 1920s and 1930s. The first theme I have in mind derives from the problem of "what went wrong," and sets out to analyze the inherent intolerance of modern enlightenment and rationalism. The late Jacob Talmon dealt with these problems in *The Origins of Totalitarian Democracy,* and Arthur Hertzberg, more specifically with modern antisemitism in *The French Enlightenment and the Jews.*[7] Baron's critique of modernization concepts dates back already to his 1928 essay "Ghetto and Emancipation."[8]

In those writings and elsewhere, Baron attacked the conception that contrasted in bold forms the bleak suffering and limited outlets of the Middle Ages with the advantageous opportunities provided by the modern period. In Baron's view, neither description represented historical reality. In much of his writing, he sought to recast the lachrymose image of medieval times, while frequently warning in his essays and lectures of the great dangers modernity presented to the future of Jewish life.

A second theme that has preoccupied Jewish historians in recent decades revolves around the debate of Jewish passivity and naivete in the face of external threats. The "sheep to slaughter" portrait of Jewish behavior in the concentration camps has frequently been projected backward to describe the lack of a cogent Jewish response to antisemitism whether in politics or during a pogrom. Hannah Arendt was the most

8

visible and outspoken representative of the political critique, although she distanced herself from defamation of the Jewish masses. Yet her prosecution of Jewish leadership during the Holocaust, put forth most explicitly in her reports of the Eichmann trial, reflected accusations she had been making since the 1940s on political ineptness in Jewish history.[9]

Baron had tremendous personal admiration for Arendt. When she emigrated to the United States during World War II, Baron helped her publish some of her first articles in English. After the war, he engaged her as director of the Commission on European Jewish Cultural Reconstruction, of which Baron was the chairperson. Her first task in that capacity was to gather a register of educational institutions and cultural treasures that had existed in Europe before the Nazi era. Ironically, Arendt's compilation provided the basis for at least part of Baron's own testimony at the Eichmann trial on Jewish life in Europe just before and right after the Holocaust.

At times, they had been close friends. On the occasion of his seventieth birthday, a group of friends and associates sent Baron a set of personal wishes. Arendt wrote as follows:

In the unlikely event that you'll see fit to take a few hours off at the occasion of "threescore years and ten" to permit those who admire and love you to grow a bit solemn, let me tell you what under ordinary circumstances is being thought, perhaps whispered behind your back, but must remain unsaid in order not to embarrass you.

Even before I met you in this country, about twenty-five years ago, I knew that the Jewish people had at long last found its historian. In three volumes, which today look like the poor relatives of your present monumental work (ironically called a "Second Edition, Revised and Enlarged") you had begun to tell the story in a way no one had even attempted before—neither Jost nor Graetz nor Dubnow.

Undisturbed by any apologetic side-glances, consciously in opposition to the "lachrymose conception of Jewish history," equipped with all the paraphernalia of modern secular scholarship and, at the same time, deeply and firmly rooted in the tradition of Judaism, you brought to your task the perennial shining marks of the great ones in the profession—those gifts of head and heart that permit to cut through to the essentials and to see, in full mastery of the details, the unfolding grandeur of the whole. The old adage that every generation rewrites the history of the past does not apply to you; future generations will be able to do this thanks to what you did. For you became the first Professor of Jewish History in this country because you have been indeed the first to establish the history of your own people as an academic discipline.[10]

And yet, despite their personal friendship, Baron's position on Jewish political history was the diametric opposite of Arendt's. Baron explained the very question of continued Jewish survival through the millennia through a combination of external forces and Jewish adaptability to changing environments and circumstances. Jewish legal status in medieval times, bemoaned by so many writers, was described far more positively by Baron, especially when compared to such large population sectors as peasants and—for that matter— women. Once liberated from the lachrymose view of Jewish history, the historian owed communal leadership a proportion of the credit for achievements along with some of the culpability for suffering. Much recent Jewish historiography revolves around this debate on political maturity, with Baron and Arendt representing the two polar positions. In the case of

Baron—although my impression is that this would be true for Arendt as well—the main lines of his position were already in place long before the Nazi period.

Let us juxtapose their respective views. Here is Arendt in *The Origins of Totalitarianism:*

Jewish history offers the extraordinary spectacle of a people, unique in this respect, which began its history with a well-defined concept of history and almost conscious resolution to achieve a well-circumscribed plan on earth and then, without giving up this concept, avoided all political action for two thousand years. The result was that the political history of the Jewish people became even more dependent upon unforeseen, accidental factors than the history of other nations, so that the Jews stumbled from one role to the other and accepted responsibility for none.[11]

It was just such a position that Baron had in mind when he wrote repeatedly that some German-Jewish scholars had concluded in the 1930s that Jews have always been objects and not active forces in their own history.

Their own overwhelming experience of the tragic fate of European Jewry for reasons entirely beyond its control taught them . . . that Jewish destinies throughout the history of the dispersion have in the ultimate sense been controlled by such external forces. They readily overlooked the fact that were the Jews mere objects of the general historical evolution, they could not possibly have survived the successive waves of hostility throughout the ages.[12]

Of course, just mentioning the Holocaust raises many questions about the viability of the antilachrymose critique. These questions aren't answered easily. Baron himself explained in later years—quite accurately—that he had never intended to deny the extent of persecutions in the Jewish past. His concern had been with the proportion of space devoted to the description of suffering, and even more, with the dominant position that suffering had seized in the Jewish historical Weltanschauung.

But it is also true that Baron, who frequently was called upon as consultant to major U.S. Jewish organizations and who was certainly considered an expert on the European scene, totally misread the gravity of the Nazi threat against the Jews. Quite late in the day, Baron wrote of the rehabilitation of European Jewish communities in their old homes and espoused his analysis of the limits of the Nazi threat with his usual total self-confidence. The question remains as to whether Baron's poor judgment had been clouded by his strong personal identification against lachrymosity, although it is perhaps more accurate to consider the effects of wishful thinking concerning his remaining family in Europe.

When Baron did realize there would be little opportunity for a renewal of European Jewry, his thinking on Jewish survival underwent a truly profound metamorphosis. This was somewhat true of his attitudes toward Israel, and much more so concerning the future leadership role of American Jews. For the first decade that he lived in America, he was dubious about the prospects of American Jewry resisting the powerful temptations of assimilation. Indeed, it was during these years that he wrote of emancipation as provoking the greatest challenge to Jewish survival since Nebuchadnezzar destroyed the first Temple and exiled the Jewish people to Babylon. But during the war, Baron became more optimistic about America's place as a world power and about American Jews as future leaders of a shattered and demoralized Jewish people. Like so many other forces in Baron's life, his fascination with America had both academic and social implications.

Baron was one of the first pillars of Jewish studies to encourage scholarly research into American Jewish history. Now a blossoming field, thirty years ago its study was viewed primarily with disdain, challenged by arguments that events were too recent and historians were therefore too closely attached to the events. Perhaps most important, the argument was raised that American Jewry doesn't have a real history; that their history is American history because American Jews aren't Jewish enough and they don't suffer enough. Compared to earlier periods laden with persecutions and more closely entwined with traditional rabbinic scholarship, the Jewish experience in America seemed to lack the classic ingredients of the Jewish historical experience.

Such arguments stood in diametric contrast with Baron's perspectives not only on America, but on Jewish history as a whole, as being more than the history of suffering or the history of scholarship. It is the history of Jewish society, of their religion, and also the history of their well-being.

Thus, it becomes clear why the study of American Jewish history was so important to Baron. It provided a laboratory for what the study of Jewish history could look like if it went beyond antisemitism and beyond the lachrymose conception of Jewish history. American Jewish history was an ideal setting for exploring new avenues of historical inquiry precisely because the American setting provides new avenues of Jewish experience.

In later years, Baron would frequently recall his frustrations in trying to encourage students to specialize in the new period. But he eventually succeeded, and among his early students were some of the pioneers of the fledgling field. Baron did not establish the discipline, but he stamped it with legitimacy, and in so doing proved himself again a scholar with forward vision. His tenure as president of the American Jewish Historical Society in the early 1950s coincided with the 1954 tercentenary celebration of American Jewish settlement, in which Baron played a leading role. Like so many other immigrants from Central Europe, Baron emerged as a cogent spokesperson for American Jewry's new role in the long saga of Jewish history.

The academic assessment of Baron's contributions to the study of Jewish history is just beginning.[13] The following work represents a study of Baron's life and an introduction to his historical thought. His major works are treated within their proper chronological framework, and the study ends with some reflective comments on the second edition of *Social and Religious History of the Jews* and on his basic thinking. The study at hand concentrates almost exclusively on Baron's career after his move to America in 1926. Perhaps his unpublished memoirs and other sources will complete the picture of the earlier period. The biographical narrative ends with Baron's retirement from Columbia University in 1963 at the age of sixty-eight, at which time he began to devote even larger amounts of time to his writing. It seemed appropriate, therefore, to switch the focus from his illustrious and fascinating career to his writing and thought.

I have not attempted to trace the subsequent impact of Baron's writings beyond the contemporaneous responses and disputes that arose. Thus, whereas his bitter arguments with Solomon Zeitlin are discussed, the historiographic disagreement with Jacob Katz over the beginnings of modernity and with Yitzhak Baer over the nature of the medieval Jewish community belong to the professional literature of those fields.

I began this study with considerable empathy for my subject and for his importance in the field to which I so proudly belong. Yet I believe I am sufficiently distanced from the subject to provide a balanced perspective. I was not his student except in one marginal setting. And, on occasion, I have differed with Baron in my writings. I think the combination of my positive inclinations with a healthy distance produces a cautious and sober analysis.

CHAPTER 1

GHETTO AND EMANCIPATION: THE MOVE TO AMERICA

Beginnings in Europe

SALO BARON WAS BORN in 1895 to one of the wealthiest Jewish families in the Galician community of Tarnow. Located in what is now the southern part of Poland, Tarnow lies some forty-five miles east of Cracow. From 1772, with the first of the three eighteenth-century partitions of Poland, until the end of World War I in 1918, Tarnow and all of Galicia was under Austrian rule. During the modern period, the Jewish population in Tarnow, which can be traced back to the fifteenth century, hovered around forty percent of the general population. This number increased gradually so that on the eve of World War II there were an estimated twenty-five thousand Jews in Tarnow, amounting to some fifty-five percent of the total population.[1]

Whereas fifteenth-century Jews engaged almost exclusively in money lending, the transition to commerce was well underway by the seventeenth century. By the twentieth century, Jews were engaged in industrial work as well.

Dating back to the eighteenth century Haskalah movement in Germany, Tarnow managed to combine its Hasidic majority with a continual presence of the Enlightened spirit. Moses Mendelssohn's close disciple Naphtali Herz Homberg, brought in by Austrian authorities to supervise Jewish education in Galicia, established a school in Tarnow in 1788. That institution closed in 1806. The Baron Hirsch Foundation established a school in 1890 that continued until 1914. During the nineteenth and early twentieth centuries, a number of prominent intellectual figures came from Tarnow.[2]

Baron's father, Elias, was not from Tarnow, but his mother, Minna Wittmayer, came from a prominent Tarnow family. There was wealth on both sides of the Baron family. Elias had several significant sources of income: an oil field located in Sloboda in the Kolomea region, which by Baron's estimate brought in the equivalent of one thousand dollars a month; a mill; and large tracts of real estate. His father sold a section of a village in eastern Galicia when Salo was a child, and later bought a large estate of several thousand acres in Dulcza, a three-hour buggy ride from Tarnow. The estate was managed by a resident foreman. In addition, his mother's family, the Wittmayers, owned a department store located in the main square of the city.

The Barons and the Wittmayers lived in two adjoining houses in the center of town. Baron himself concentrated on a wholesale banking business, which he conducted from his home. Private banks formed the primary sector of his clientele. He also played a leading role in communal life before and right after World War I. For a time he was president of the community and also a member of the city council. The Barons' house was large and had a traditional decor; the furniture was heavy, but it was comfortable and complete in supplying conveniences for the family. Salo lived there with his older sister Gisela and his younger sister Tanya.

In his various interviews, Salo Baron described his family as religious but enlightened. In a fascinating juxtaposition of descriptions of Baron's father that emerged during Zvi Ankory's interview with Baron, the two recalled strikingly different portraits. Ankory, who knew the family well in his youth in Tarnow, described Elias Baron as a Jew with a beard dressed in traditional attire. Baron, however, responded that his father was a Central European liberal. Then Ankory replied that he knew him to be a traditional Jew and a learned man in later years. But Baron rejoined that, as a youth, his father had demonstrated some rather unusual interests for a traditional Jew.

In my interview, Ankory described the elder Baron as a man with a reddish beard, who wore a traditional, but not black, frock and sat at his desk kneading a piece of bread between his fingers. Ankory explained that in his mind this picture symbolized the father's sense of self-importance. Another source commented that Elias Baron was very careful with money.

Minna Baron is described as a short woman with a rather square face, who was progressive both in fashion and in her outlook. Baron described his mother as a "distinguished lady," who usually wore stylish clothes and ordered the latest fashions from stores in Paris and Vienna. She herself was active in communal affairs: for example, a charity designated for poor, expectant mothers. She wore a sheitel (a religious wig) to cover her hair and had several in different colors. Minna was also active in the children's education. Despite his father's objections, she insisted that Baron's sister Gisela study at a gymnasium.

A rather vivid description of the household is found in letters written at a much later date and under somewhat strained circumstances. In 1937, Baron and his wife Jeannette spent a sabbatical year in Europe and Palestine, while Jeannette's mother took care of their daughter Shoshanna. During that time, Baron traveled alone to archives and libraries in Russia while Jeannette stayed with Baron's parents in Tarnow. Her letters to him depict her unhappiness with the situation. Elias, Baron's father, is portrayed as a dominating man, who instructed Jeannette on what to wear so as not to attract undue attention. Moreover, financial matters were frequently at issue and bitter disagreements soon followed.[3]

Jeannette's letters portray three such incidents. On one occasion, Jeannette was particularly embarrassed by a discussion about her mother spending summers in Canaan. Elias commented that she would not be able to manage financially without their help. Jeannette explained to Salo that the matter "got under her skin" and so she fabricated a lie that her mother still had substantial independent means. She urged Salo to assist her in this "fib," if necessary. On another occasion, the father inquired about Salo's salary and asked if it had been increased after they were married. When he was informed otherwise, Elias then instructed her not to have any more children because "they weren't worth the trouble of bringing them up."

The most unpleasant discussion concerned the parents themselves. The father reported that Salo had examined the books and concluded that the family was spending beyond their means. A heated debate ensued between father and mother, causing Jeannette considerable discomfort. Baron responded to Jeannette on this last point:

As to Papa's expenses you need not worry. Although they are considerably larger than I had thought, he is still able to save a larger portion of his income than I am likely to be {sic} for many years to come. Please tell them—again in my name—that, if they must quarrel, they should do it during your absence because it is evidently painful to an outsider.

The descriptions provided by Jeannette's letters graphically illustrate the atmosphere and some of the major concerns in Baron's home.[4]

Baron's father leaned in the Hasidic direction, but, nevertheless provided his children with an enlightened education. Polish, German, and Yiddish were spoken at home. Baron stated several times that he had learned Polish from his nurse and that it was his first language. He learned Yiddish and Hebrew later from a private teacher. On the other hand, Baron's niece, Shoshanna Eytan—who lived in the house during the early 1920s, commented that German was the primary language spoken in the house, but she also learned to speak and read Polish there. Baron recalled speaking German at the

Czech spas over summer holidays. It was also at these spas that he became acquainted with leaders of various Hasidic groups.

Several anecdotes indicate some of the differences between the Baron family and the more traditional elements of the community. As a young boy, Baron wore a traditional caftan and a dark velvet hat. But he also wore Western attire during the summers when the family visited the spas. When Baron was ten he registered for gymnasium. It was decided that he would walk to school in traditional attire accompanied by his tutor and change to Western clothing once he approached the school building. Due to a mishap, Baron and the tutor ended up running through the streets with Baron dressed in the Western outfit. As a result, according to his memoirs, he was taunted for years in the synagogue. In another incident, when Baron's older sister Gisela married a religious Jew who was a lawyer, several people in the small synagogue painted the Barons' regular chairs in protest to the groom's secular education. Baron's father, who was a leader of the synagogue, consequently walked out and resigned.

Baron's love of learning apparently derived most especially from his grandfather's influence. Wittmayer was a prosperous businessperson who taught the young Baron the importance of good deeds and traditional learning. As a child, Baron accompanied his grandfather early in the morning to open up the store and then to synagogue. There, Wittmayer would freely dispense charity to those in need.[5] Baron's love for his grandfather found expression some thirty years later when he adopted Wittmayer as his middle name.

Baron began his study of Talmud with a private teacher at

the age of five and a half. Then around the age of eight, he was sent to a Heder, a traditional school, where he was placed with teenage boys. But his mother objected to the social situation and the difficulties that resulted. Eisig Wrubel, Zvi Ankory's father, was consequently engaged as Baron's young tutor. He lived in the Baron house in that capacity from 1904 through 1912. Even after Baron began his university studies in Cracow, Eisig stayed on to teach Baron's sisters and to do various chores for Baron's father.[6]

Baron began his studies at gymnasium at the age of ten, studying with a private tutor from age ten to fifteen. For the next three years, Baron was designated a "privatist," meaning that he studied privately but took his semi-annual exams at the end of each semester together with his class. Baron concentrated on math and physics at this point in his studies.

Baron was extremely proud of his math and chess skills. He related stories of how as a youth he could perform complicated calculations in his head and how he had so excelled at chess that he stopped playing for a number of years so as not to be tempted to compete in tournaments. In his later years, he regretted the decline in his mathematical abilities.

Baron's father trained him in the family businesses, and by the age of fifteen, both his father and his grandfather left him in charge when they were away. When he began to contemplate his future occupation, the family enterprises were a definite consideration. The sciences, at which he also excelled, were another possibility.

Baron showed an interest in political thinking at an early age, at first identifying himself as a Polish nationalist. At age fifteen, he came under the influence of a teacher named

Umansky, who instructed him in modern Hebrew grammar and literature. This teacher also influenced him in the direction of Zionism, and as a young teenager Baron began to write political articles in Hebrew for Zionist periodicals. It was around this time that Baron's academic interests moved from the sciences toward history.

Baron started publishing newspapers articles in 1912 at age seventeen. Almost all of these appeared in the Galician Hebrew paper *HaMizpeh*, which was edited by Simon Lazer, former editor of the better-known *HaMaggid*. *HaMizpeh*, which appeared from 1904 to 1921, was closely identified with the religious Zionist position of the Mizrachi. Baron's articles fit in well with the paper's general position, opposing both the assimilationists on the one hand and the Hasidic camps on the other. He wrote in a clear and fluent Hebrew style that far surpassed the eloquence of his later English writing—even in its edited format.[7] Several articles dealt with sensitive political issues, and because gymnasium students were prohibited from publishing political articles, Baron used the pseudonym *Shevah,* representing his Hebrew name Shalom Ben Eliyahu.

The first of these pieces, "A Sad Phenomenon," published in 1912, is of particular interest for its reflections on the political status of the Jews.[8] Concerned with the ongoing war between Turkish and Serbian forces, he was upset that Jews were found on both sides of the conflict, which put brother against brother, and that they even volunteered to do so. This article conveyed Baron's feeling that Jews required their own state. Already reflecting on the basic forces in Jewish history, Baron explained that Jews had survived as a people over the ages because of three factors: the ghetto, Jewish culture, and the unceasing national political aspirations expressed through Messianism. But conditions were changing rapidly: the ghetto walls had fallen; general culture was increasingly permeating Jewish society; and thus, only the political hopes remained. Zionism now provided the answer for Jewish survival.

In the meantime, however, Jews found themselves living temporarily in countries where equal rights had been granted on paper. This required that the Jews fulfill their civil duties, including taxes and army duty, even though they had not been granted equality in practice. But, under the circumstances, volunteering for the army was beyond what should be expected of Jews and what they should be ready to do; the request was unfair given the inequality of their situation and the tragic pitting of Jew against Jew.

The other articles dealt with political and economic problems facing Galician Jewry. One of his basic themes concerned the need for a reform of the Austrian electoral system; this would provide the appropriate proportional representation for the Jews of Galicia. He also believed in educational reform that would empower the Jews of the area to improve their economic status. Baron was particularly incensed at the ultra orthodox sector that had refused to undertake reforms that would provide basic skills in commerce and skilled labor.[9]

In 1913, Baron began traveling to Cracow to study at the university and to pursue his Talmudic studies at a higher level. He moved to Vienna during the summer of 1914, around the outbreak of war. The details of this move are somewhat obscure, but his family apparently also came to

Vienna during the Russian occupation of Tarnow.[10] Baron remained in Vienna from 1914 until his departure for America in early 1926. He studied at the university and at the rabbinical seminary known as the Israelitisch-Theologischen Lehranstalt headed by Hirsch Perez Chajes.

When Baron went to Vienna he was somewhat undecided about his career. However, he seemed to have abandoned the idea of becoming an engineer and managing the family oil field. His decision to study law apparently derived from the possibility of future connections with the family bank. While in Vienna, he earned three different degrees at the university and pursued his rabbinical studies at the Israelitisch-Theologischen Lehranstalt. His degrees were in history (1917), political science (1922), and jurisprudence (1923).

Baron had studied independently in his youth, and in his various interviews, he indicated that he continued to study as an autodidact in Vienna as well. Still, he named several teachers who had influenced him: Hans Kelsen, a prominent professor of jurisprudence who later moved to America, and economist Carl Grünberg. Baron wrote his political science thesis on Ferdinand Lassalle under their supervision. Baron's claim that he primarily taught himself seems to be confirmed by the contradiction between Kelsen's emphasis on an independent logic of law and Baron's own continual emphasis on context and social forces as the dominant forces in the shaping of the status of the Jews. His book on the Jewish question at the Congress of Vienna makes no reference to faculty supervision.[11]

While at the rabbinical school, Baron was particularly influenced by the rabbinic scholar Victor Aptowitzer, who suffered from seriously impaired vision. Baron became his close assistant and spent many hours aiding Aptowitzer in his work.

Around 1919, Baron started to teach Jewish history at the Jewish teacher's institute, also headed by Vienna's dynamic rabbi, Hirsch Perez Chajes. From the outset of his career, Baron was expected to teach the entire gamut of Jewish history, an approach he continued throughout his tenure at Columbia.

In the study on the Jews and the Congress of Vienna, Baron placed his theme in the broad framework of the history of Jewish emancipation. When examining his writings so closely, it is possible to take his erudition and accomplishments for granted; nevertheless, his study on the Congress of Vienna still evokes a very special reaction. The book was published in 1920 when Baron was twenty-five years old; it was based—or perhaps was in its entirety—a doctoral dissertation concluded three years earlier. True, Baron primarily employed printed sources. But the wide spectrum of materials, including some archival additions, reveals a rather remarkable accomplishment not only in its vast erudition, but in its understanding of the nuances and variations of the different conditions facing Germanic Jewry in different settings. Much of the work summarizes diplomatic initiatives deriving either from Congress participants or from various Jewish circles, spiced with Baron's insights and brought together into a coherent superstructure. More lively and more original was Baron's description of the social encounters and political efforts initiated by prominent Viennese Jewish families. Here Baron was able to take advantage of materials close at hand to extend his narrative beyond the diplomatic pale.

Baron discussed both the diplomatic handling of the question as well as Jewish efforts to secure more positive results. He was particularly emphatic that a number of notable Jews— who were influential in political circles either because of their economic importance or their intellectual accomplishments— were actively involved in these diplomatic endeavors.[12] The outcome was generally negative in that favorable Jewish legislation adopted during the Napoleonic period in many of the German states and independent cities was now reversed; still, Baron remained positive about the long-term influence of the congressional debates. The most significant result of these deliberations, according to Baron, was that with the Congress of Vienna the Jewish question became a European question. All of the major European powers, with the exception of France, were actively engaged in attempts to alleviate conditions for Jews in several particularly difficult circumstances.[13]

His other publications during his Viennese years included his first essay on Heinrich Graetz (1918), which is discussed later in this study. Additional articles and several reviews on related themes helped establish his reputation, but Chajes provided the crucial recommendation that resulted in Baron's move to New York.

Jewish Institute of Religion

Stephen Wise, founder and president of the Jewish Institute of Religion (JIR) rabbinical school in New York, brought Salo Baron to America. A brief description of JIR's early years will help set the stage not only for Baron's life and career in America, but for several significant broader phenomena as well. The history of JIR is integrally tied both to the migration of Jewish scholars and to the early seeds of academic Jewish studies in America.

Wise founded the JIR with the intention of providing a new approach to rabbinical education focusing on professional training, with an emphasis in the curriculum on homiletics, practical experience, and social involvement.[14] Admission to the institute required a university degree.

Wise encouraged a diversity of religious viewpoints and perspectives on issues facing the Jewish community. Thus, for example, in 1926 he invited Claude Montefiore, leader of England's Liberal Judaism and anti-Zionist spokesperson, to address the first JIR commencement. He explained to critics that the institute was demonstrating the very openness to contrary ideas that was missing from the official seminary of Reform Judaism, the Hebrew Union College (HUC) in Cincinnati.

For many years we have been looking with abhorrence upon the attitude of the Hebrew Union College toward Zionism and Zionists. . . . The Institute was founded in some part, in order that there might be a place where every viewpoint in Jewish life could secure a hearing. . . . Ought I permit my Zionism, however much it means to me, to prevent me from inviting to the Institute the foremost living Jewish liberal because he happens to be a non-Zionist?[15]

To illustrate Wise's vision of openness, honorary degrees were given out at that first commencement to Montefiore, who was ill and could not attend, and to the Hebrew poet laureate, Hayim Nachman Bialik.[16]

The idea of a new rabbinical school appealed to those who, like Wise, were dissatisfied with the Reform status quo, especially with HUC. Wise's pro-Zionism was a hallmark of contrast between the two schools. He also emphasized that New York provided extensive opportunities for the professional training of the students and for their academic studies that could not possibly be matched in Cincinnati.

The first classes met in the fall of 1922, and the institute was soon housed within the facilities of Wise's Free Synagogue. The library was established on the basis of the private collections of Marcus Brann of Breslau, Emil Hirsch of Chicago, and Wise's personal library as well. Joshua Bloch served as the first librarian before moving on to head the Jewish division at the New York Public Library.[17]

Under Wise's strong leadership, JIR attracted distinguished faculty members from both America and abroad. Thus, from the outset, several notable scholars were identified with its program. Ismar Elbogen, one of the leading historians of Judaism in Germany at the time, signed on for the opening semester and for one semester the following year before deciding to remain at Berlin's Hochschule für die Wissenschaft des Judenthums.[18] In addition, Israel Abrahams came from England. But Wise sought out younger talent as well. Shalom Spiegel taught there before moving to the Jewish Theological Seminary, and Harry Wolfson taught for several years when his position at Harvard was in jeopardy.[19]

Although Wise himself was no academic scholar, he possessed both a deep respect for scholarship and an academic vision of the faculty he was building. When soliciting essays for a volume in memory of their former colleague Israel Abrahams, Wise wrote to the members of the faculty in 1926: "This request may be put the more firmly, in view of the fact, for reasons which it may not be profitable at this time to discuss, that members of the Faculty have made a minimum of contributions to the literature of their several subjects during the years of their association with the Institute—a matter which is one of profound significance."[20]

Several objectives guided the selection of faculty in the early years. The desire to establish its reputation by attracting older, well-known scholars was matched by the need to bring in younger teachers as well. Wise explained that he was seeking "three or four outstanding men as heads of departments, giving much of their time and strength to research, and then . . . a staff of men to do the day-by-day teaching."[21] Although most of the professors had been born in Europe, the faculty itself expressed the desire to secure English-speaking scholars for its teaching ranks. At the time, this meant primarily trying to locate suitable candidates from England, for there were few American-trained scholars in Judaica.[22]

Still, it was self-evident to Wise and his colleagues that qualified scholars would have to be brought from Europe. Wise, as a leader of the Zionist movement and the American Jewish community, traveled regularly to Europe and Israel, and on those occasions sought out potential faculty for his young seminary. In July 1922, he wrote from Berlin:

Of one thing I am persuaded . . . namely, that my coming to Europe ought to be richly productive of good to the JIR for years to come. I am enabled to make my program clear, Lehrfreiheit as the atmosphere of Jewish study and Jewish loyalty. I have the feeling that before another week I shall have most of the great scholars of the four seminaries [Berlin, Vienna, Budapest, Breslau] enrolled as members of the visiting staff and perhaps some of the best of them as our permanent teachers.[23]

Wise maintained especially close contacts with the Viennese community, having studied there as a young rabbinical student under the personal supervision of Adolf Jellinek, a leading nineteenth-century rabbinical figure. In particular, Wise was in contact with Hirsch Perez Chajes, chief rabbi of Vienna and a leader in the Zionist movement and of many of Vienna's Jewish institutions; he was director of the rabbinical school known as the Israelitisch-Theologischen Lehranstalt, and the Pedagogium, or teachers' seminary.[24]

By 1925, Wolfson's difficulties at Harvard had been alleviated with the establishment of the Littauer chair.[25] Judge Mack of the U.S. Circuit Court of Appeals and Chairman of the Board of Trustees of the Jewish Institute of Religion then consulted with Chajes on the Institute's need to hire a Jewish historian.[26] Chajes recommended Baron, who was then teaching at the Pedagogium. That fall, Wise invited Baron, as well as Cecil Roth of England to each come for a semester. According to the faculty minutes,

Dr. Wise described at length and read from several letters concerning Dr. Cecil Roth of Oxford University, one of the brilliant young Jewish scholars in England. Dr. Roth . . . will be succeeded by Dr. Salo Baron of Vienna, another promising teacher. . . . Both men were highly recommended to Wise by several prominent authorities. Dr. Wise announced that he considered the Institute very fortunate to secure the services of two such scholars.[27]

31

Simultaneous with Wise's overtures, Baron was also invited to teach at the rabbinical seminary in Florence, but he found the opportunity to come to America particularly attractive. In the aftermath of World War I, he had begun to admire America's power and the great contribution it had given to the Allies. In discussing this move, Baron told Professor Zvi Ankory that he had always been an Anglophile, so it was "just one step" to America. Furthermore, as the 1920s unfolded, Baron knew he would not find a permanent position in Vienna or elsewhere in Austria, and certainly not at a university where Jews faced considerable difficulties. Apparently, he also saw no long-term future with the Jewish institutions because of their great financial burdens.[28]

Joshua Bloch resigned as librarian in early 1924, and the position was filled only on a temporary basis. As the institute entered the 1926–27 academic year, it was vacant once again. In early September, Wise announced to the faculty that Baron would join them for the entire year. He also reported that Cecil Roth was interested in becoming the librarian and a teacher of Italian and Spanish history at the institute. The minutes report, "Dr. Wise said that he thought Dr. Roth would be a great bibliographer and would fill the post well." Yet, no decision was reached at that time concerning Roth and, less than a month later, Baron was appointed acting librarian as well.

No reasons for the choice of Baron over Roth were given. However, Roth's intended specialization in Renaissance Italian and Spanish history paled alongside Baron's breadth.[29] Baron's first courses at the institute, offered during the winter semester of 1926, were the history of the Jews in the Second Temple Period, the Jews in medieval Europe, the Jews in the period of Reformation and the rise of capitalism (sixteenth to seventeenth centuries), and the economic history of the Jews in the Middle Ages. The last course was given in Hebrew.

In subsequent years, Baron offered a number of new courses, in addition to those already established in his cycle. These included: "Contemporary Jewish History"—a survey of the chief movements in contemporary Jewish life in their connection with the Jewish past; "A History of the Jews in the period of the Kings"—a course in political, economic, social and intellectual history; and an elective course—"The Talmud as a Source of History."[30] Baron was committed to offering the students a broad overview of the Jewish historical experience, and his courses indicate a balance between the various periods.[31]

From the outset of his association with JIR, Baron earned the appreciation and friendship of George Kohut, JIR trustee and Wise's close collaborator in many endeavors. Yet at the same time, several leading faculty members were hesitant or even hostile to Baron's appointment. When Kohut informed Wise of Baron's imminent arrival in January 1926, he wrote that he was optimistic that "you and I are going to like him and get a great deal of satisfaction out of him . . . , [but] I don't quite like the attitude of the Faculty toward him.[32]

Kohut and Baron became friends and frequent allies. Together they urged Wise to establish a *Journal of Jewish Studies* to promote the good name of American Jewish scholarship in general and of JIR in particular. Although faculty and trustees alike were reluctant to invest scarce funds for the adventure, the idea of an American-based scholarly journal had been firmly implanted in Baron's thinking and reemerged a decade later with the founding of *Jewish Social Studies*.

But some other faculty members remained negative toward Baron, and when the question of a long-term commitment arose in late 1926 and early 1927, Wise was concerned about the opposition. He wrote to Kohut: "I ought to tell you in strictest confidence that the Dean [Slonimsky] is not quite happy about Baron. He thinks we might get a bigger and stronger man. I do not know."

Slonimsky recommended another possibility, but Wise remained in favor of Baron: "I do not want any prima donnas. Heaven knows the whole chorus is full of them." The positive decision on Baron's appointment was delayed until just prior to his return to Europe in late May, by which time Slonimsky approved and maintained that he had done so from the start.[33] Baron's responsibilities at the institute now increased rapidly. He became acting librarian in October 1926 and in 1928, became director of the Department of Advanced Studies, which was responsible for postgraduate training.[34] He was also appointed to various tasks concerning curriculum planning and scheduling.

The turning point in Baron's advancement at JIR seems to have coincided with the position offered to him in 1928 by the Jewish Theological Seminary of Breslau. For the rest of his life — in his writings, letters, and conversations — Baron loved to refer to the invitation to accept the chair in Jewish history first occupied by Heinrich Graetz.[35] It thus came as a total surprise to me when working on the archival collection housed at Stanford to discover that the offer put forth by Breslau was not the one that Baron had boasted about for the next sixty years.[36] The position differed from Baron's description in at least three major respects. First, the letter emphasized that a new teaching position was being created. It certainly did not refer in any way to Baron being appointed as successor to Graetz and Marcus Brann—the immediate successor to Graetz's position, who died in 1920.

In addition, the appointment was to the lower rank of lecturer (Dozent), with the appropriate salary and teaching hours. Finally, the position offered to Baron was intended to cover the period beginning with the year 1040. Graetz's area of specialization was actually in the rabbinic periods. Consequently, in this sense as well, Baron was not viewed as Graetz's successor.[37]

There is no indication in the sources that Baron gave any serious consideration to accepting the invitation to Breslau. But, already in letters from the period, he referred repeatedly to the great honor he felt at being named Graetz's successor. In a letter to Herbert Solow of the *Menorah Journal* a month after the offer was posted from Germany, Baron expressed his gratification as well as his intention to remain in New York: "Although I regard a call to a chair occupied once by Graetz as very honoring indeed, I practically decided to remain at the institute for the years to come."[38] In fact, Baron wrote to Wise almost immediately after receiving the letter from Breslau: "Although I feel indeed very honored by a call to a Chair occupied once upon a time by Graetz, I think just the same that I shall stick to the old flag of the JIR."

Wise was enthralled with the implicit honor bestowed upon the institute and wrote Kohut that he planned to publicize the offer to Baron. The publicity issued by the institute is interesting on two grounds. First, Wise's language concerning the connection with Graetz was far more cautious than that used by Baron. "To Professor Salo Baron . . . has come a call from the Jewish Seminary of Breslau to fill the Chair of Jewish History, which place is associated with the name of the greatest of Jewish Historians in Modern times, Professor H. Graetz." The release issued sometime in May also indicated that Baron had not yet reached a decision concerning the position. This was not accurate, but apparently sought to emphasize—perhaps overly so—the attractiveness of the offer.[39]

Baron's advancement at the institute precipitated continued sniping,[40] but again Kohut was gratified with Baron's presence. When the Jewish Theological Seminary's esteemed historian Alexander Marx heard of Baron's appointment as head of advanced studies, he wrote to Kohut to express his pleasure. Kohut turned Marx's rather modest comments into a rave review of Baron's accomplishments:

He is the one man on our Faculty who has been universally appreciated as a scholar of distinction, with a wholly original outlook upon the field of his work and a unique approach as to method and style of approach. Altogether, we can congratulate ourselves upon having a man affiliated with us who is not only a great scholar, but a remarkable teacher. He will rear a band of disciples who will bring great credit to us and will achieve something really distinctive in the field of original research.[41]

As was quite natural in a new institution, curricular issues arose regularly at faculty meetings. Very early in its history, the institute faculty debated whether too much emphasis was being placed on the study of Hebrew literature and Midrash. Elbogen defended the current position, while others sought a more professionally oriented curriculum. In this instance, as he seems to have done frequently, Wise placed representatives of both sides on a committee to resolve the dispute.[42]

Baron became active in such discussions. In a comprehensive review of the curriculum, Baron prescribed stricter admission standards, especially regarding background in Judaica, and specifically in Hebrew grammar, history, and some Mishna. He suggested that students planning to come to the institute prepare themselves while attending college, but the feasibility of such a requirement was questionable in 1927. Later in the discussion, it was indicated that Columbia and "California" provided such opportunities. Baron also suggested that the institute program be increased to five years.[43] At another meeting he stated that the requirements for admission to a rabbinical school should be higher than those for admission to a law or medical school. Rabbinical students require not only academic preparation, but self-reliance and courage as well "to deal with problems which will face them in the ministry."[44]

Baron's respect for those already in the ministry and those preparing for such a career was sincere and profound. He continued to teach and maintain administrative responsibilities at JIR even after his appointment to Columbia. Baron indicated to Columbia's president Nicholas Butler that he felt committed not to leave JIR without adequate coverage. In fact, he continued to teach for a number of years and to serve for some time as director of advanced studies. He was last listed in the annual bulletin for the fall term of 1936–37.

Baron thought quite well of his students at JIR and was particularly pleased with the group attending his advanced seminars.[45] He maintained correspondence with these men after they left New York to undertake rabbinical positions; these writings also reveal considerable patience and understanding for their difficulties in pursuing their writing tasks due to a lack of free time and inadequate library facilities. The JIR students had clearly earned his respect and cooperation.

Even in a 1987 interview, Baron still spoke highly of his students at JIR in the 1920s and 1930s, and, in fact, referred to some ambivalence about the move to Columbia because he was less sure about his new students. The discussion on curricular matters at JIR mentioned above revealed that Baron was not particularly interested in teaching students who lacked a sufficient Judaic background, however intelligent they might be.

Indeed, Baron's continued high regard for the quality of the program at JIR should be considered when measuring the accomplishment at that institution. It is true that many of the leading scholars who taught there left for other institutions, though Baron's continued commitments and Wolfson's return to Harvard once his position was secured were hardly adverse comments on JIR. Wise may have failed to convince Elbogen to move to America and join the faculty permanently, but remember that five years later Elbogen also turned down Columbia University. In other words, as long as the main pool of Judaic scholars was still located in Europe, any American institution, whether seminary or university, could expect difficulties in recruiting the best faculty.

What I find particularly striking is that more than any other seminary in America, Wise selected scholars who would go on to play a leading role in the teaching of Jewish studies at American universities. Many of the names that appear in the history of JIR appear in the context of the development of university programs as well—Baron, Wolfson, Ralph Marcus, even Elbogen must be mentioned in this connection. The other seminaries certainly had their outstanding scholars, but Wise's criteria seem to have been closer to university requirements. In fact, Columbia also had considerable difficulty in filling positions and faced many problems similar to those encountered by Wise Perhaps, Wise's achievements at JIR, considering the state of the field at the time, should be viewed in a more charitable light.[46] For one, it was Wise who had brought Salo Baron to America.

First Impact

In 1928, Baron published one of his best-known and most cited essays, "Ghetto and Emancipation: Shall We Revise the Traditional View?" This essay introduced Baron to the English-reading public, while adumbrating many of his major ideas on Jewish history; these ideas would appear later in expanded and more cogently argued presentations.[47]

The contributions made by Baron to Jewish historiography in his essays can easily be overlooked because of the towering position of his multivolume monographs and histories. But it was through the genre of essays that Baron put forth some of his most significant, innovative, and sweeping interpretations. "Ghetto and Emancipation" was a prelude of ideas to appear later in more fully dressed formulations, primarily on the need to revise accepted conceptions of modernization and its implications for Jewish life. It also laid the broad, conceptual basis for one of the central components in Baron's historical thinking—the need to correct the undue emphasis in Jewish historical writing on the sufferings of the past.

By invoking the images of ghetto and then of emancipation, Baron was calling to mind primary symbols of Jewish life first in the medieval period and then of the modern. In the popular mind these two periods were distinctly different, one perceived as a time of persecution and wretchedness, the other of equality and opportunity. This historical perspective enjoyed wide influence and had permeated not only Jewish views of their past, but also of the future.

Emancipation, in the judgment of Graetz, Philippson, Dubnow and other historians, was the dawn of a new day after a nightmare of the deepest horror, and this view has been accepted as completely true by Jews, rabbis, scholars and laymen, throughout the Western world. It is in terms of this complete contrast between the black of the Jewish Middle Ages and the white of the post-Emancipation period that most generalizations about the progress of the Jews in modern times are made. . . . If in so short a time the Jew has risen from such great depths, is it not logical to hope that a few more years will bring him perfect freedom?

But Baron argued that because the contrasts are not so great, the hopes built on them should also be qualified. "If the status of the Jews (his privileges, opportunities, and actual life) in those centuries was in fact not as low as we are in the habit of thinking, then the miracle of Emancipation was not so great as we supposed."[48]

Here, Baron demonstrated one of the strengths of his popular writing. He was able to turn his scholarly ideas into an analysis of Jewish affairs relevant to contemporary leaders, while issuing veiled warning of the potential pitfalls of the blessings of modernity. First, however, he set out to revise the established conceptions of the Middle Ages.

In the medieval world, in which each separate corporation had its rights and obligations, the legal status of the Jews was closest to that of the urban citizens. And it was certainly superior to that of the peasant majority, who had fewer rights and more duties than the Jews. In light of their status as a separate corporation, the disabilities effecting the Jews were parallel to restrictions placed on any corporation. Thus, because the Jews fulfilled certain economic functions, it was natural that they could not own land or join most guilds—all corporations were restricted in certain ways.

One truly distinctive aspect of the legal conditions of the Jews was their status as *servi camerae*. Here too Baron maintained that their position as serfs of the throne was far more desirable than that of the peasants as serfs of their local masters. This legal conception of the Jew as property of the monarch had generally worked to their advantage.[49]

The ghetto had come to be symbolic of the evils of the Middle Ages, but Baron sought to remind his readers that the ghetto had originated voluntarily within the Jewish community as an agency of social and religious cohesion. Furthermore, Jews had used the ghetto as a means of defense, securing themselves inside walls that they themselves had erected: "there were locks inside the Ghetto gates in most cases before there were locks outside." It was only later, during the period of the Counter Reformation, that the ghetto was imposed on the Jews with increased restrictions on Jewish mobility. In fact, the ghetto had facilitated the development of autonomy and "the preservation of Jewry as a distinct nationality" ("Ghetto," p. 519).

Having discussed what he called the legal and theoretical aspects of Jewish existence, Baron next turned to the question of Jewish suffering during the Middle Ages. "But did actual events—persecutions, riots, pogroms, monetary extortions— reduce their theoretical legal privileges to fictions in practice?" Baron turned for evidence to one of his favorite historical sources: population figures. "It is certainly significant that despite minor attacks, periodic pogroms, and organized campaigns of conversion, the numbers of Jewry during the last centuries preceding Emancipation increased much more rapidly than the Gentile population" ("Ghetto," p. 521). Admittedly able to provide only "reasonable" estimates of prerevolution statistics, Baron still felt confident to assert that the Jewish population had grown much more than non-Jews.

Going even further, for all the accepted emphasis on violent persecutions during medieval times, Baron could state—even writing before World War II—that the modern record demonstrated little improvement. "Between Chmielnicki and Human, the two great pogrom movements of earlier East European Jewish history, more than a century intervened, whereas three major pogrom waves have swept Eastern Europe between

1880 and 1920, despite the coming of Emancipation." Furthermore, whereas emancipation had apparently not relieved the Jews of the dangers of pogroms, it had brought with it the extra burden and danger of military service. "During the continuous wars of the sixteenth, seventeenth, and eighteenth centuries, . . . the Jews were neutral and suffered few losses. If they had been combatants they might have lost more than in all the pogroms" ("Ghetto," p. 522).

In presenting this argument, Baron ignored the ideological implications of military service as understood by the proponents of Emancipation, as well as the origins of the argument from antisemitic claims (going back at least to the eighteenth century) that Jews benefited unfairly from military exemptions. For Baron, the numerical argument stood independently: the separate medieval status of the Jews provided significant protection from physical harm and for group survival, in some ways more protection than resulted from the emancipated status of modern times.[50]

Also within the economic sphere, Baron argued that medieval Jews were, on average, better-off than Christians. And whereas there were many impoverished Jews, there were, even relatively, more impoverished peasants. Baron referred to the rise of a number of wealthy banking families to support his claim. The Jews fared well economically in part because of the very restrictions that had been placed on them. Forced into the money trade, Jews were well prepared for the emergence of early capitalism. As is discussed later, Baron had some sympathy for Sombart's thesis on the role of the Jews in the emergence of modern capitalism. In this essay, he phrased it this way: "One need not accept Sombart's exaggerations to see that the Jew had an extraordinarily large share in the development of early capitalism, and received corresponding benefits."[51]

The other side of Baron's main argument was, of course, that certain benefits enjoyed by medieval Jewry had been lost with the advent of modernity. Foremost was the loss of internal autonomy with powers ranging over educational, taxation, and judiciary matters. As Baron turned to a discussion of the modern state and emancipation, he hinted at a number of ideas that would subsequently appear in expanded form. These include the notion that Emancipation was even more necessary for the modern state than it was for the Jews. "Left to themselves, the Jews might for long have clung to their corporate existence. For Emancipation meant losses as well as gains for Jewry." The negative side of Emancipation implied that Jews would lose their communal autonomy and were now subject to military service. Through this process, the path was being prepared for what many hoped would be the complete assimilation of the Jews.

Within this environment, Reform Judaism emerged to reduce the differences between Jews and Gentiles, partly by stripping Judaism of its national elements. "The reality of the living Jewish ethnic organism was to be pared down to the fiction of the Jewish 'Confession.' " The growth of Reform also paved the way for the appearance of the scholarly movement known as Wissenschaft des Judenthums. Anxious to demonstrate that Jews were fully capable of integration into the broader society, these scholars adopted the explanation that whatever defects may exist among contemporary Jews resulted from the way Jews had been treated in the past.[52]

Thus, the worse the treatment of the Jews historically, the clearer the explanation of their faults, and the brighter the hopes for improvement as a result of changed conditions.

Reform Jews adopted these ideas, extending them at times to the entire period of Diaspora and especially to the Talmudic period. Ironically, Baron saw a close connection on this point between the Reform and Zionist movements, as Zionism also sought to reject the Diaspora Jewish experience. "They differed only in that the Zionists denounced the post-Revolutionary period as equally bad." Baron concluded the essay with the hope that Jews were coming closer in their positions and that common bonds were being built on a more accurate assessment of the historical past.

The significance of "Ghetto and Emancipation" lies not in the cogency of its arguments, but in its basic conceptualization of the two periods of Jewish history. In fact, the arguments are occasionally fallacious and even at times flippant. For example, Baron sought to demonstrate the economic well-being of medieval Jewry by referring to the emergence of the Rothschilds: "But is it not remarkable that the most typical Ghetto in the world, the Frankfort Judengasse, produced in the pre-Emancipation period the greatest banking house of history?" As proof that the average Jewish income greatly surpassed the average Christian income, this was hardly the trickle-down theory at its best.

Elsewhere, as indicated earlier, Baron used the above-average increases in Jewish population of pre-Emancipation days to suggest that violence against the Jews in medieval times had been overstated by historians. Conversely, there was a decline in Jewish population growth subsequent to the French Revolution. Baron didn't actually assert that this reversal in growth processes resulted from increased violence in modern times. However, he came close when referring to the increased tempo of pogroms in the period since 1880, while he totally ignored the question of what other social and economic causes stood behind the fluctuations in growth rates between traditional and modern conditions.

In fact, there was also, at least at the time—a decade prior to Nazi occupation of Europe—a serious contradiction in Baron's argument that Emancipation had not protected the Jews from violence; having specified that the pogroms in question had taken place in Eastern Europe, Baron had also just written that "it must be borne in mind that Emancipation did not come to Russia, Romania or Turkey until the present century, while in Austria (including the Jewish masses of Galicia and Hungary) it postdates 1867."[53]

In the essay's concluding section, Baron extended his more sober analysis of the benefits of Emancipation into a veiled caution against overconfidence regarding the Jewish future.

At any rate, it is clear that Emancipation has not brought the Golden Age. While Emancipation has meant a reduction of ancient evils, and while its balance sheet for the world at large as well as for the Jews is favorable, it is not completely clear of debits. Certainly its belief in the efficacy of a process of complete assimilation has been proved untenable.[54]

A basic reassessment of the benefits and shortcomings of modernity should, in Baron's view, provide the opportunity for the diverse poles of Jewish movements to move closer to each other. Specifically, Baron asserted that Reform Judaism and Zionism, two movements that had frequently clashed in the past, actually shared common ground in their critique of medieval Jewish life. Reform leaders had emphasized the negative effects of excessive suffering, while Zionists had declared in general that a normal Jewish life was virtually an impossibility in the Diaspora. In fact, Baron noted that recently the two movements had started to move toward a more central position. Whereas Zionists like Martin Buber had rediscovered the values of the ghetto and of the autonomy it represented, some Reform leaders had reconciled themselves with Zionism.

Of course, the reconciliation described by Baron was unbalanced. Zionists had hardly embraced the values of Reform at all. Perhaps Baron's immediate environment at JIR under Stephen Wise's aegis had influenced Baron's perceptions of significant change. It would be more accurate to suggest that such a common reevaluation of the Jewish past was what he sought, and this indeed was a position that Baron continued to stake out for himself both in Jewish historiography and in communal politics in the turbulent years to come.

The weakness of some of its arguments aside, the essay offered a fundamental critique of how historians had perceived the Jewish past, and without doubt, "Ghetto and Emancipation" helped establish Baron's reputation in America. In subsequent writings Baron provided an extensive formulation of how he thought the medieval period should be presented, but this earlier essay suggests that suffering had been overstated and the Jews had enjoyed relative economic and legal prosperity in comparison with the bulk of the general population. The historiographic revision of the modern period was less developed. The ideas that Emancipation was a mixed blessing and that it was granted to the Jews by the modern states out of their own needs would become major components of later articles on the themes of Emancipation and modernity.[55]

Baron had first presented "Ghetto and Emancipation" at a meeting of rabbis in New York with the title, "Ought We to Revise the Traditional View of Modern Jewish History?" This title was rather misleading, however, because it was really the medieval period that was subjected to revision in Baron's talk. Baron submitted the manuscript to the *Menorah Journal,* the leading intellectual periodical in Jewish life at the time.[56]

At first, the editorial process apparently moved quite rapidly, for within two weeks Baron was returning the manuscript to the editors "with considerable additions." But then matters slowed down, and a little more than two months after the first contact had been made, Baron wrote to the editors expressing considerable anger at the delays.

I am highly astonished that I have not heard from you until now. Indeed the continual delays caused that I have lost any further interest in having my paper published at the present time. Please, therefore, kindly return to me my original manuscript with all additional notes I sent to you to supplement it.

E. E. Cohen, the managing editor, responded immediately: "I am sorry you feel as you do. . . . There have been delays to be sure, but certainly not of exceptional length, as editorial offices go. We are still anxious to print your paper, and I hope you will reconsider your letter."[57]

Baron's relations with his editors and publishers were often strained. The themes observed in this brief episode recur frequently in subsequent encounters. Whether or not Baron actually intended to withdraw his article, he continually pressured and made heavy demands of those involved in the publication of his writings. Two recurring sources of tension involved time tables and the number of reprints. In this case (as in most) his editors acquiesced. Two weeks later, Herbert Solow of the *Journal* extended his apologies to Baron: "I certainly regret that this delay has occurred, and I do not wonder that you have been annoyed." Solow assured Baron that a June publication would still be possible.

In response, Baron described at some length the difficulties posed by the delay.

As things stand, a June issue is for me rather inconvenient in more than one respect. At the first place I leave for Europe June 9th, and so I may not even see the paper for many weeks after its publication. Furthermore, in the case of this article there may be a favorable or unfavorable reaction in the public, as it touches somewhat delicate matters. It might even become necessary for me to enter into a further discussion, although with an utter dislike. Finally, the distribution of the reprints, at least as far as this country is concerned, could no longer be done under my supervision.[58]

It would seem that the delicacy of reprint distribution has changed with time. Nevertheless, Baron took advantage of the accommodating mood to stipulate new conditions regarding reprints; the editors agreed.

49

Later, Elliot Cohen explained to Baron that the delays resulted from the necessary level of editing. "We regard your article as both interesting and important, and feel that every point that you make should come to the reader with the utmost clarity."[59] Baron responded positively to the changes and expressed his appreciation for the efforts. Cohen had apparently also suggested a new title, which Baron rejected. "It may be that the longer and seemingly too 'scientific' title will appear less attractive to certain readers. But, to tell the truth, I care very little for that kind of readers."[60] Nevertheless, the title was soon changed to "Ghetto and Emancipation."

When Baron traveled to Europe that summer, he found the reprints awaiting him in Vienna.

Many thanks. Until now I heard only from a few people about it. Their reaction was mostly a compromise between a helpless astonishment and a half-hearted approval. Of course, there are some enthusiasts who, like George Alexander Kohut, exaggerate this affair infinitely. Was any echo of it in America? I would appreciate it very much if you would be able to send me a few extracts, if their {sic} are any. Particularly the unfavorable ones interest me most.[61]

Baron was pleased with the effect of his essay, and whereas his relationships with the *Menorah Journal* were frequently tense, it provided Baron with an appropriate forum to communicate his sometimes controversial ideas to the public. He promised to send a new contribution upon his return from Europe. The reference was to a long essay "Nationalism and Intolerance," which appeared in two installments in June and November 1929. In the meantime, the editors began to turn to Baron for his advice on manuscripts submitted by other authors, and at his own initiative, Baron occasionally suggested articles for publication.

Near the end of 1929, Baron wrote a letter on the importance of the *Menorah Journal* in response to a request by Elliot Cohen, who hoped to use the letter to help raise funds to secure the journal's future. The letter also provides a glimpse of how Baron viewed American Jewry at this point in time.

I still cannot believe that American Jewry should give up one of its finest means of expression on account of a lack of funds.

Indeed the "Menorah Journal" has been for years not only a fine intellectual organ for America, but one of the best in World Jewry. . . . Just now, when the period of philantropic *{sic}* or financially reconstructive activities is drawing to a close and a new leadership, leadership primarily also in the cultural sense, is being assumed more and more by the American section of the Jewish people, the need of a Journal of this kind is more urgent than ever before. . . . As a writer and as a reader, I should miss the *Menorah Journal* perhaps more than any other single publication. As a writer I found there courteous understanding and intelligent collaboration in problems of Judaism which troubled me and which I desired to discuss in public. As a reader, I often delighted in the lucid presentation of sometimes very complex problems treated by men who felt that they had something to say.[62]

This letter was sent on 13 December 1929. The next day, Baron was appointed to the Miller chair in Jewish history at Columbia University. From that position, he continued the process of becoming not only one of the leading scholars in Judaica, but also one of the leading spokespersons of the American Jewish community.

The Migration of Jewish Studies

By the mid- to late-1920s, the centers of Jewish learning in Central Europe were emptying out their resources. Scholars were departing regularly to Palestine and America, and even library collections were being sold to the New World.[63] The economic chaos in Europe and the growing threat of antisemitism were the determining factors in this passing of the scepter. The files of JIR are laden with appeals and discussions on how to help the floundering European seminaries. Wise, Kohut, and Baron were particularly concerned to help the Vienna seminary maintain its aging but venerable scholars, several of whom had been Baron's teachers. With Chajes's death in early 1928, the situation in Vienna deteriorated rapidly. Weakened by hyperinflation and bereft of leadership, even the renown Viennese community seemed unwilling to contribute in order to prevent the collapse of the legacy of the Wissenschaft des Judenthums in Europe.[64]

From his arrival in America in 1926 until his marriage in 1934, Baron returned to Europe each summer, dividing the period between work, vacation, and time spent with his family. Berlin and Vienna were standing fixtures of these annual trips. In 1929, Baron wrote to Stephen Wise about what he had heard and the mood he found in Berlin, especially at the Hochschule für die Wissenschaft des Judenthums, the citadel of European Reform Judaism:

Here I saw many of our mutual friends. The Hochschule looks forward with some anxiety to the future. Gutman is leaving for Cincinnati (second term), Albeck for Jerusalem (maybe next year too). Elbogen may go to Columbia, and if Torczyner would come to the Institute they would have to provide for a whole faculty. I understand that Torczyner wrote to you recently.

Not all of these developments actually took place right away, as Wise responded: "What you write about the Hochschule is tremendously interesting. I hear that Elbogen will not accept the Columbia call." Wise was also doubtful that Torczyner would come to New York. But the portrait of imminent decimation of one of the leading institutions of Jewish life in Europe reveals a great deal of the trying climate in which Jewish scholars were living even before the Nazi rise to power.[65]

The background to Baron's own migration to America demonstrates that a similar scenario was playing in Vienna. Chajes allowed Baron to accept Wise's invitation to visit the institute and subsequently agreed to a permanent move. In addition, Chajes also agreed to allowing philosophy professor Zevi Diesendruck to be absent from Vienna. Moreover, Chajes himself was considering leaving his multiple responsibilities for either America or Israel, and JIR actively considered offering him a leadership position. The difficulties faced by the seminaries were not caused by decreasing enrollments. In fact, Jewish consciousness was increasing during this period, and, with it, student enrollment. At the Hochschule, the student body grew from 61 students before World War I to a peak of 155 in 1932. Its orthodox counterpart fared less well, but still showed a small increase—from 31 at the end of the war to 38 in 1924.[66] Numbers were not the problem; but ever-decreasing sources of financial support hindered these academies of learning, while the growing threat of antisemitism clouded the prospects for continued vitality.[67]

Several American Jewish leaders sought to provide support, and Wise was particularly active in these efforts to provide assistance for the modern rabbinical seminaries in Germany, Budapest, and especially Vienna, regardless of movement orientation. In 1923, he expressed his frustration at the hesitations of both HUC and the Jewish Theological Seminary (JTS) and so forwarded to Chajes $5,000 that he himself had raised to be divided among the five institutions: "Nothing has given me more pleasure in making the collection for the European Seminaries than the thought that it would give you some pleasure and lighten by ever so little the heavy burden which you are finely and bravely carrying for the Jews of Austria."

But concurrent with these concerns lay the question of Chajes's own future. From the outset, Wise mentioned to Chajes the possibility of inviting him to the institute.[68] Chajes came to visit America in late 1924, and the leaders of the institute then debated the role he might fill permanently. Wise was convinced that Chajes would accept nothing less than being head of the seminary. Not only was Wise personally reluctant to step down, but others participating in the discussion did not feel that Chajes was the appropriate person for the position.[69] Chajes's readiness to release his faculty to accept positions abroad and his own apparent interest to migrate indicate that the seminary in Vienna like the Hochschule in Berlin were consciously facing an unsure future.[70]

The orthodox seminary in Berlin faced a similar crisis in

academic leadership. Joseph Wohlgemuth left in 1931, because of poor health, and Moses Auerbach settled in Palestine in 1934. The chronicler of the closing years of what was popularly called "Hildesheimer's Seminary" referred to three vacancies in pivotal positions during this same period and to an attempt by the seminary's leadership to relocate the institution to Palestine.[71]

These migrations during the 1920s and early 1930s represent the second of three stages of the migration of Jewish studies out of its nineteenth-century European center. Around the turn of the century, several young scholars, such as Talmudist Louis Ginzberg and historian Alexander Marx, were part of the enormous influx of Eastern European Jews to America. Others, like George Kohut and Harry Wolfson, came at a younger age and later played a prominent role in the development of American Jewish scholarship. Few Judaica scholars in America — such as Louis Finkelstein — were natives.

The wave of the teens and twenties brought to America such personalities as Solomon Zeitlin, who immigrated during World War I, Jacob Mann, and Shalom Spiegel, as well as Baron. Several other scholars settled in Israel at this time: including Yitzhak Baer, Ben Zion Dinur, Yehezkel Kaufmann, and Gershom Scholem. Some of these participated in the early years of the Hebrew University.

What did Jewish Studies in America look like at the time of these movements? Almost all Judaica scholars were based in Jewish institutions, especially the main rabbinical seminaries and colleges devoted to Hebrew studies. In 1935, a committee was formed under Baron's leadership to organize celebrations of the eight-hundredth anniversary of the birth of Maimonides. A published list of those involved provides a reliable register of Judaic scholars. Other discussions in this study confirm that this list provides a rather complete picture of the situation: Boas Cohen, Israel Davidson, Z. Diesendruck, Louis Finkelstein, Louis Ginzberg, Richard Gottheil, Isaac Husik, A. Z. Idelsohn, Jacob Mann, Jacob Marcus, Ralph Marcus, Alexander Marx, Abraham Neuman, Henry Slonimsky, Shalom Spiegel, Chaim Tchernowitz, Harry Wolfson, and Solomon Zeitlin. Including Baron, five of those named taught at universities; others were connected with HUC, JIR, JTS, and Dropsie College. Their fields included history, philosophy, rabbinics, and Semitics. Although only three were native Americans, this distinguished assembly demonstrates how the first two waves of migration had already brought a core of Judaica scholars to American shores.[72]

With the annexation of Austria, followed later by Krystallnacht, those scholars remaining in Central Europe now sought to flee the Nazi terror. During this third stage of the migration of European Jewish scholarship, refugees like Hannah Arendt, Martin Buber, Ismar Elbogen, Abraham Heschel, Guido Kisch, Franz Rosenthal, Isaiah Sonne, Selma Stern, Eugene Täubler, and Max Wiener found new homes in America and Israel.[73]

During the war years, Salo Baron maintained his optimism that Jewish scholarship in Eastern Europe remained strong enough to lay the basis for a cultural reconstruction in the postwar period. But Baron had no such illusions about the future of Jewish studies in Central Europe, and as this wave

of immigration made its flight to American shores, Baron—
by then forty-five and an established fixture in American
Jewish life—served as beacon and support of a generation of
refugees, many of whom were considerably older. His role as
a central address for these refugees is discussed further in a
later chapter.

In sum, Baron's own migration was not an isolated event,
but rather part of a wave that enriched the academic reservoirs
of the two communities that would dominate Jewish life
in the postwar period. Neither the Hebrew University nor
American institutions could have established their Judaica
faculties without this migration. In early 1939, HUC president Julian Morgenstern, addressing the Union of American
Hebrew Congregations, spoke of the new role to be played by
HUC specifically and by America and Palestine in general in
replacing Europe as the center of Jewish Wissenschaft.[74] In
fact, by that time both communities had already greatly
prospered by the ongoing migration process—which helped
form the basis for the new faculty of the Hebrew University
of Jerusalem on the one hand and the expansion of Jewish
studies in America on the other.

CHAPTER 2

JEWISH HISTORY COMES TO THE UNIVERSITY

The Search

On 9 may 1928, Linda Miller of New Rochelle, New York, wrote to Nicholas Murray Butler, president of Columbia University, expressing interest in endowing a chair in Jewish history, literature and institutions in memory of her husband who had died some six months earlier.[1] She also stipulated the way she wanted Judaism to be presented through the chair: "I should like to make it clear that it is the spiritual and intellectual aspects of Jewish life that I should hope to see accented in the courses, rather than the nationalistic ideas which have recently become popular in some quarters." This stipulation would reappear several times during the subsequent search for an appropriate incumbent for the chair. The negotiations over the establishment of the Miller chair and the ensuing search procedure are described at some

58

length because they indicate some of the continuing difficulties faced in the establishment of Jewish studies in American universities.

The original contacts with Columbia concerning the chair were carried out by Rabbi Hyman Enelow of New York City's prominent Temple Emanuel.[2] Some aspects of these discussions were considered delicate because the family feared that publicity might result in adverse remarks in the press. Butler seemed somewhat perplexed as to the proper course of action and suggested to Enelow ways to reduce the accompanying attention.[3]

When the preliminaries were concluded, Butler responded to Miller's initiative and explained that an incumbent of such a chair would receive a salary of $9,000 to $10,000, requiring a capital sum of $200,000. In order to make available additional funds for the library and for research assistance, Butler requested a total endowment of $250,000.[4]

An intensive pace of correspondence ensued. Miller agreed to the terms set forth by Butler, but now expressed herself more directly on the question that deeply concerned her. Although "the sum you mention exceeds the amount I had been under the impression it would require, I think your explanation so much in keeping with the high character I should wish the Foundation to possess that I should be willing to advance that amount if I could put aside any uneasiness as to the personality of the professor in charge."

She wondered "at which stage of the negotiations it is customary for a donor to state his wishes and of the deference that would be accorded to them." She continued, "My wish would be to have the chair offered to Dr. Enelow, as I think he is exceptionally well qualified." With some understatement, she concluded:

I can readily understand that I must seem presumptuous in daring to make suggestions as to the personnel of your faculty. I am not insensible of the impression I may create. My excuse is that in recent years numerous conflicting visions have sprung up on the subject of Judaism. Among them one which construes Judaism chiefly in political terms, and I am eager to see the spiritual and religious element emphasized.[5]

Butler assured Miller that her generous gift would allow Columbia to secure a distinguished professor and to enable him to conduct advanced scholarly work. He then addressed the problem posed by the attempt of a donor to stipulate an academic appointment.

You will, I am sure, see the embarrassment that would result from naming a professor at the instance of a generous benefactor. No matter what the competence of such a man might be, his colleagues would regard him as one apart, and his power for University service would be gravely diminished, if not destroyed. Columbia has never made an appointment of this kind and I feel sure that you will understand the embarrassments in the way of attempting to do so.

Butler then assured her that Enelow would be given earnest consideration, but concluded that the university's purpose "would be to strengthen the University by the addition of a truly fine and productive scholar, able to represent this important field and to develop it along the finest University lines."[6]

In her reply, the donor expressed her understanding of Butler's position: "I want to say, in all candor, that in principle I am heartily in accord with your attitude regarding the appointment of professors at Columbia." Still, she remained worried about certain questions in practice:

There are, both within and without the Jewish group, scholarly individuals who put an interpretation on Judaism that seems to me subversive of all that is finest in the Jewish tradition. I feel that I might get a good measure of unhappiness out of certain conceivable appointments. It is this apprehension which causes me to tax your courtesy with one more question: would you not favor the suggestion that I might be allowed to select one of two or three who would be acceptable before the initial appointment be made?[7]

Of course, Butler could not agree to the request that she be allowed to select from a list of candidates acceptable to the university, but he did assent that "I should make it my business to see that any two or three names suggested by the University's proper officers and advisers as those from which a final selection should be made were submitted in confidence to you for your suggestions and criticism before any final steps were taken." Miller agreed to these conditions and made the necessary arrangements for the donation to be transferred.[8]

Butler indicated in an internal memo his suspicion that Enelow himself stood behind Miller's various objections and suggestions. If that was so, then Enelow may have been influenced by certain specific precedents and the historical connection in general between Temple Emanuel and the teaching of Judaica at Columbia. In 1887, Richard Gottheil had been appointed to a chair at Columbia in rabbinic literature and Semitic languages, and the funds for that position had been provided by Temple Emanuel. The rabbi of this East

Side citadel of Reform Judaism at that time was Gustav Gottheil, father of the endowed professor. At other times— 1868, 1892, 1903—the congregation provided support for library acquisitions and research in Judaica.[9]

While Enelow sought to further his own candidacy, Butler's commitment to keep Miller informed about the search's progress proved fruitful for Columbia as well. During the course of subsequent developments, Miller repeatedly insisted that Columbia had committed itself to the appointment of a distinguished scholar. Her involvement kept Butler to his word, and the search committee was compelled to resist compromises or temporary solutions.

With these negotiations concluded, Butler instructed F. J. E. Woodbridge, the dean of the faculties of political science, philosophy, and pure science, to begin consultations toward filling the new position, indicating that "it is important that we find for the chair an outstanding scholar who will not be a functionalist but who will command respect both within and without the University. Such a chair might easily be made the beginning of very elaborate work in the comparative history of religions." Butler mentioned the possibility of considering the chief rabbi of England, Joseph H. Hertz, "a very brilliant and able Columbia man who went to England as Chief Rabbi. How he would fit into the picture, I do not know, but I should naturally include him in any list of those to be considered."[10]

About two weeks later, Butler issued a formal announcement of the chair and moved to form a search committee.

It is in my judgment important that we choose for this chair the ripest and most distinguished scholar available no matter from what land he be taken. The Faculty of Union Theological Seminary stands in the front rank of those who expound the history, literature and institutions of Christianity, and in other parts of the University we have made a substantial beginning in the study and interpretation of the history, literature, and religions of China and of India. The new chair, therefore, may well prove to be a strong and helpful addition to this group of scholars and of studies, inviting us to strengthen and develop in the largest possible way our opportunities for advanced instruction and research in the whole field of religious history, literature and institutions.

Among those appointed to the committee were Richard Gottheil, professor of rabbinical literature and Semitic languages, James Shotwell, professor of history, Virginia Gildersleeve, dean of Barnard College, Herbert Schneider, then assistant professor of philosophy, Robert MacIver, professor of social science, Raymond Knox, chaplain of the university, and Henry Sloane Coffin, president of Union Theological Seminary. [11]

Most prospective members of the committee received Butler's announcement with enthusiasm. Raymond Knox saw the position as "a substantial and valued addition to the work already begun in providing instruction and research in the whole field of religion." Robert MacIver wrote of the appointment "to be made in furtherance of a study so important in itself and so crucial for the historical understanding of our civilization." A distinctly sour note came from Semitics professor Richard Gottheil in a letter from Paris:

I am very glad to learn that the arrangements have been made, making it possible to have the Chair established at Columbia about which you write. I can well imagine where the money comes from and have already taken the matter under serious consideration.

Of course, the Chair will be in the department of Oriental languages and litteratures {sic}.

I trust that the first meeting of the commitee {sic} will not be held until I return, as I—which is quite natural—know more about the subject than any other member of the committee. I have been teaching these subjects for 41 years. You will remember that, with your permission, I am not leaving here before October the 3rd in order to avoid any possible attack of hay-fever.[12]

The committee began its deliberations in the fall, and it seems that Gottheil did indeed have considerable influence at the outset. The initial selection of the committee, made at Gottheil's suggestion, was Michael Saul Ginsburg, a Russian-born scholar then living in France. Ginsburg, a specialist in the ancient period, had studied at Petrograd and later at the University of Paris. He had been recommended to Columbia by Rostovtzeff of Yale and Reinach of Paris, among others. Dean Woodbridge informed Butler that Ginsburg "appears to me the most promising of the men suggested," but then added somewhat curiously, "I wonder if you have any means of securing additional information about him?"[13]

Butler immediately informed Miller of the committee's choice, describing Ginsburg as a man coming from "a most excellent Russian Jewish family, who has a fine cultural background and who has already made himself a distinguished reputation as a scholar." Having provided a synopsis of Ginsburg's credentials and recommendations, he concluded:

The impression of our committee is that there is no other scholar of his standing and that he would be a great ornament to this new chair and to American scholarship in his chosen field. The suggestion would be to appoint him for a limited term of years, say, three, in order that he might have opportunity to display his qualities and personality to his American colleagues.

The suggestion of a trial period seemed to reveal that Butler and the committee were aware that they were on unsure ground in conducting this search. This may also be attested to in Butler's suggestion to Miller that she could read of the candidate's family in *The Jewish Encyclopedia*.[14]

Mrs. Miller responded right away in a hand-written letter that was transcribed and forwarded to Woodbridge for the committee's consideration. Her letter argued strongly against their selection. Her arguments must have impressed the committee sufficiently, for the Ginsburg nomination was soon dropped.

I am very much afraid that your committee is being misled. If this Mr. Ginsburg were anything like the eminent Jewish scholar he is represented to be surely something would be known about him or his writings by people familiar with the field. I have asked three men, two of whom are amongst the most distinguished and learned professors at the Jewish Theological Seminary, (without revealing the purpose of my inquiry) and all of them said they have never heard of the man. I can't see why a person so obscure in this field should be considered for this post when it is known that, even in this country, there are several eminent Jewish scholars, any one of whom, I am sure, would be very glad to receive this call.[15]

Butler was concerned enough to send Miller's letter onto the committee and to request "a careful memorandum, supported by the testimony of the scholars which you have before you, as to the competence of this particular man? I fear the good lady is being advised by some one who is himself hopeful of getting the post." Butler was obviously referring to Enelow as the source of Miller's objections, but it would seem that Miller herself deserved some credit for her basically intelligent inquiries.[16]

Butler answered Miller the following week, this time describing Ginsburg as "a young scholar of fine training and the greatest promise." Butler elaborated on the candidate's accomplishments and the appropriate recommendations, and then provided a list of the other names considered by the committee: Joseph Hertz, chief rabbi of England; Herbert Danby, bishop of Jerusalem; Rabbi Bernard Drachmann and Rabbi H. G. Enelow, both of New York; Louis Ginzberg, professor at the Jewish Theological Seminary; and Julian Obermann, professor at the Jewish Institute of Religion.[17]

Miller responded with considerable disappointment.[18]

My impression is that of a promising young man who is just beginning his career. I certainly hope that, as such, he will be given a chance somewhere to prove his mettle, but I can see no reason whatever why he should be appointed to a chair, the endowment of which at your suggestion provided the means for the selection of the most eminent scholar in the field. You may recall that at your request I added fifty thousand dollars to my original offer for the Endowment so as to enable Columbia to secure the service of the most prominent scholar available. Certainly, this can not be said of the young candidate tho {sic} he may have published, or be about to publish, several papers on Jewish subjects. I think such a selection would mean not only a disappointment to me but would react unfavorably upon the future of the chair.

This was followed by a detailed discussion of most of the names disclosed by Butler. Miller expressed surprise that Hertz and Drachman should be brought up in an academic context. Miller wrote highly of Louis Ginzberg, but was concerned over his opposition to liberal Judaism, "and I, for one, would rather see a man appointed whose sympathies would embrace all types of Judaism." She then recommended Jacob Mann of the Hebrew Union College: "Professor Mann is as eminent a Jewish scholar as there is in the field and he is sure to be fair to all types of Jewish thought." She dismissed Obermann as unsuitable because his work was in "Semitic languages or Comparative Religion rather than in Jewish History and Literature."

Considering the extent of her judgmental comments in this letter, which indeed does seem to have been informed by outside advice, Miller found it appropriate to conclude with the assurance that "I should like to add that I earnestly hope that in making this appointment only the actual merit and achievement of the man will count, and no other consideration." However, it should again be observed that Miller's arguments raised viable questions about some of the names that had been considered by the committee. Of course, the academic authorities would presumably not be concerned about whether or not Louis Ginzberg was opposed to Liberal Judaism, but Miller correctly observed that they were at times finding it difficult to distinguish between rabbinical practitioners and university scholars.

Butler defended the appointment of a younger scholar,[19] but despite his rebuttal the nomination of Michael Ginsburg was dead. Moreover, the search committee now seemed to be at a loss as to how it should proceed.

The Columbia files leave considerable room for questions about this first phase of the search. For some time I was unable to identify this candidate. But then, somewhat by coincidence, the Baron papers at Stanford shed considerable light on this whole incident. In early October 1928, George Kohut sent a lengthy letter to Stephen Wise discussing the possibility of engaging for JIR a young, poor scholar of the ancient period named Michael Ginsburg. From other documents, I was able to ascertain that Ginsburg—then living in France—was the son of the better-known historian of Eastern European Jewry, Saul Ginsburg. Although the son was destitute, he was responsible for supporting himself and his parents. Michael Ginsburg was determined to migrate to America; he had been in contact with Cyrus Adler and Louis Marshall, but nothing seemed to come of those attempts.[20]

Kohut was impressed with Ginsburg's potential, although concerned that he did not know Hebrew very well. Significant for the development of our own story, Kohut suggested to Ginsburg that he contact Richard Gottheil so that Gottheil could decide on a recommendation. Returning to what we know from the Columbia files, Gottheil must have in very short order recommended the somewhat unknown Ginsburg for the Miller chair, presumably seeking to guarantee his continued influence on the chair's direction. Somewhat remarkably, the search committee acquiesced—a rather clear indication of its own confusion. Almost three months after the

Ginsburg nomination was dropped, Woodbridge suggested to Butler on behalf of the committee that the endowment be used to bring visiting lecturers to Columbia.[21]

Simultaneous with Gottheil's efforts on behalf of Michael Ginsburg, a group led by Kohut and Wise sought to organize support for one of the best-known scholars of the day, Louis Ginzberg, professor of Talmud at the Jewish Theological Seminary. Kohut wrote to Ginzberg, who was spending a sabbatical year in Jerusalem, to convince him of the importance of the affair.

There can be no question as to any other candidate. You are easily the outstanding Jewish scholar of the present day, and it would be unthinkable that any other incumbent should be considered.

It is no longer a question of loyalties. The matter has assumed a much larger and wider aspect. Indeed, it becomes not only a civic but a national duty to accept so important a call.[22]

The support behind Louis Ginzberg's candidacy soon found a sympathetic ear when the committee decided on a visiting appointment.

The search committee's new proposal, submitted in late February 1929, revealed some of the continued difficulties involved in the search.[23] Indeed, Woodbridge opened his letter by referring to "the problem raised by the recent endowment." He continued: "The Committee have {sic} made an effort to secure information with regard to the most prominent scholars in the field, both here and abroad, but have been unable to decide with the desired confidence upon anyone to appoint at the present time to a permanent position." They proposed that distinguished scholars be invited as visitors at Columbia, and that part of the income from the fund be used to support the research of younger people.

The committee preferred scholars already located in America, but had also found that the best of these "are among those who have already had considerable foreign experience." They recommended Louis Ginzberg as the most distinguished possibility. Perhaps anticipating potential objections from the donor, Woodbridge added, "The Committee make {sic} no alternative suggestion at this time because there appears to be no equal in America to Professor Ginzberg in this field. Indeed, he seems to enjoy here the reputation of being one of the greatest living Jewish scholars." Butler wrote to Woodbridge that he would "present this matter to the benefactress in question before taking it to the trustees so that, if possible, we may have her concurrence and approval."[24]

Once again Miller responded with criticism of the committee's plans, and again, her critique served a constructive role. There seems no doubt that the search committee was by that time somewhat exhausted and certainly confused by the task it had undertaken. Woodbridge had said as much in his proposal for turning the position at least temporarily into a rotating, visiting appointment. But Miller had given a considerable amount of money to fulfill a clear vision of how the chair should function.

It seems very far removed from the purpose I had in mind when I endowed the Chair. It was my aim to enable the University to appoint a permanent professor who would maintain an interest from year to year and who would try to reach the student-body along spiritual lines. What your Committee proposes, it seems to me, is to engage a visiting lecturer and to appoint fellows, which is an entirely different project. The latter may be quite commendable but it was not what I contemplated. Surely it does not seem to be what you had in mind, either, when you first wrote to me about your plan to secure the most eminent scholar available for this Chair.[25]

She referred again to the possibility of appointing Jacob Mann of Hebrew Union College. She would have no objections to the appointment of Ginzberg to a permanent position "except that I personally should prefer a scholar belonging to the liberal school, such as Dr. Mann, as I think he would be more likely to do justice to the various aspects of Jewish life."

Again, it is clear that the academic authorities at Columbia were quite sensitive to Miller's criticisms, and a letter from Woodbridge to Butler revealed more of the difficulties facing the committee, and perhaps, especially Woodbridge himself as chairperson.

I think you can make it clear to her that the Committee has worked in the best interests of the endowment which she has created. It is undoubtedly the most considerable endowment for the purpose in any American university. It gives us the opportunity to go far in establishing here a center for Jewish studies of the highest character. If we are to succeed and make the endowment yield the results which she has at heart and which are so important, we must move slowly and with caution. We find among those interested in the work such a difference of opinion regarding emphases that there is great danger that any permanent appointment made at this time would not be regarded with general favor. There are a number of distinguished scholars in the field representing different points of view of whose scholarship we might avail ourselves without any commitment regarding their particular bias. The plan proposed by the Committee, therefore, seems to offer the maximum of scholarly interest without emphasizing sectarian bias. The Committee recommended Dr. Ginzberg because it was confident that his appointment would be immediately recognized by all Jewish scholars as an appointment of great distinction and because it believed that a temporary appointment in his case would indicate that the University was not committed to an orthodox as over against a liberal position. His appointment could be followed by another representing a different point of view.[26]

Woodbridge was hoping to benefit from the experience that would be gained by a series of visiting appointments, "both of the men involved and of the progress of the work." The committee had concluded that the field of Jewish studies was in need of encouraging younger men and that was the reason for recommending that the endowment provide fellowships. "The time seems particularly opportune for this because among the younger men there are several who are approaching the whole matter with a distinctly scholarly and university spirit."

Woodbridge promised to have the committee examine the possibility of Jacob Mann and concluded his letter to Butler with the interesting observation that it was precisely because a permanent appointment of Ginzberg "might appear to prejudice the interests of the liberal school" that the committee had not recommended a permanent appointment.

Meanwhile, Butler answered Miller's critique of the plan to invite visiting faculty.[27] In explaining the need to move slowly on this matter, Butler observed:

Our advisers have developed such differences of opinion that the reconciliation of these is a matter of some difficulty as well as of large importance. We are of opinion that a permanent appointment made at this time might not be regarded with general favor, since there are a number of distinguished scholars in this field who represent different points of view and a number of whom might be found useful in connection with the work of the chair at one time or another. Our advisers desire to try out various modes of approach to the subject and thus by experience come to a result which will be widely if not universally accepted as sound.

A few weeks later, Woodbridge again explained: "Our great difficulty in the whole matter has been that of finding a man who will look at the development of the subject as a university enterprise as distinct from a sectarian one."[28] Butler decided to proceed with a visiting appointment for two years, setting the salary at $7500, considerably below the $9,000 to 10,000 mentioned earlier in his letters to Miller.[29]

Whatever the background to Butler's instructions, a lapse in the files leaves us unaware of why the appointment of Ginzberg as a visiting professor did not proceed. But on 1 June 1929, Woodbridge wrote to Butler, "I could tell you a long story about this but will come to the situation as it now exists. The Committee is now quite convinced, in spite of their former report, that we should ascertain whether Professor Elbogen . . . would be available for a permanent appointment."[30] Ismar Elbogen was currently professor at the Reform Hochschule für die Wissenschaft des Judenthums in Berlin. Woodbridge explained that he thought this appointment "would be more agreeable to the donor than the appointment of anyone here with the exception of Rabbi Enelow whom the Committee does not feel justified in recommending." He then added, somewhat cryptically, that "furthermore, I think that the appointment of Professor Elbogen would free us from other local difficulties." Both Woodbridge and Butler had previously hinted at conflicts within the search committee. It seems possible that Richard Gottheil, who had raised certain assumptions at the very outset of the search and whose first candidate had been vetoed by the donor, may have been involved in some of those problems.

Concerning appointments both in Chinese studies and in Jewish history, Woodbridge indicated that he wished to make a higher offer in order to attract his current candidates. Butler, however, insisted that the lower offers stand.[31] Concerning the suggestion of Elbogen for the Miller chair, he wrote that "if the donor is agreeable, that would be a good solution of the problem."

The negotiations with Elbogen were conducted from June to November 1929.[32] In July, Irwin Edman met with Elbogen in Berlin and reported him to be apparently quite interested in the Columbia position, but hesitant primarily because of pension considerations related to the move from Germany to America. Elbogen was fifty-five years old and concerned about the support of his wife and two teenage children in the event of his death or incapacity. He was also reluctant to give up his current level of income and the respect of Berlin's Jewish and general intellectual communities. Edman recommended that the proposed salary be increased to $10,000 and requested precise information concerning the pension situation.

He then commented in German, "Ich habe mich mit dieser Sache schon zwei Wochen den Kopf zerbrochen und ich wünsche dass sie schon erledid sei." ("I have racked by brains over this matter for two weeks already, and I would like it to be finally settled.") The two were scheduled to meet in late August, by which time Elbogen was to reach his decision. But Edman made little of the fact that Elbogen had requested an official letter "to show the faculty of the Hochschule."

The position was officially offered to Elbogen in a letter from Butler of 20 July.[33] The salary remained at $7,500 with an additional $2,500 for travel expenses. Somehow Butler hoped that Elbogen would still arrive for the current academic year and promised to commence the salary retroactively as of 1 July. A month later, Elbogen expressed his interest in the position, indicating that he would be unable to leave Berlin before August 1930 and requesting a salary of $10,000. He wondered whether teaching assignments would include graduate work and, probably thinking of German models, whether this professorship would form a department of its own.

Butler responded in mid-September after conferring with Woodbridge and Edman, who had since returned to New York. "In our opinion, the chair of Jewish History and Institutions at Columbia University may easily become, and should become, the chief instrument on this side of the Atlantic for the promotion of the subject matter with which it deals." Butler explained that, by his understanding, most, if not all, of the instruction would be at the graduate level. On the question of salary, he wrote that "in view of your distinction and relative age," the salary would be raised to $10,000. Information about pensions would be sent separately; and

Butler added, "I can only say that it is the well-established tradition of Columbia University to permit none of its distinguished servants to suffer if old age or disability should overtake them."[34]

If Butler and Woodbridge thought they had finally settled the matter of the chair in Jewish history, they were quickly unsettled by a brief telegram stating simply "Awfully Sorry Cannot Accept Letter Follows. Elbogen." It required some clarification to ascertain that the telegram had been sent prior to Elbogen's receipt of Butler's letter of 12 September. Nevertheless, even after receiving the letter, Elbogen wrote on 28 September to explain his refusal of the position. He expressed his appreciation of the offer, but continued:

But I must regretfully tell you that my decision expressed in my cable of September 19, can not now be reversed. It is a question of loyalty to the Hochschule in which I have been teaching during the last twenty seven years. My students have implored me to remain, the trustees have urged me and placed the responsibility of the continuance of the college upon my shoulders. You will understand, my dear President Butler, that I was unable to resist these pleas and the unanimous solicitations of my pupils, colleagues, collaborators and friends.[35]

Butler fell back on the plan to bring visiting faculty. He offered such an arrangement to Elbogen in an "urgent invitation" to come as a visiting professor for the spring session of 1930 and to remain for half or all of the next year. Elbogen turned down the offer in two telegrams, dated 28 October and 13 November. A letter of regret from Frank Fackenthal on 15 November closed the negotiations.

During the fall of 1929, the relationship between Columbia and Miller entered a new stage of difficulties. In fact, Butler's almost desperate attempts to hold onto the Elbogen appointment should probably be understood in light of the growing impatience of the donor. On 30 September, Butler wrote to Miller of the contacts with Elbogen.[36] His letter was less than forthright in several respects. The phrase that Elbogen "was the best possible man for the post" by this time must have sounded a little thin. But most questionably, Butler forgot to mention that Elbogen had already declined the invitation in his telegram received in New York on 19 September. Of course, Butler still held out some hope that Elbogen could be convinced to accept the position, but he was obviously unwilling to reveal that six more months of efforts had ended in failure.[37]

Miller's reply indicated that she had read about the negotiations with Elbogen "in the papers."[38] Because of Elbogen's affiliation with Reform Judaism, one might have expected her to be considerably satisfied with these efforts; but still, her response was restrained. She had heard only the highest praise of Elbogen's scholarship, so that "there can be no cause to complain in that regard. However, I cannot help regretting that the Committee seemed to find it impossible to find an American, who, I think, might have reached the student body in a spiritual way in addition to the pursuits of scholarly research."

During the coming weeks, Butler pressed Woodbridge to continue the search. A year and a half had now passed since the endowment had been placed. Obviously disappointed with Columbia's inability to make the desired appointment and with the fact that the endowed program was not yet functioning, Miller turned to her financial advisors at the Equitable Trust Company of New York. On 13 December 1929, they wrote to Butler on her behalf, recalling that they had been responsible for the transfer of funds. The letter continued:

We were greatly surprised to learn from Mrs. Miller that the Chair has not yet been established, and we know that she is both disappointed and grieved. On her behalf we are writing to ask what you propose to do in the matter. If you cannot fill the Chair, then we think it only proper that you should return the monies paid to you.[39]

Fortunately, Butler could report that despite the delays caused by "a distinguished professor in Berlin," the committee had now offered the position to an appropriate candidate whose "favorable answer is confidently expected in the very near future." This time Butler was accurate. In fact, the date on Butler's letter to the bank may have been changed to allow the official offer to Salo Baron to be mailed first.[40]

Following the breakdown of the Elbogen negotiations, the search committee undertook a renewed and intense wave of activity and consultations, which resulted in Salo Baron's nomination. These steps were outlined in a report sent to Butler on 12 December. Schneider and Edman were responsible for most of the contacts, which included Cyrus Adler, head of several major Jewish institutions; Harry Wolfson; and G. F. Moore of Harvard. As a result of these consultations, the committee concluded that Baron and Louis Finkelstein, professor of theology at the Jewish Theological Seminary, were the leading nominees.[41]

The preliminary report by Schneider and Edman described Baron as follows:

Dr. Salo Baron, Professor of History at the Jewish Institute of Religion. Age 45 {sic}.[42] He is recognized by almost all our informants as the leading Jewish historian in this country. Students report him to be an excellent teacher. His work has been primarily in the economic and social history of the Jews, but he has a thorough training in Rabbinic literature (Vienna) and a special interest in conducting researches in the field of the interaction between Persian and Hebrew cultures. Especially recommended by Wolfson, Marcus, Elbogen, Rabbi Wise.

An instructive contrast is provided by their report on Finkelstein, who also came highly recommended:

Louis I. Finkelstein, Professor of Theology at the Jewish Seminary. Age 35–40. Though a comparatively young man, he is said to be the most promising of the scholars at the Seminary. He has made contributions to the history of Jewish self-government in the Middle Ages and to a new interpretation of the conflict between Sadducees and Pharisees. His training has been in American institutions. Especially recommended by Cyrus Adler, Wolfson, G. F. Moore.

Woodbridge explained in his cover letter that "Dr. Baron was selected in preference to Dr. Finkelstein because of his foreign training."

It is curious that none of the names mentioned in this report—the others were David Blondheim of Johns Hopkins University and Isaak Husik of the University of Pennsylvania—had appeared in any of the committee's previous communications. But whereas it is impossible to know why these scholars seemed to come to the committee's attention only at this point, we can make several inferences from their deliberations as the final decision was made.

First, the committee considered only candidates already located in America. Obviously it could no longer afford the time or the potential disappointment involved in trying to relocate a scholar from Europe. Perhaps, Miller's recurring preference for an American scholar also played a role. Nevertheless, the committee explicitly considered European training to be an advantage, a preference stated several times in their reports. When, it came to the question of the research fellowships to be provided by the endowment, all three of the younger men nominated were trained in America. This would seem to reflect the desire to encourage and train a new generation of American scholars in the field of Jewish studies.

There is another striking contrast between the assessments of Baron and Finkelstein, a contrast that underscores the significant change in Jewish studies represented by the Baron appointment. Finkelstein was presented as a professor of theology who had worked primarily in the area of rabbinics. No other comments of explanation were necessary. Concerning Baron, the report indicated his primary interest in the economic and social history of the Jews and then continued "but he has a thorough training in Rabbinic literature."

Despite the fact from the outset the chair had been designated for the study of Jewish history, literature, and institutions, most of the scholars considered by the committee had been scholars of rabbinic literature. Louis Ginzberg and Ismar

Elbogen are leading examples. Even on this last list, Blondheim was a philologist and Husik a historian of medieval philosophy. None of these men could have been placed in a history department, and, in fact, both Ginzberg and Elbogen were intended to be affiliated with religion and philosophy. That Baron, who was described in the report as undoubtedly "the leading Jewish historian in this country" was considered by the committee only late in the search process must have resulted in part from a reluctance to consider a historian for the position.[43]

Butler wrote to Woodbridge the next day, thanking him and the committee for their efforts: "I feel confident that you have found the best possible solution under all the perplexing and somewhat difficult circumstances."[44] The position was offered to Baron in a letter of 14 December with the salary set at $7,500.[45] Baron and Butler met a few days later and a letter from Butler summarized their agreement. As a result of their discussions, Baron was granted permission to assist the Jewish Institute of Religion on a visiting basis for a year or two to help them overcome his departure.

In the meantime, Butler had written to Miller on 16 December to bring her up to date on the developments.[46] Butler's response to the bank was also dated that day. Butler formally notified her of Elbogen's negative reply and proceeded to discuss the Baron appointment. Based on the previous contacts between Baron and the committee, Butler stated, "We have tendered him an invitation to accept appointment to the new professorship, and confidently await his acceptance."

Miller initially responded with pleasure at the appointment. Based presumably on the Elbogen experience, she requested that no publicity be given to the invitation until Baron actually accepted.[47] But a few days later she was deeply distressed. And again, Columbia's oversights had compounded the problem.

> Dear President Butler,
>
> I spent part of last evening reading Professor Baron's article in the November Menorah and spent a sleepless night thereafter.
>
> I do hope he will pay some deference to my wishes on the subject of the so-called ethnic Jew. This is the doctrine which, of all in the world, I believe most dangerous to Judaism as a spiritual force in the world.
>
> Of course, Zionism is dead, but the doctrine of the ethnic Jew goes on to express itself in further dangerous forms.
>
> I noted from the Who's Who in Menorah that the gentleman is not forty-five years old but thirty-four. I am wondering by whom you were so badly misinformed, however!
>
> I do wish I could learn not to care about the Chair. Since that has seemed impossible I can but hope it will not stand for such doctrine.
>
> With regrets for the unavoidable necessity of further attention to this matter from you, I am
>
> > Cordially yours,
> > Linda R. Miller[48]

Again, it would be easy to conclude that Miller was merely a pest by her interference in the academic process, but she had indeed indicated from the outset that she was totally opposed to Jewish nationalist efforts and obviously did not want such ideas propagated from a chair bearing her husband's name. Columbia's careless mistake regarding Baron's age, which was repeated in memo after memo even while giving his correct birthdate of 1895, only aggravated her anger and fueled her doubts; recall the original concerns with the issue of the experience of the chair's incumbent. In short, there is little point in judging Miller's constant criticism, but there is some point in learning about the various pressures involved in effecting the decisions at hand.

Of course, Miller was not wrong in her understanding that Baron's position was influenced by nationalist thinking. But Butler sought to set her mind at ease:

You may depend upon Columbia University to set an example of the highest and broadest minded scholarship in dealing with every question which it undertakes to illuminate. I have been assured by men whose judgment I firmly trust that Dr. Baron is without any partisanship in reference to the matters which he will have to undertake to present. Judge Mack of the United States Circuit Court of Appeals has just written me a most unqualified letter of approval of Dr. Baron, and my own talk with him was satisfactory in high degree.[49]

Understandably, Butler didn't mention the age question. However, if Miller was appeased on the questions she had raised, Butler set off a new area of concern by enclosing to Miller a copy of Mack's letter, indicating that Baron would be allowed to continue his relation with JIR.[50]

In a telegram sent on Christmas Day 1929, she protested

Baron's continued affiliation with JIR "while occupying the Miller Chair. If so I most strongly protest. Can I have your prompt reassurance in this regard." In a subsequent letter, Miller further explained her position to Butler: "My sole concern was to know that the Chair would remain an independent source of instruction and that its Professor, once he had severed his connection elsewhere, would no longer be considered as not having done so {sic}."[51]

Again Butler was placed in the position of explaining at some length Columbia's policies. It is interesting to note that Butler did not see any reason for special concern over Baron's continued connections with a theological seminary. Of course, Columbia already had its own seminary. Butler explained that after the transitionary period Baron "will have precisely the same freedom, no more and no less, that every other professor in Columbia University has in regard to literary work, to occasional lectures, or to cooperation with other scholars and scholarly bodies." Butler continued that in fact, Columbia had close relationships with more than a score of other institutions in order to advance "the general interests of learning in New York and in the nation."[52]

Joining the History Department

Over the next several months following announcement of Baron's appointment, letters of congratulations poured in from scholars, family, and friends in America and back in Europe. Several of the notes of congratulation are of special interest, including those from among the candidates at various stages of the search. Ismar Elbogen was among those with whom Baron had discussed the position the previous summer. Now Elbogen wrote: "In my opinion, it is far more appropriate that a young and fresh scholar as you, who already lives in the country and has the confidence of the academic youth, should occupy the new Chair, than a man of my age." In fact, Elbogen went on to talk about his poor health.[53]

Louis Finkelstein, who was also seriously considered in the last stages of the search, wrote as well:

Every friend of Jewish learning must be rejoiced that the position is to be filled by a man of your extraordinary capabilities and achievements. I am sure that under you the department will be of great value to Judaism and to the Jews, as well as an inspiration to the students. My gratification on your appointment, I hope you will do me the justice to believe, is not in any way tempered by the fact that I had heard from different people that I too was being considered by the Committee. I do not think that I really was. And in any event there was so much danger that the appointment might go to someone unworthy of it, that I felt very happy when I heard that it had come to you.[54]

With the conclusion of the search, some of those active in Jewish studies and its advancement in America took the opportunity to celebrate what was widely perceived as a major stride forward both in the pursuit of the discipline and in its status in academic life. Finkelstein's letter to Baron and Kohut's letter to Ginzberg a year before indicate some of the seriousness with which the Miller chair was viewed. When the appointment was confirmed, Baron's friends at JIR expressed jubilant gratification that one of their own had been chosen. Wise expressed his pleasure and acknowledged Baron's contributions to the institute.[55] Kohut was the closest of these friends.

It goes without saying that we are all very, very proud of you and especially so since thus far your head has remained strangely normal in size. Good fortune spoils many people, but I am persuaded that you are far too sensible and level-headed to become either arrogant or exclusive, and that all your friends who have come to love and cherish you will always feel a sense of close fellowship with you.[56]

Kohut also took the initiative to plan a dinner party in honor of the occasion at his home. Among the guests were Wise, Judge Mack, Dean Woodbridge, and Schneider and Edman, as well as a small group from JIR and JTS. Notes of regret were sent by Butler, Carlton Hayes, and Harry Wolfson. Kohut commented in a note sent the following day: "It was a great compliment to you to be able to get together at such short notice such an array of distinguished gentlemen, and I am sure they appreciated to be asked to do you honor." The careful planning of the guest list indicates that the arrival of Jewish history at the great American university was an underlying theme to the celebration.[57]

A similar theme was struck in a more public pronouncement when leading Reform Rabbi Solomon Freehof wrote an editorial in *The American Israelite:*

The Littauer and Miller Chairs are somewhat different in purpose from the general gifts by Jews to the universities. They have a specific intent. Jewish culture should be recognized as part of world culture. . . . A proper appreciation of the Jewish element in western thought must be attained by anyone claiming to understand the growth of the mind. Any university which is Humanistic enough to be more than merely a professional training school should have a Chair of Jewish Studies.[58]

As Baron responded to the various letters of congratulations, he repeatedly emphasized how his appointment was "particularly gratifying to me, because I personally did nothing in order to obtain the nomination."[59] Indeed, during the summer of 1929, he indicated to several friends and confidants in Europe that he was not particularly interested in the post.[60] Still, Baron's account of his own passive role in the search was not accurate—he certainly had taken steps to advance his candidacy for the Columbia position. In January 1929, Baron went to meet Herbert Schneider of Columbia's philosophy department and a member of the search committee and subsequently sent him copies of a number of his articles.[61]

Any of us may at times consciously or otherwise alter the course of events in our own memories or in the way we recount them to others—historians are humans and of course no exception. Baron too had a flare for the dramatic and the occasional exaggeration, and in this study, we encounter several examples in which the account of events as codified by Baron in oral and written testimonies does not fit the record from other evidence. This particular case in point has no wide-reaching consequences for our story except to indicate that Baron did occasionally misrepresent how developments occurred even right after they had taken place. We turn now to a far more interesting and significant case of such reformulation.

With the appointment in place, there now arose the question of departmental affiliation. Baron repeatedly indicated in interviews and oral testimonies that Butler was in favor of Baron joining the history department and that he also preferred such an affiliation, but that because of resistance from the history department itself Butler was required to insist on their agreement. Baron's account is reflected in Eli Ginzberg's statement that "it took a lot of arm-twisting by the president to get the History department to accept Baron as a member, just as he had to force the English Department to promote Lionel Trilling." The material I have found confirms Butler's attitude on the matter, but not that of the history department or, for that matter, of Baron. Indeed, it would seem that Baron's later version of the story was almost an exact adaptation of the Trilling account.[62]

A few days after the appointment had been finalized, Frank Fackenthal, secretary of the university, wrote to Baron that Butler suggested that Baron's courses be listed with the Department of History. Baron seemed both confused and hesitant, as he had planned to list his courses with both religion and Semitic languages.[63] Fackenthal concluded that Baron did not favor an affiliation with the history department. A few days later, Fackenthal wrote to Howard McBain, who had been serving since 1 July as dean of the faculties of political science, philosophy and pure science: "The President wants us, you and me, to discuss the departmental affiliations of the Miller Chair. The President's preference is for History. I think the account would like to be independent but that is hardly practical."[64] Following a meeting on the question that involved Carlton Hayes of the history department, Schneider of philosophy, Baron, and McBain, McBain wrote to Fackenthal and seems to have presented Baron's position in describing how the proposed courses would cross departmental lines between history, religion, and Semitics. "It would perhaps be best for the present to let this Chair remain in an anomalous and semi-independent status. In another year or two we would know more about where his students are drawn from and this would indicate the logical departmental affiliation."[65]

Butler, however, repeated his position in a memo sent to Fackenthal:

I do not think it wise to let the new Jewish Chair remain anomalous and unidentified. If we do, it will grow quickly into a separate department, which is much to be deprecated. My preference is to frankly put it into History as a matter of classification, and, of course, to announce the appropriate courses also under Semitics and under Religion.[66]

McBain then asked Hayes about the position of the history department. "I gathered from Dr. Baron himself that he was rather disinclined to have his work categorized under History." Hayes in turn immediately wrote to Baron:

Before I present the matter to my colleagues in the Department of History, I hope that you will express quite frankly your own preference. . . . I feel certain that if you wish to join the Department of History my colleagues will welcome you most cordially, but we certainly do not wish to insist on your joining us, if you believe that your joining the Department of Semitic Languages would be preferable for your future work at Columbia.[67]

In his response, Baron indicated that he had originally understood from Butler that a new department was to be created, but that objections arose about having a one-man department.[68] Butler had indeed written in his letter of appointment of the hope "to build up the strongest possible University department in this field of advanced instruction and research." Baron continued:

I hope that you will believe me that I am not guided in these considerations by any petty ambitions. On the contrary, I regard it as a higher distinction to teach within a great department, in close cooperation with a number of distinguished scholars, than to head a small department somewhat in a corner of the University life. As far as my personal predilections go, I should feel happy to be affiliated with the department of history where I do my own chief research work. However, I may be succeeded by a man who is chiefly interested in Jewish Philosophy, Biblical Literature or in Hebrew Philology.

Baron recommended a postponement of the decision for a year or two.

Hayes consulted with Butler once again and reiterated in his response that Butler was adamantly opposed to the creation of any small departments, but explained that he personally "would be most reluctant to urge you in any way whatsoever to become a member of the Department of History." The problem raised by Baron concerning his successor—in any case a strange objection to be raised by a thirty-five-year-old newly appointed incumbent—was easily answered that each case would be judged in its own right. Hayes assured Baron that the department "exercises no restraint upon the courses offered by its members" and explained that the university's policy was intended for administrative convenience. He added that a subsequent change in affiliation could be brought about in the coming years if experience so indicated.[69]

Baron's preferences toward independence may have resulted from a classic European conception of the autonomous senior professor. There also seems to have been a real question as to which department was most appropriate regarding subject matter and which students would enroll in Baron's courses. Perhaps, Baron's insistence that he not be pinned down to a single disciplinary approach also played a role.

But it still remains a puzzle why, if a departmental affiliation was necessary, Baron was not adamant about an appointment to the history department and, in fact, seemed rather cool toward the idea, apparently favoring that it be with either religion or Semitics. Baron's academic background in history, law, and political science pointed to neither of these other directions. Neither did his later image as the champion of writing the social and economic history of the Jews. Perhaps in the meetings that took place, Baron sensed some hesitancy by the history department and reacted accordingly. But, even if this was the case, it certainly did not require the kind of high-pressure tactics by Butler that Baron described. Butler's pressures were applied to Baron, not to the history department.

There is abundant room for speculation on the personal dimensions involved. Carlton Hayes was later known for the lack of assistance he provided to Jewish refugees during the Nazi era when he was American ambassador to Spain. In his historical writings as well, Hayes was hostile in remarks on the Jews. Yet I should add that Baron spoke of Hayes only in the most cordial terms and described him as a good friend. Both Edman and Schneider of the philosophy department had played significant roles in the search, and it is certainly possible that Baron found them to be supportive and committed to development of the program. But the opposite would be said about Gottheil's role in Baron's appointment, yet Baron seemed to prefer Semitics over history as well. In sum, the best explanation would seem to be that Baron preferred an independent status and mentioned the other departments to demonstrate the problem most clearly.

Still, Baron quickly understood the uniqueness and opportunity that had been paved. This is best demonstrated by a rather remarkable letter written by Baron to the academic secretary Frank Fackenthal in late December, which under the advice of Herbert Schneider, was never sent. In it, he wrote in defense of being placed in a separate department: "After all Judaism is primarily a religion and culture. The political, economic and social history of the Jews, although doubtlessly of supreme importance, is only one part, and perhaps not even the most essential in the subjects included under the heading of Jewish History, Literature, and Institutions."[70]

The primary position of religion and culture over the various contours of social history grates hard against the portrait of Baron's historiographic emphases. We shall meet these tensions in later discussions as well—both historiographic and biographical. But Baron adjusted his outlook quickly and soon after the decision for a history affiliation had been cast, he wrote to Frank Gavin of New York's Central Theological Seminary: "The novelty of the experiment is externally emphasized by the fact that my Chair constitutes a part of the Faculty of Political Science so that the purely historical part of Jewish culture outside of pure philology will come more to its rights." Over the years, Baron increasingly became the model and spokesperson for placing the study of Jewish history within its disciplinary context. And yet, the tension we have described here between the cultural and social aspects of Jewish life reach to the very heart of the polarity that defined for Baron the parameters of Jewish existence. These poles play a prominent role in the two major monographs Baron wrote during the course of the next decade.[71]

CHAPTER 3

A SOCIAL AND RELIGIOUS HISTORY

Precursors

RIGHTLY OR NOT, Baron is most frequently identified with his multivolume *Social and Religious History of the Jews,* originally published in a three-volume edition in 1937 and subsequently revised, reaching the end of the medieval period in eighteen volumes. The central importance of this work in Baron's career requires that attention be given to the development of the very genre to which it belongs and to those historians who preceded Baron in such an undertaking.

The modern-day enterprise of writing a comprehensive history of the Jews began in the early eighteenth century with the publication of Jacques Basnage's five-volume work covering the period from Jesus to his own day. Basnage was a member of the group of French-Protestant exiles who had moved to Holland after the Edict of Nantes was revoked.

Ideas of religious toleration began to emerge within these circles of French expatriots, and for some, these ideas applied to the Jews as well. Basnage's work has generally been evaluated as important primarily because as a popular work in its time, it contributed to greater understanding and toleration of the Jews within the enlightened circles of Europe.[1] Ben Zion Dinur also expressed his historiographic appreciation of Basnage's writing: "His books are important as the first comprehensive and truly erudite history of the Jews in the Christian era, filling a gap between early Jewish historical writings and modern Jewish historical research."[2] Baron wrote in a similar vein, describing Basnage as "the Frenchman, whose synthesizing endeavor represents a real milestone in Jewish historical literature and whose very shortcomings acted as an incentive towards improvement and progress."[3]

For well over a century, Basnage's history served as the leading source of information for Christians on Jews and Judaism. A little-known one-volume work published in 1820 by Solomon Löwisohn of Vienna was the first such history written by a Jew, but that same year also saw the publication of the first volumes of Isaac Jost's multivolume *History of the Israelites*.

Jost's *History*, which covered the period from the ancient Hasmonean dynasty through 1815, appeared in nine volumes between the years 1820 and 1828.[4] Thirty years later, Jost published an additional three-volume set covering the most recent developments; it was counted as the tenth volume of his history.[5] Although Jost's work preceded that of Graetz by thirty years, his work has been of only limited interest and he is only reluctantly accredited as the father of modern critical

Jewish historiography. In fact, Baron was the primary force behind reviving Jost's place in the development of Jewish historical writing.[6]

Although he had a stronger basis in university studies than Graetz, Jost was not as conversant with Jewish sources as either Graetz or his childhood friend Leopold Zunz. Consequently, Jost was often criticized for misreading his sources. Even more important, he has been portrayed as the most dispassionate of nineteenth-century Jewish studies scholars, although not all writers have assessed that characteristic negatively. Twentieth-century critics have agreed that Jost lacked a system to organize and present his material.

His contemporaries already raised the question of whether such an ambitious project as a total history should be undertaken when critical research into Jewish culture and history was just beginning. Johann Eichhorn, a leading biblical scholar and Jost's former teacher at Göttingen, came to his defense:

How long has the scholarly world waited in vain for these preliminary studies! Why should we not try the reverse! To arouse enthusiasm for such monographs by an overview of the scattered sources, as far as one diligent scholar can bring them together, even though from the viewpoint of method they should first be worked over piecemeal by individual scholars.[7]

This classic scholarly tension between monographs and sweeping history was also reflected in the strained relationship between Jost and Zunz. Given that Jost's first nine volumes are rarely cited or even consulted today, Jost's primary legacy is to be found in the very writing of such a comprehensive work.[8]

A surprisingly sympathetic rendering of Jost's significance can be found in the assessment by the nationalist Jewish historian Ben Zion Dinur. According to Dinur, the lack of organic unity in Jost's writing derived from Jost's denial "of the one living and unifying factor—the nation." Yet, whereas Jost represented the epitome of the Jew in pursuit of emancipation at the price of national consciousness, Dinur maintained that historiographically, Jost accomplished far more and had greater influence than is usually thought.[9] But Jost denied more than just the national element in his history. Baron argued that Jost never found a substitute for the kind of theological or teleological structure he was rejecting. Both Baron and Dinur, however, appreciated Jost's enlightened secularist style.

What drove Jost, Graetz, and others in the nineteenth century to write comprehensive histories of the Jews was a combination of inner and external forces that required the full breadth of Jewish history to demonstrate that certain interpretations— whether theological or even rationalist, whether Christian or Jewish—lacked the validity of scientific inquiry. Jost was encouraged to write his history by friends closely identified with the now aged Haskalah movement in Berlin. For decades, the Haskalah had sought to harness history as a didactic tool to be implemented within the Jewish community to liberate Jews from a strictly rabbinically dominated perspective on what forces had forged the nature of the past and

97

present Jewish situation. Reward and punishment would no longer be called on to explain the swings of history, but rather had to be replaced by the dynamics effecting all nations. Jost has been described in terms that cast him as the Voltaire of Jewish historiography because his writings and attitudes embodied an anticlericalism reminiscent of the French master.[10]

Of course, neither the Haskalah, whose influence had already passed its heights, nor Jost himself intended their endeavors only for internal consumption. The title, *Geschichte der Israeliten,* reveals a motivation to repair a damaged image. In this title, Jost noticeably opted not to use the unpopular term *jüdische,* which at the time was seen as having derogatory associations. And whereas Jost's work is still seen primarily as that of an enlightened educator of the Jews, it fared far better with Gentile academic circles than that of Graetz. Although Graetz strove to provide a comprehensive historiographic response to Christian conceptions of Jewish history, he wrote primarily for a Jewish audience.

Heinrich Graetz was born in 1817 in the Posen section of Prussia.[11] When Samson Raphael Hirsch's *Nineteen Letters of Ben Uziel* first appeared in 1837, Graetz, aware of the new opportunities of the times, was impressed by Hirsch's approach to Jewish tradition. Graetz wrote to Hirsch to request permission to become his student and lived and studied with Hirsch for three years between 1837 and 1840. The split between the two came gradually over the next decade. In several respects, Hirsch was not fulfilling Graetz's expectations. Graetz saw Hirsch move far closer to a strictly observant

Orthodoxy, whereas Graetz was more inclined toward adaptation. In addition, Graetz had expected Hirsch to undertake a stronger position of leadership within German Jewry, which Hirsch did only after the split between them was complete.[12] Yet Graetz, treading the already well-known path of the Jewish intellectual without possibilities of employment and either unwilling or incapable of entering the rabbinate, faced difficult financial problems. He continually turned to Hirsch over the course of the 1840s for help in finding employment, and this perpetuated their already strained relationship.

In 1842, Graetz moved to Breslau for studies at the university, but this period does not seem to have played a pivotal role in his development, as he continued to rely primarily on his own studies. In 1845, he received his doctorate from the University of Jena, writing his thesis on "Gnosticism and Judaism." Over the next six years, Graetz was employed primarily as a school principle, at first in Breslau, later in Nikolsburg with Hirsch, and then in a small town nearby. In 1852, Graetz moved to Berlin. He was near completion of a history of the Talmudic period and contemplating a complete history of the Jews. One biographer suggested that Graetz may have realized the need for extensive libraries for these purposes. More generally, it would seem that Graetz felt the need for more stimulating surroundings. He also had lost his job in Lundenburg.[13] But the move to Berlin accomplished other objectives for Graetz as well, as he now earned some part of his sparse income from lecturing to rabbinical students on Jewish history. Within a few months, he was offered a position at the new Breslau seminar to be headed by Zacharias Frankel.

Frankel, a traditionalist in favor of moderate reforms, had hoped to pursue his program within the orthodox framework, but after an initial outburst of enthusiasm, he failed to attract support within their ranks. His attempt to convene a conference of "theologians" in 1846 as a traditionalist alternative to the Reformers' rabbinical conferences was continually frustrated and finally aborted.[14] Graetz did appear for the scheduled conference, but more importantly, the closeness in their positions and the positive impression he made on Frankel eventually resulted in his appointment to the Jewish Theological Seminary of Breslau, opened in 1854 under Frankel's directorship. Graetz taught there for the rest of his professional career.[15]

Graetz's "The Construction of Jewish History," which appeared in 1846, represents the preliminary thinking of a scholar under the age of thirty and near the very beginning of his historical research and conceptual analysis.[16] Yet, this essay previewed some essential characteristics of the historiography to come. On the whole, I would suggest that such a "philosophy of Jewish history" produced early-on in the career of writers like Graetz and Dubnow, not yet ripened in their methods and thoughts, or even influenced by the very fruits of their own research, is not as critical for the understanding of a historian's outlook as an analysis of their later historical writing itself. What, nevertheless, is striking about Graetz's essay is the extent to which it set the agenda for the future metahistorical discussions of both Dubnow and Baron.

Judaism itself, according to Graetz, combines two basic elements—the political and the religious—with one or the other of these elements dominating at different times in history. At the end of the essay, Graetz suggested that there had been three periods in Jewish history, each characterized by a different combination of the basic social and religious elements of Judaism:

1. The pre-exilic period, dominated by political-social characteristics, until the Babylonian Exile.
2. The post-exilic period, characterized by religious elements, until the loss of national independence, identified by Graetz with the destruction of the Temple.
3. The period of Diaspora, still religious, but now more philosophically inclined.[17]

At the time of the Construction essay, Graetz clearly had only a vague notion of how the periods of Jewish history should be divided. In fact, based on the structure of his multivolume history, it could be argued that he never achieved a well-developed sense of periodization.

Graetz's history of the Jews appeared in eleven volumes between 1853 and 1874. Publication began with Graetz's work on the Talmudic period. Some writers have suggested that he intentionally commenced publication with the period following the destruction of the Temple in 70 A.D. as a response to Christian belief that Jewish history had come to an end with that very event.[18] Others have commented on Graetz's intention to portray rabbinic literature and Talmudic personalities in a far more positive light than was being presented by writers from the Reform movement.[19] Neither formulation would be contradicted by the observation that Graetz seems to have begun with the period in which he was most interested. Actually, Graetz apparently wrote this volume independently and only late in the process decided it would be the fourth volume of a complete history.[20]

In fact, the Construction essay dealt primarily with the ancient periods of Jewish history through Gaonic times and only barely mentioned certain intellectual developments in the medieval and early modern periods. Strikingly, even near the end of his life, long after he had completed his multivolume history of three millennia of Jewish history, Graetz was still primarily interested in the more ancient periods and especially the Talmudic period; for just as this period stood at the core of his early essay, it totally dominated the Retrospective essay he wrote decades later for the conclusion of the English edition.

In the introduction to the fourth volume of his history, Graetz indicated how he wanted Jewish history to be presented: "The long era of the dispersion, lasting nearly seventeen centuries, is characterized by unprecedented sufferings, an uninterrupted martyrdom, and a constantly aggravated degradation and humiliation unparalleled in history—but also by mental activity, unremitting intellectual efforts, and indefatigable research."[21] To illustrate his point, Graetz referred to the graphic image of Judah as the mournful wanderer on the one hand, but also as proud and content scholar on the other. "The one represents the external history of this era, a history of suffering, the like of which no other people has endured in such an aggravated degree and to such an immense extent; the other exhibits the inward history, a comprehensive history of the mind, which, like an immense river, springing from the knowledge of God as its fountainhead, receives, appropriates, and blends all the tributary sciences—again a history peculiar to this people alone."

But despite the emphasis on suffering, it was also Graetz's objective to break Jewish history out of the doldrums of martyrdom. In the past, Jews had produced memorial books to commemorate the victims of persecution; they had also compiled lists of scholars indicating the links by which rabbinic learning had been transmitted from one generation to another. Graetz was consciously seeking to combine these two traditions.

In this formulation, the greater the sense of tragedy conveyed, the more remarkable the marvel of Jewish cultural achievement. Thus, it was ironic that Graetz should have been attacked by both Dubnow and Baron for the resulting overemphasis on suffering, for Graetz had carefully delineated the contours of his history to include the positive. In fact, he was explicit: "It is not even difficult to show that Judaism, during its period of dispersion which has still not ended, has produced, in addition to a passive history of severe trial and martyrdom also an active history which gives the most striking evidence of infinite vitality and flexible energy."[22]

One of Graetz's truly significant accomplishments was the inspiration he provided to at least two generations of young Jews as the gateway to the world of Jewish studies. In a deceptively subtle, but cogent bibliographical essay entitled "From Graetz to Dubnow," Ismar Elbogen outlined something of the explosion in historical scholarship that was produced in the generation following Graetz. To attribute this productivity to Graetz would ignore the multifaceted constellation of forces that led not only to an invigorated Jewish scholarship at the end of the nineteenth century, but also to a comprehensive and creative outburst of communal and intellectual activity that resulted in new national and international movements in Jewish life. As disappointed and frustrated Jews turned inward and still-hopeful Jews reassessed their strategies, Graetz's *History* provided a tone of consolation and hope by emphasizing that past suffering had not stifled the Jewish spirit. The work could easily be ridiculed by emerging scientific standards, but as a literary tour de force it survived well into the twentieth century. And if it was deemed outdated by the middle of this century, then that was not because of enhanced critical criteria as much as it was a result of the massive weight of powerful developments. Among those who turned to Graetz in their youth—and who later turned away from him—was Simon Dubnow.[23]

Dubnow's life (1860–1941) transcended evenly between the nineteenth and twentieth centuries, and almost evenly between Heinrich Graetz (b. 1817) and Salo Baron (b. 1895). Although raised in a traditionalist environment in White Russia, Dubnow was exposed early to the Haskalah critiques of Jewish law and thought. By the age of Bar Mitzvah, Dubnow was known in his hometown as a rebel. As a young adult, he contemplated rabbinical studies at the Breslau seminary formerly headed by Frankel, to be followed by a career as a religious reformer. But the wave of reaction of the 1880s that decimated optimistic spirits throughout the Pale also effected Dubnow's outlook on the potential integration of

Russian Jewry. It was at this point, as indicated in his autobiography, that he chose his life mission of guarding Jewish identity through Jewish history. Part of the credit for that decision goes to Graetz, who influenced Dubnow through the pages of his history.[24]

Graetz's influence was strongest in Dubnow's early writings, most especially in his essay "Jewish History," which was originally planned as an introductory essay to a Russian translation of Graetz's *History of the Jews*. But gradually, Dubnow moved away from Graetz's emphases and approaches. By the time Dubnow's own history of the Jews appeared in 1925, his introductory comments were still respectful but critical of both the content and structure of Graetz's history. He recalled his earlier "immature" fascination with Graetz, but now maintained that Graetz's historiography was but a one-sided presentation.

In the treatment of the medieval and modern history of the Jews, we likewise find the dominance of a one-sided spiritualistic conception that is based on the axiom that a people deprived of state and territory can play an active role in history only in the field of intellectual life, while elsewhere, in its social life, it is condemned to being a passive object of the history of the peoples among whom it lives. Jewish historiography initiated by Zunz and Graetz thus paid attention mainly to two basic factors in presenting the history of the Diaspora: it dealt mostly with intellectual activities and with heroic martyrdom (Geistes-und Leidensgeschichte).[25]

Dubnow also criticized Graetz for what he called a synchronistic arrangement by which he treated the history of the Jews in all countries concurrently, thus presenting "a chronological record of events that coincide in time but differ fundamentally in character and local conditions. . . . With Graetz the confusion is further augmented by his method of throwing together political, socio-economic, and literary data in the narrowest sense of the word into a single chapter."[26]

Nevertheless, Dubnow expressed his continued respect for the founding efforts of his predecessors: "Even though I differ from my predecessors in my general conception of Jewish history as well as in many details, I am always conscious of the fact that, without the labor of a century of scholars of the school of Zunz, Geiger, Graetz and Frankel, we could never have reached the present stage of Jewish historiography."[27]

In the introduction to his *World History of the Jewish People,* Dubnow set out some of the principles guiding his own approach to Jewish history, beginning with the selection of the somewhat paradoxical title. The notion of a world history would hardly seem appropriate for what was in fact the history of a single people, but it was Dubnow's intention to underscore that Jewish history reflected both geographically and chronologically the full gamut of the history of civilization. "It embraces in a physical sense almost the entire civilized world (except India and China) and it coincides chronologically with the whole course of the historical existence of mankind. Judaism represents a true historical microcosm."[28]

Dubnow termed his approach to Jewish history "sociological," although he understood that term in his own specific sense as applying to the history of the Jews as a nation: "The subject of scientific historiography is the people, the national individuality, its origin, its growth, and its struggle for existence." Thus, Dubnow specifically chose the term *sociology* in order to imply a scientific approach to history and sought to identify himself with the recent methodological developments introduced by Max Weber and others in pursuit of that objective. Still, he admitted that he was not using the term in the same sense as Weber. For Dubnow, sociological stood in contrast with the theological approach of earlier Jewish historians who as part of their program of integration had emphasized the concept of Judaism as a religion at the expense of proper emphasis on the people itself. As Dubnow explained, the process of secularization had now made possible the development of a scientific approach that was free of the artificially imposed nineteenth-century limitations. [29]

In explaining the implications of his approach, Dubnow emphasized the significance of the autonomous institutions of communal structure. To Dubnow, an autonomous community meant social vitality, thus confirming that in the social sphere as well as the religious, the Jewish people had always been an active agent in the shaping of its own history. "Basic to this conception is the idea derived from the totality of our history, that the Jewish people has at all times and in all countries, always and everywhere, been the subject, the creator of its own history, not only in the intellectual sphere but also in the general sphere of social life." [30] Economic factors were also part of his understanding of sociological history. Indicating that the older school had sorely neglected economic considerations in their emphasis of the spiritual, Dubnow, however, explained that he would not reduce all of history to materialistic causes. "We do not reject the antiquated, spiritualistic conception of history only to become captives of the opposite doctrine, the no-less-one-sided materialistic view of history which equally obscures all historical perspective."[31]

In search of a system based on national and social factors in place of religious or literary criteria, he chose to divide historical periods "primarily [on] the historical environment of the Jewish nation." This formulation suggested a major revision, because Dubnow rejected the term "Talmudic Period" and its obvious ties to a purely cultural perspective, as well as the notion of a "First Temple Period" and "Second Temple Period." In their place, Dubnow referred to these periods as "the Kingdom of Judah under Assyrian and Babylonian Sovereignty," "Babylonian Exile and Persian Rule," and "Roman Rule and the Fall of the Jewish State."

This emphasis on the environment resulted in the system of cultural hegemonies that is usually identified as one of Dubnow's primary innovations.

The history of the stateless period . . . after the Jews had lost their unified center, must be subdivided in accordance with clear-cut geographical considerations and along lines corresponding to shifts in the center of national hegemony within the Jewish people. Each epoch is determined by the fact that the dispersed nation possessed within this period one main center, or sometimes two co-existing centers, which assumed the leadership of all other parts of the Diaspora because they were able to achieve far-reaching national autonomy and a high state of cultural development.[32]

Dubnow's history appeared when he was in his late sixties and at a point when Baron was already formulating some of his basic historical ideas. In 1931, two years following the publication of the last of Dubnow's volumes, Baron presented a series of lectures on which his own history would be based. Proximity in time was accompanied by proximity in substance, as Dubnow had anticipated several of Baron's criticisms of Graetz and more generally, some of Baron's basic approaches to Jewish history. Such closeness provoked an emphasis on differences, but it would be more accurate to say that Baron never really included Dubnow as a full partner or even prominent precursor in the enterprise of writing a history of the Jews. Still, his criticism of Graetz and Dubnow were tied to the development of his own style of Jewish historiography, and these criticisms are among our concerns in the next section.

Baron and His Predecessors

During Baron's first years in America, he published a number of historiographic essays on his predecessors in the writing of Jewish history. In some ways these presentations hint through his criticisms of others at the guidelines Baron proposed for himself. Let us begin with his 1928 discussion of Isaac Jost.[33]

Baron had a penchant for commemorative anniversaries — some, as in this case, rather artificial. The lecture on Jost was delivered at the American Academy for Jewish Research to mark the centennial of the final volume of Jost's *Geschichte der Israeliten,* which was published between 1820 and 1828 with a supplementary work on contemporary developments published in 1846–47. To understand the timing of Baron's essay, it would be more to the point to observe that during this period Baron was quite involved in the study of earlier Jewish historians.

While Baron sought to restore Jost to his proper place in the annals of Jewish historiography, his assessment of Jost's accomplishments was actually quite bland.

Now we can restore Jost to his rightful position in the historical literature of the Jewish people. Although not a great spirit, he was certainly a pioneer. Although not a man of genius and high aspirations, he was a solid, quiet worker who tried to lay solid, reliable foundations for the development of Jewish historical knowledge, and succeeded in doing so to a large extent.[34]

Such muted enthusiasm concluded an essay loaded with such attributes as "a belated offspring of the Enlightenment," or describing his work as full of "contradictions and hesitations, in weakness and sometimes even in confusion." But Baron did not write this essay in order to belittle Jost; there was no need of that because Jost was being virtually ignored by the successive generations of historians.[35] Whatever else its purposes were to have been, it allowed Baron to explore some of the potential pitfalls in the writing of a history of the Jews.

Primarily, Baron criticized Jost for insufficient vision to see the grand opportunity lying before him. Caught between the Enlightenment and the period of Romanticism, Jost "if he had been a much greater man," should have used rational criticism to attack traditional forces while rebuilding what remained "into a new comprehensive structure." On Jost's lack of a philosophy of history and conception of Judaism, Baron commented:

He has no notion whatever of the existence of certain leading ideas and tendencies peculiar to every period such as Ranke emphasized later. To him history seems a straight line of development which he judges very much from the point of view of his own age. In general, Jost's philosophy of history is very simple; he is not even a theologian like most of the other Jewish historians of the nineteenth century. It is perhaps one of his essential weaknesses that, treating a subject like the history of the Jewish people, he had no definite view as to what this Jewish people really was. Personally almost an agnostic, a man who boasted of not having gone to a synagogue for more than twenty years, because, as he said, he "did not go to theater," he could hardly feel deep sympathy with Jewry as a purely religious group. On the other hand, in his eyes the Jewish people was no longer a nationality. . . . Although his work was description rather than definition, this weakness and the resultant inner contradiction could never be fully overcome.[36]

Much in this description echoed difficulties in Baron's own conflicts, but a discussion on Baron's religious life will be saved for later on. What resounds in Baron's critique of Jost is the absence of a systematic conception of Jewish history, and it was that failure, according to Baron, more than any other that resulted in the weakness and incoherence of Jost's presentation. Also noteworthy is the reference to Jost's belief in the advancement of progress. Baron had just published his essay "Ghetto and Emancipation" in which he had profoundly questioned the validity of such an approach for Jewish history.

Jost had undertaken the first multivolume history of the Jews since that of Basnage over a century before. Despite the abundance of earlier literature on the Jewish past, most interest had generally been confined to the periods around the rise of Christianity and even then, the treatment had been primarily theological or philological. Jost indicated that his predecessors—both Christians and Jews—were of little help, and

Baron was in general agreement. Only in the case of Basnage did Baron feel that Jost had underplayed earlier contributions: "Nevertheless he is really much indebted to the Frenchman."[37]

With considerable literature beginning to appear on various aspects of Judaism, Jost was criticized for his apparent superficiality. Anticipating later criticisms of his own work, Baron came to Jost's defense:

> It is an utter injustice to demand from Jost a thorough criticism and compilation of sources like that of Rapoport. To compare a monograph of Rapoport on one single personality . . . with corresponding passages in Jost and to declare Jost's narrative "superficial talk," as Graetz does, is anything but fair. The author of a broad synthesis cannot be as accurate on individual points as the investigator of a narrow field.[38]

In sum, Baron's attitude toward Jost and his work displayed fundamental ambiguity, as considerable criticisms were combined with an underlying sympathy for the accomplishments of a historiographic pioneer. "Pioneer" was Baron's word to describe Jost, and it was a word used by Baron in various contexts to express deep personal praise.[39] Baron, who also rarely, if ever, entered a synagogue for religious observance, must have identified as well with Jost's antipathy toward religion. After all, it was Baron who chose to describe Jost by reference to his absence from synagogue, and unknowingly, his daughter described Baron to me years later in virtually identical terms.

Near the end of his analysis of Jost, Baron returned to his point of departure, but with some contradiction. Baron had

accused Jost of writing his history unsystematically and especially without a coherent perspective, partly because he was
not "even a theologian"; but Baron later defended Jost for
being essentially impartial in his writing. In fact, Baron
felt that this objectivity probably encouraged considerable
criticism of Jost during the nineteenth century. Geiger accused Jost of presenting a dry account of Jewish history;
Graetz called it a *Philistine* presentation, "despoiling [Jewish
history] of [its] brightness." According to Baron, Jost's apparent nonpartisanship did not fill the needs of the contemporary
agenda in which Jewish scholars had joined the battle for
emancipation. "In such a period impartiality could hardly be
tolerated. A non-partisan was almost an enemy." And then
Baron concluded in 1928 that "these struggles are over now.
The turmoil of those dissensions and quarrels and vicissitudes
has quieted down, and although new conflicts have arisen, the
old ones are so far from ours that we are not prevented from
getting the right perspective for historical judgment." It may
have been time for a proper historical perspective on Jost's
contribution; more significantly, it was also time for a new
and proper perspective on Jewish history itself.

Even before his essay on Jost, Baron had begun a series of
studies on the much earlier sixteenth-century Italian Jewish
historian, Azariah de' Rossi. Three essays on his life, thought,
and historical writing appeared between the years 1927 and
1929.[40] Baron explained that his interest in de' Rossi derived
from his appraisal that the sixteenth century marked a new
beginning in Jewish historical writing and that de' Rossi's
works represented the most significant of such works of his

time. Baron referred to de' Rossi specifically as the "founder of historical criticism."

As with his essay on Jost, Baron used the opportunity provided to discuss several elements that were beginning to play an important role in his own historical thinking, most especially the attitude of the historian toward the forces of nature and the possibility that history was not—certainly Jewish history was not—moving in a straight-line direction of progress. Baron himself would discuss the role of nature in Jewish history in the introduction to the *Social and Religious History,* but he was, as we have seen, already concerned with the concept of progress. Thus, his remarks on de' Rossi's attitudes reinforced the possibility of alternative positions:

Moreover, one of the fundamental points in the philosophy of life of the period was the thought that the best things belong to the past. In modern times, our watchword is progress and we instinctively regard human history, notwithstanding its ebbs and flows, as a development from lower to higher forms. This idea of evolution and progress was entirely strange to the mind of a Renaissance man. On the contrary, since the Middle Ages the dominant idea in this regard had been rather of continual degeneration.[41]

Baron's fascination with this relatively unknown historiographic precursor requires some additional explanation. In Baron's view, de' Rossi combined vast erudition in secular languages and subjects with a critical technique for the examination of sources. Baron marveled at his wide-ranging reading and praised his analysis of sources. Baron emphasized that whereas de' Rossi had paved the way for modern historical writing, the emergence of the Counter Reformation reversed

Renaissance trends toward cultural integration, and as a result, Jews became increasingly ghettoized, intellectually as well as physically. Three centuries later, with the birth of Wissenschaft, the work of critical historical scholarship was continued. During the interim, de' Rossi's works were ignored. This view, of course, fits with Baron's general perspective on the beginnings of modernity. Primarily, however, the essays on de' Rossi formed an integral part in Baron's considerable interest in precursors, in their lives, their writing, their strengths, and their weaknesses as historians. This was further revealed in a new essay on Heinrich Graetz.

One of Baron's first essays, published when he was twenty-three, presented a methodological comparison of Graetz with the leading German historian of the nineteenth century, Leopold von Ranke. After writing on de Rossi and Jost, Baron now returned to the most important figure in Jewish historiography to date, when he wrote the entry on Graetz in the 1931 *Encyclopedia Judaica*.[42] But these items alone do little to demonstrate the power that Graetz held over Baron specifically and for that matter over twentieth-century Jewish historians in general. Indeed the world of Jewish studies still has a deep fascination with Graetz almost a century after his death, although that interest has begun to turn away from the historian and toward Graetz as a participant in Jewish history.[43]

The nature of Baron's attitude toward Graetz can best be described by beginning with two overall observations. First, Graetz was for Baron the father-figure of Jewish historiography, even though the father concept had actually been applied by Baron to de' Rossi and Jost, but not to Graetz. The contradiction is not serious. In essays specifically devoted to those earlier scholars, Baron accredited them with their pioneering efforts, and yet, Graetz represented the most significant lighthouse of the past. Indeed, de' Rossi and Jost were rarely mentioned in Baron's writings, including the *Social and Religious History,* and Graetz was for Baron his most significant precursor.

Moreover, after 1928, in his writings, letters, and conversations, Baron loved to refer to the invitation extended to him that year to accept the chair in Jewish history at the Jewish Theological Seminary in Breslau first occupied by Heinrich Graetz. We have already seen that this rendition was not precisely accurate, but the distortion underscores the significance Baron attributed to Graetz. As formulated, the offer was viewed as a great honor at the time, and early-on Baron may have felt that the fact of the invitation would help establish his own prestige in America. Yet, Baron continually referred to this episode long after these purposes were objectively relevant.[44] For Baron, even more important than this offer was his more fundamental ambition to be Graetz's successor in Jewish historiography as well.

But then it must be noted that the honor implied in this anecdote was compromised by Baron's frequent attacks. There were several common criticisms of Graetz. However, Graetz was often excused for one reason or another, whereas his successors were not entitled to the same leniency. Already in his 1918 essay comparing Graetz and Ranke, Baron wrote that as opposed to Ranke's broad multinational orientation, Graetz was "the historian of a single people," who wishes to explain its evolution mainly through internal factors. The dominant trends determining the Jewish developments originate and disappear, according to him, only within the Jewish people as a separate entity. As if it were possible completely to isolate any community or individual from the rest of the world and deny any external influences upon it![45]

The tendency to view Jewish history as isolated from its surroundings was a recurrent theme in Baron's critique of his predecessors, as was his emphasis on the need for historians to make greater use of archival sources. This latter criticism also appeared in the 1918 essay and again with special dispensation for Graetz because of the enormous quantity of undistilled primary sources he had to cope with.[46]

But Baron's central criticism of Graetz was neatly summed up in bi-lingual alliterative phrases describing Graetz's writing as the history of "suffering and scholars," or in German, as *Leidens- und Gelehrten-geschichte*.[47] In a different phrase, Baron referred to such writing as representing the lachrymose conception of Jewish history, meaning that view placing great emphasis on persecutions at the expense of appreciating the rich and varied nature of the Jewish historical experience. Baron's understanding of the lachrymose conception and what implications it bore for his own writing of Jewish history are discussed at a later stage in our analysis of the major principles in Baron's writings. But it was with regard to the lachrymose conception that Baron drew the clearest lines of demarcation between himself and his predecessors; Baron primarily identified this mode of writing with Graetz.

After discussing the criticism in general in "Ghetto and

Emancipation," Baron singled out Graetz, beginning most clearly in his 1931 biographical essay. Baron was perfectly aware that Graetz was the least responsible and the least guilty of the indicated distortion. In 1949, he wrote: "Graetz did not invent the conception of Jewish history as that of an uninterrupted succession of scholars and martyrs. The entire Jewish historiography of the Middle Ages and early modern times consisted of chronicles recording dramatic events, mostly persecutions, massacres, or expulsions."[48] Moreover, it was specifically to avoid overly emphasizing the sufferings of the past, that Graetz gave such pivotal attention to scholars and scholarship. Nevertheless, in the same sentence of pardon quoted previously, Baron refers to the lachrymose conception as "the Graetzian conception of Jewish history." I cannot help but wonder whether it was with tongue in cheek or mere flippancy that Baron wrote in 1939: "To be sure, the accusation frequently heard that Graetz, for example, had placed exclusive stress upon the biographies of rabbis and the story of anti-Jewish persecutions is clearly contradicted by his own programmatic formulation of the 'national character' of the entire history of the post-talmudic period." The accusation came from no other source more frequently than it did from Baron himself.[49]

Of course Baron could claim that Graetz, though intending to avoid the emphasis on suffering, was unable to do so. But the same accusation could be applied to Baron as well. For that matter, any historian might well find that it is not so easy to become liberated from antisemitism as both subject and cause in Jewish history. These points will concern us at later stages. In the case of Graetz, there seems little doubt that Baron had created a strawman, placing him in too narrow a box, apparently in order to better define their differences in approach. But other aspects of his critique—such as the isolation of Jewish history from the world around it—would have accomplished the same objective with greater accuracy. That criticism, however, was reserved for Dubnow, not Graetz.

Although Baron wrote two essays specifically on Graetz, he wrote little that was comparable on Dubnow—a brief review notice, a three-page reflective celebration of Dubnow's eightieth birthday, and an essay in a volume in honor of Dubnow that did not deal with the man or very much with his work, but primarily with his major criticism against the isolationist approach to Jewish history.[50] Of course, Dubnow was mentioned by Baron frequently in bibliographic footnotes dealing with the Jews of Eastern Europe, but he was usually treated as a relatively ineffective writer who had failed to surpass the quality of Graetz's pioneering efforts.[51]

In 1926, when Baron was thirty, he wrote a short but highly critical review of the first volume of Dubnow's *World History*.[52] Baron explained that even if one accepted in principle Dubnow's understanding of a world history of the Jewish people based on the dispersion of the Jews, such a conception would still not apply to the ancient period which was the focus of this volume, when Jews were physically concentrated in a single region, the Near East. Worse, Baron faulted Dubnow for bringing insufficient material in this volume relating to the world background in which the Jewish people emerged. Thus even if approached from a traditional understanding of what a world history would imply, Dubnow's work came up short. Finally, Baron contended that despite the claims of a new sociological approach, there was little in this volume that had not been said before and in basically the same way. Baron concluded that Dubnow had written about a period blessed with considerable scholarly literature that Dubnow had not mastered, having devoted his earlier efforts primarily with modern Russian-Jewish history.

Baron's fundamental criticism of Dubnow's work was rooted in Dubnow's concept of a world history. Just as Baron identified the lachrymose conception with Graetz, he associated what he called the isolationist approach to Jewish history with Dubnow.

Both Jewish and world scholarship have long recognized that Jewish history, particularly during the two and a half millennia of the dispersion, cannot be fully understood without the background of the various civilizations under which Jews happened to live. By giving his ten-volume Jewish history the telling title, *Weltgeschichte des jüdischen Volkes,* Simon M. Dubnow announced that he wished to treat his subject within the framework of world history. . . . In practice, however, neither Dubnow nor most of his contemporaries have greatly advanced in this respect beyond their predecessors, including Graetz. This older treatment of Jewish history which may, perhaps uncharitably, be designated "the isolationist approach to Jewish history" still had a modicum of justification at the time when Graetz and the other nineteenth-century historians were chiefly interested in the intellectual history of the Jewish people.[53]

Again, Baron's criticism of Graetz was milder, this time because intellectual history perhaps could better justify an approach that isolated Jewish developments from what was happening outside the Jewish world. But Baron eventually criticized that position as well.

Perhaps the clearest statement of Baron's own approach to history is contained in "Emphases in Jewish History." In this essay he criticizes Dubnow's failure to place Jewish history within its broader context and most especially his failure to subject Jewish history to the same rules of explanation applied to other nations. Having discussed the inclination of nineteenth-century Wissenschaft scholars to explain Jewish history primarily through internal factors, Baron continued:

Even the positivists among the Jewish thinkers, such as Ahad Ha-am and Dubnow, essentially accepted the primacy of such "inner" factors. They set up a sort of autonomous national will which was the driving force in shaping the destinies of the people and which, in the supreme interest of national self- preservation, made all the necessary adjustments required in the different periods and regions. . . .

It cannot be denied, however, that the idealistic approach no longer satisfies our present generation of scholars and students. There is a growing feeling that the historical explanations of the Jewish past must not fundamentally deviate from the general patterns of history which we accept for mankind at large or for any other particular national group.[54]

To borrow a term from Zionist ideology, I would refer to this aspect of Baron's thinking as the normalization of Jewish history. We continue this discussion at a later stage, but a few more lines help explain the choice of this term. "Every unbiased investigator will admit that general methods necessarily must be adapted to the requirements of each particular subject and that, for instance, no one can deal with the history of the United States in exactly the same way as he would investigate the history of China. There is, nevertheless, a growing sentiment that the differences in methods must needs remain limited {sic}."[55]

Baron continued his criticism in a 1940 Hebrew essay in honor of Dubnow's eightieth birthday. Despite the heading indicating this essay was written to honor Dubnow, it too was highly critical. Baron emphasized that an isolationist approach was inadequate when applied to intellectual history, but it was surely more insufficient in the case of social, economic, and political developments. Dubnow was right to criticize Graetz for fusing together events of the same time period regardless of the country being discussed. By doing this, Graetz had gravely understated the relevance of surroundings to developments in Jewish history. In defense of Dubnow, Baron explained that Dubnow was trying to compensate through his use of hegemonies. But Baron believed it was blatantly obvious to Dubnow's readers that he too followed the isolationist approach on which he had been raised; it was an approach that developed not out of conviction, but out of necessity. The budding field of Jewish history had to first gather and examine the available sources. The task of writing a history combining the inner and outer forces "was left to the next generation—our own—and the ones to come."[56]

Baron suggested that Dubnow's isolationist approach resulted from his political beliefs in national autonomy for the Jews, citing references from Dubnow's *The Minutes of the Lithuanian Council of Provinces* that the ancient Israelite kingdom had never died. Throughout the ages, enemies of the Jews had referred to a scattered and separate people, and more recently, of a nation within a nation. Dubnow concluded that the autonomous people had lived on throughout Jewish history. He even proposed national autonomy for American Jewry, disregarding that the heavy majority of American Jews would not want such "rights." Baron insightfully connected national political autonomy with historiographic isolation.

In fact, Baron's relation to Dubnow was more complicated than he had carefully led his readers to believe. His own utterances on the topic emphasized the distance between them, but it was the actual proximity between them that necessitated the camouflage. Historiographically, Baron repeatedly complained that Dubnow had failed to fulfill his declared objectives, which were frequently similar to his own goals. Dubnow's failures paved the way for a renewed attempt. But the underlying similarity of the two historians lay as well in their common appreciation of the significance of the Diaspora in the shaping of Jewish history. True, Baron could dismiss Dubnow's political notions of national autonomy in the Diaspora as out of hand, but he was nonetheless a champion of the vibrancy and contributions made by Diaspora communities in Jewish history. Indeed, the old debates between Dubnow the Diaspora nationalist and Ahad Ha'am the Zionist became more pronounced in Baron's days, for the nineteenth-century dream of a cultural center in Israel was, by the 1930s, much closer to reality. In Israeli eyes at least, Baron's resurrection of Dubnow's position seemed more out of place once Jewish history was being taught and written on the heights of Mount Scopus.[57]

In sum, during the late 1920s and early 1930s, Baron wrote at least five essays on leading Jewish historians of the past: de' Rossi, Jost, and Graetz. These articles are read today for their historiographic analysis and their portraits of intellectual history; but they also represent Baron's own musings on the task of writing a history of the Jews, presented through his assessments of the successes and failures of his predecessors. Through these essays, we see a preliminary formulation of the basic principles in which Baron sought to establish his own approach.

Especially noteworthy were Baron's insistence on presenting Jewish history with a sensitivity to the influences on its course by broader trends and the reciprocal influence—when applicable—of Jewish developments on their surroundings; the necessity to develop an encompassing structure to house the history, and, of course, a commitment to write a balanced history of the Jews that placed both scholars and suffering in proportion to other developments within a rich and varied historical experience. Finally, and related to all of these, was the basic underlying conviction that Jewish history was no more unique than the history of any other social group and that it must be described and explained using the same norms as used elsewhere in the historical profession. These last differences emerged most clearly in his scattered discussions on Dubnow's place in Jewish historiography. Still, it is interesting that these references date primarily from the years right after the appearance of Baron's own history of the Jews, in which he set out to explain—at times by inference—his own approach to the writing of Jewish history.

The Publication Process

In the spring of 1931, soon after his arrival at Columbia, Baron delivered the Schermerhorn Lecture series sponsored by the Department of Religion, entitled "Jewish Society and Religion in Their Historical Interrelation." Baron's theme was "the interrelation of social and religious forces, as exemplified in the long historic evolution of the Jewish people."[58] The lectures not only provided Baron with an introduction to the Columbia community, but provided as well the opportunity for a first run on his own emerging version of a history of the Jews. Six years later, that history appeared as *A Social and Religious History of the Jews*. Although usually identified today as Baron's classic, albeit unfinished, eighteen-volume work covering ancient and medieval Jewish history through 1650, the original 1937 edition appeared in three volumes, two of text and a third of notes and bibliography, and covered the entire scope of Jewish history through the time of publication.

The work was published by Columbia University Press, but only after a tortuous process of financial arrangements and editing difficulties. In an interview Baron recounted that the press was reluctant to publish the work, and it was the strong intervention of Nicholas Butler that guaranteed its publication.[59] But Baron was mistaken about the identity of his primary supporter. Butler was the president of the press and indeed played an active role in that capacity. His files contain numerous memos to the press offices on publication procedures and suggestions. However, I found no such memo relating to Baron's *History*. Rather, Baron's support during this period in a number of ways came from Herbert W.

Schneider, a philosophy professor and a member of the press' publication committee.

Schneider, widely known for his *History of American Philosophy,* had been a member of the search committee established to fill the Miller chair. He was also responsible for the Schermerhorn Religion Fund, which had sponsored Baron's lectures. The press files show that Schneider intervened repeatedly to secure and facilitate the publication of Baron's work. Thus, it was Schneider who provided considerable support for Baron's endeavors in his early days at Columbia and deserved considerable credit for the publication of Baron's *History.*

In early 1934, Baron submitted the work, entitled "Jews and Judaism" to Henry Holt and Company. At the time Holt was responsible for publication of the Schermerhorn lectures and was the house where Schneider served as editor of the American Religion Series. When Holt decided not to publish Baron's *History,* it explained the decision to Schneider in confidence: The reader's "opinion is that this is an excellent book of doubtful immediate value. It is, in other words, one of those ventures which we dare not risk this year."[60] Simultaneously, they wrote to Baron: "Your book is an impressive performance characterized by immense erudition and a persuasive form of presentation. Its style is more vivid than one would expect in a work of this kind. Its scope and scholarship should make it the standard book on the subject." However, they felt the first volume was too difficult for the average student to grasp and the second volume could expect a "respectable but not large" sale.

These comments effectively summarized the evaluation submitted by the reader, who spoke highly of both the erudition and vivid style of the manuscript. However, the reader concluded with caution:

Its scope and scholarship should make it the standard book on the subject. The more cultivated Jews and Gentiles interested in the disturbing problem of the modern Jew in the midst of a Gentile world will want to add this work to their libraries. Public and college libraries will have to buy it as soon as they have the funds to do so. On the other hand, I do not think that the first volume, Israel in Antiquity, will have much of a market as a college text. It is too mature a work for the average student. The second volume, if sold separately, should have a small sale as a text in the better Hebrew schools.

The report predicted only limited interest among non-Jews and public institutions, and Jewish interest alone would not justify publication. Indeed, the reader must have been thinking of some rather unusual "Hebrew schools" to project use of the work as a textbook in that context.

Irwin Edman also attempted to aid with publication of the work and on Baron's behalf wrote to a commercial press, which declined to read the manuscript because there was virtually no chance that they would want to publish a work "on a subject which interests the public only when there is a pogrom or a book bonfire."[61] Apparently at Schneider's suggestion, Baron now submitted his work to Columbia's press. A memo written by Charles Proffitt, then assistant director and later director of the press, indicated that Schneider had spoken enthusiastically about the work, but the press was still hesitant because of a lack of funds.[62]

The difficulties faced by Baron reveal the reluctance of both commercial and university presses in the 1930s to undertake publication of a book on Judaica. Eventually, however, the process of integration of Jewish studies into the university world necessitated that university publishing follow suit as well. By the time of publication, Baron's stature on the campus mandated proper treatment by the university's press.

In many ways, Baron proved to be a difficult partner in the publication process. The story of the production of the *History* indicates a stream of delays on Baron's part exacerbated by his own impatience toward others. Office files indicate continuous frustrations as Baron, although late with his own tasks, still demanded that editing be sped up, even while he revised copy after editing had been completed. He also concerned himself with minute details of the production process. Already at an early stage—before the editing of the manuscript had begun, Charles Proffitt summed up the difficulties to Herbert Schneider: "It would be fine if authors could get away from the idea that they may spend years in preparing a manuscript, but that a publisher can handle his end of the job overnight!"[63]

Indeed, Proffitt reported in May 1935 that Baron had expressed his desire to see the work published by that September in order to secure textbook use for the fall semester. Shortly thereafter, the press received a copy of the manuscript and realized immediately that considerable work lay ahead of them. The manuscript was so heavily interlined with handwritten changes that office editing could not commence until Baron had reedited the work.[64]

Meanwhile, Schneider endorsed its importance stating "that there is no history of the Jews comparable with Professor

Baron's work, except one that was published a great many years ago. . . . There have been other histories of the Jewish people in more recent times, but they have been short ones." Schneider also suggested the three-volume format later adopted for the work, with the third volume to contain the footnotes.[65] In a separate consultation, Schneider estimated potential short-term sales at between nine hundred and a thousand copies, in contrast with Baron's projection of three to four thousand copies. The press, cutting the projected sales even further, determined that an eleven hundred copy printing would be appropriate for some time to come.[66]

Proffitt informed Baron that the press, realizing the importance of his work, was prepared to undertake its publication, but required a heavy subsidy of $5,000 from the author. Meanwhile, Proffitt wrote to Schneider, "It would seem possible that Professor Baron might know of some source of funds from among the Jewish people, but we have no money in sight that will be available for a very long time."[67] Proffitt also enclosed an excerpt from the *Saturday Review of Literature* summarizing the available bibliography in the field of Jewish history.

The main difficulties behind the press' hesitations lay in the anticipated cost of printing, the condition of the manuscript, and ultimately considerable doubts concerning the potential sale of the work. Both the press and Baron proceeded to search for lower estimates. Proffitt kept Schneider informed of developments and explained that the high subsidy was partly the result of Baron's insistence for speed. "From the beginning, we have told him that we should have a considerable amount of time to secure the most favorable estimates, and to consider carefully the probable extent of sales income. However, he was in a great hurry, and we did what we could in the short time allowed." Apparently, the amount of subsidy being requested now convinced Baron to give the press additional time to examine the situation once again.[68]

A few days later, Proffitt explained to Schneider:

I should tell you in confidence that our rather tentative attitude toward the whole matter is conditioned not only by the fact that a very large amount of money will be involved, but also by the condition of the copy of the manuscript which has been placed in our hands, and which, in some places, is so difficult to decipher that Geddes commented that reading it was like trying to read an unfamiliar foreign language.[69]

What Geddes, sales and advertising manager of the press, had actually written to Proffitt was that "once one catches on to this author's revision and correction techniques, this manuscript becomes quite interesting. (It is like discovering suddenly that one can read a foreign language.)" But Geddes still decided that he could not foresee much lay interest in the work.[70]

After the summer months, Baron secured a lower estimate and indicated to Proffitt that he was sure "that the manuscript will probably require little, if any editorial revision by your staff." Proffitt transmitted that remark without comment, but it would hardly prove the case, and the press was quite aware of the situation.[71]

An agreement was finally reached in December 1935. The press preferred to work with one of its own printers, but managed to secure an estimate more in line with that submitted by Baron. The subsidy was reduced, and Baron agreed to the terms, expressing the hope that production work could start immediately in order "to have the work published by May." Part of the subsidy was to be provided by the Schermerhorn Foundation under Schneider's influence.[72] About a week later, it was discovered that Baron had neither submitted nor planned a bibliography for the work—production problems were just beginning.

The manuscript was actively edited between December 1935 and August 1936 by G. W. Read, a freelancer closely affiliated with the press, under conditions of internecine warfare between author and editor, with officers of the press walking a diplomatic tightrope between them. Questions concerning Baron's command of the English language took a secondary place alongside complaints concerning his working procedures, his insistence on having all material returned to him for additional verification, and his misjudgment of his own working schedules. By the time the volumes were nearly ready for publication, the press was actually organizing "ammunition" to be used against Baron if the need should rise. Even Herbert Schneider, Baron's staunchest supporter for publication, at one point referred to the business as "both tragic and amusing."

Much of the difficulty actually derived from the preparation of the bibliography, which, because of its comprehensive breadth, has through the years astounded readers regardless of specialty. In fact, Baron agreed to include a bibliography only under strong directives from Proffitt in accordance with press policy.[73] But now, preparing the bibliography at the last moment, Baron submitted his citations on index cards based on a few chapters at a time. Both editor and press attempted to convince Baron to finish the work in toto, but the efficiency they were advocating was outweighed in Baron's mind by the time that would be lost in waiting for the entire project to be completed. The piecemeal approach, however, made the task of assuring uniform references throughout this long and complicated work all the more difficult. An even worse blow came with the corrections and omissions that were submitted even after the cards had been edited. Thus, Baron could innocuously mention in a letter to managing editor Henry Wiggins: "In going over the bibliography of the first seven chapters I have discovered certain omissions and incorrect titles. Kindly forward the enclosed cards to Miss Read for inclusion in her bibliography." Yet, a few lines later, Baron was pressing to know when the editing of that section would be completed.[74]

The editor complained and Wiggins attempted to explain to Baron the difficulties involved in this procedure. Responding to a copy of Wiggins's letter to Baron, Read wrote that the letter "seems to me admirably designed to serve its purpose. However, I may say confidentially that I doubt if anything serves its purpose in this connection, and I expect that in page proof our friend will wish to change, enlarge, revise, recast, eliminate, add—your fancy can complete it."[75]

In the meantime, Baron continued to reconstruct publication schedules, while commenting on many aspects of production.[76] Hoping to be ready for publication by the opening of the academic year in September, he elaborated:

In order to have a bound copy on August 1st, we should, in my opinion, start with the actual printing not later than April 15th. Assuming that the entire galley of the two volumes of text could be returned to the printer with the necessary corrections within a month, we could expect the page proofs of these volumes to arrive in quick succession after May 15th. The work on the index could then immediately begin. I assume that it will take 4–6 weeks to complete it. In the meantime, the final copy of the third volume could be set up by the printer and both corrected galleys and page proof thereof returned to him by the end of June. July would then be left for the reading of the final proofs, press work and binding. I hope that this tentative schedule will meet with your approval.

Certainly no less remarkable was his discussion of page length and margins, the spacing of the notes through an additional "hairline," and increasing the spacing between sentences. Characters chosen for chapter headings and subheadings were too large and too pronounced in comparison with other books published by Columbia. Subheadings should commence at the beginning of the line, and of course, the question of page headings for even numbered pages arose as well. A long discussion then followed on headings for the pages of notes, in which Baron discussed three possibilities, stating his preference for placing "on the left hand top: Ch. III, followed in the middle by the heading and at the right hand by volume and page, relegating the number of the page in the third volume to the bottom." This discussion was concluded with the—by now—somewhat gratuitous remark: "I have made these suggestions largely from a layman's point of view. Of course, you know much more about these matters and I shall be glad to accept your superior judgment."

Wiggins decided not to engage in debate with Baron on the question of scheduling and responded that "with regard to schedule, we definitely have the feeling that this matter should be left for discussion until the manuscript for the first two volumes has been sent to the printer for typesetting."[77] Obviously, so tight a timetable as that proposed by Baron must have seemed improbable in that he was still compiling his bibliography and revising sections that had already been edited. Meanwhile, Wiggins wrote to Read: "No amount of explaining seems to make clear to the gentleman the fact that, in proposing such a schedule, he is simply biting off more than he can possibly chew. We have written strong letters to him without avail, and nothing seems to be left save to let nature take its course."[78]

Although the difficulties with Baron were increasing, causing considerable hardship on the editor, the press simultaneously found that its position was seriously limited. Even by 1936, Baron's stature was such that they dared not alienate him. Proffitt explained their position in a letter to Miss Read written in April after, at her insistence, they had acted to limit Baron's changes in the notes and bibliography.

Professor Baron is a very distinguished scholar, and the critics who have examined this manuscript have been very generous in their praise of it. As a consequence, we have to be careful, in dealing with him, not to insist upon a course of action which would enable him to do things which impaired the scholarly value of his work. At the same time, of course, we must not surrender our own standards or make any larger than absolutely necessary the loss to the press which will probably be involved in the editorial work on this manuscript.[79]

During the month of May, relationships approached the point of explosion. Baron complained repeatedly that the editing was not finished, but continued to supply index cards for inclusion in the bibliography. Then at the beginning of May, Read was informed that Baron wanted to make a change in the format of the bibliography.[80] Wiggins candidly explained the situation to Read:

I am afraid that you may feel that you would have more success with this particular author if you were in direct contact with him. I hope this is not the case, as those of us who have been working with him down here have done about everything that we could think of to get him to comply with our reasonable requests. Mr. Proffitt and I have repeatedly discussed the difficulty which Professor Baron is causing you by his piecemeal manufacture of his bibliography.[81]

Wiggins then repeated Proffitt's explanation that Baron justified his changes on the impregnable grounds of scholarship. "We cannot afford to have him report to his faculty colleagues that the press is putting obstacles in the way of his turning out a piece of good scholarship."

Read assured Wiggins that she did "not think anyone could deal with Dr. Baron more successfully than yourself and Mr. Proffitt. I believe him to be very difficult, perhaps because very ignorant about our side of the bookmaking game. I have no doubt that when it comes to knowledge of Jewish history, he may be a ranking scholar. . . . He is not, however, scholarly in his work—nor does he know the English language."[82]

Meanwhile, Baron became increasingly impatient to see the remainder of the manuscript. Telegrams were exchanged between the press and Read, and as Wiggins subsequently explained, "Our difficulties with the author were approaching

'boiling point.' Mr. Baron is not a very considerate gentleman, and, in spite of the many delays he has caused us, he
seems to think that we must rush our work as soon as he is
ready for it."[83]

In early June 1936, the office compiled a memo on the status
of the work, based primarily on a report submitted by the
editor together with the finished manuscript and the bibliography as it then stood. The office version that was sent to
Baron represented a mellowed adaptation of what Read had
herself written.[84] Baron responded at length and in detail.[85]
One point of his reply concerned the comments on his style in
English. "I wish to say that some of the comments are grossly
unfair, not so much to myself—for whom English is not
really a native language—as to the expert editor who had
gone over the manuscript before." The reference was presumably to Herbert Solow, whom Baron had met at the *Menorah
Journal,* and who is listed in the preface as assisting with
editorial preparation.

Baron claimed that few corrections had been made in his
manuscript by the editor. He also wrote that he had "foreseen
that the preparation of such a complicated bibliography under
pressure would lead to some errors and inconsistencies." He
also referred to the difficulty of not having the manuscript at
his disposal while preparing the bibliography. Read naturally
jumped on these points: "I may point out that Mr. Baron
took about three months to prepare his bibliography (which
he insisted would be ready in two or three weeks) and now
excuses himself for errors on the ground of pressure in its
preparation, and not having all the text at hand during his

work, though the press could not convince him in advance that the latter would be a handicap."[86]

Of course, Read was surprised that the substance of her remarks had been sent to Baron, and Wiggins apparently felt that he owed her an explanation:

I quite agree with you in your feeling about Professor Baron. He has always been a difficult and unreasonable person to deal with and his attitude toward the editing is of a piece with his attitude toward schedule and financial problems. . . .

Mr. Proffitt felt that it would be good for Professor Baron's soul to see certain sections of your report and, since reading Professor Baron's reply and your letter, he has told me that he still thinks it was good for Professor Baron's soul. . . . Your letter leaves us with some good amunition {sic} in our arsenal, to be used as occasion demands.[87]

One more shot in this struggle is worth examining. In late July, a month after the previous exchanges, Read wrote to Wiggins that Baron had now introduced revisions in the style of the bibliography, affecting the entire work. "At least a week's extra work will be required to repair so far as possible the damage done. . . . Is Mr. Baron to continue indefinitely to destroy the editorial work done on his book?" And then she continued: "Throughout Mr. Baron's work runs a sort of naive wonder as to the possible cause of what he refers to as 'anti-Semitism' or 'Judenhass.' Can it be that I have an inkling as to the answer—which, I am afraid, however, will always elude Mr. Baron? "[88]

At no time, despite the considerable animosity that was brewing, did any official of the press give written expression to any similar thought. But Wiggins's reply to Read's letter does indicate a truly ludicrous scene. Wiggins apologized for the delay in writing to her, as he had his "own troubles with this particular book." The author had been with him for over two hours a few days before. There is no indication of the topic of discussion, but over the next three days, at Proffitt's instructions Wiggins counted the corrections that had been made in Baron's manuscript by the editor and recorded how many had been accepted by the author. The point of this exercise was to be prepared "in the event of Professor Baron's making criticisms at some later date of the work done by the press."[89] One certainly must give Baron credit for reversing the usual situation and making his publishers so paranoid.

Baron had long expressed dissatisfaction with the title, *Jews and Judaism: A Study in Social and Religious History*.[90] As the editing came to a close, the title was changed, at Baron's suggestion, to *A Social and Religious History of the Jews*.[91] Baron had also suggested titles for each volume, *Israel in the Orient* for the first and *Western Jewry* for the second. Proffitt was opposed, however, because "the arrangement of your work is fundamentally chronological rather than geographical" and so as not to encourage sales of separate volumes in place of the entire set.

After the new title was accepted, Baron suggested a new subtitle: *A Social and Religious History of the Jews: An Interplay of Socio-Economics and Religion throughout Three Millennia*. Baron explained:

I realize that the main title is long enough. But I can see numerous advantages in turning the attention of readers avid for an economic interpretation of history to the inclusion of economic materials in this book, and that of all readers to the main theme of the entire work, namely, the interrelations between social and religious history.[92]

The main question was whether the term *economics* should appear somewhere in the title. Proffitt responded, however, that "social" included economics as well. "The word 'social' in the main title will suggest to practically everyone who might be a reader of your book that you give proper emphasis to economic factors." Proffitt rather emphatically opposed a long subtitle after a long title.[93] With these various discussions completed, production apparently proceeded routinely and the work finally appeared in 1937.

This chapter in Baron's life, the story of the preparation of the *SRH* for publication, provides a detailed description of Baron's complicated personal interactions in a professional context. Perceived on the one hand as unreasonable and closed-minded, he was also regarded with esteem for his stature and his scholarship. Of course, there was also a serious anxiety over the troubles he could cause within the Columbia academic community. It is also interesting to note how the man admired for his broad powers of conceptual thinking was at the same time perceived as a man unable to get beyond the specifics of printers' estimates to see the problems at hand. But then again, Baron acted to solve what might easily have been seen as overwhelming difficulties with the result of publishing a work that not only established his ranking position in the field, but also proved his own estimates of sales to have been the most accurate. Columbia University Press for its part also transcended the difficulties posed by this undertaking, and somewhat against its own financial judgment, committed its resources to what became one of the great pioneering efforts in the American publishing of Judaica.

The Meaning of a Social and Religious History

Recall that Baron took very seriously the title selected by Dubnow for his history, criticizing Dubnow for not providing what was expected from a work entitled *World History of the Jews*. Virtually every word in Baron's title, including the opening *A*, could be subjected to exegesis—and was by the reviewers. But the primary task must be to understand the significance of the combination of *social and religious*. And surprisingly, there was little discussion about the title until Baron's own recent methodological discourse.

The tendencies of twentieth-century historiography toward multifaceted presentations found expression in titles as well. Some of the more significant works of the early century include Rostovtzeff's *Social and Economic History of the Roman Empire* (1926) and his *Social and Economic History of the Hellenistic World* (1941). Significantly, among the best-known works with similar titles are those of Columbia's Carlton Hayes: *A Political and Social History of Modern Europe* (1923) and *A Political and Cultural History of Modern Europe* (1936). In his foreword to the latter work, Hayes commented on the difference between them:

The content [of the second work] is considerably richer. Into the story of how modern Europe has earned a living and been ruled is now woven a story of what it has thought and achieved in science and philosophy, in literature and art. The new synthesis is intended to present not a one-sided, but the many-sided, aspect of modern Europe.[94]

Of course, Baron's title revealed that here too the reader would find a work of history examined from multiple perspectives. If in the mainstream of world historiography, the new approach came to correct an overemphasis on political, diplomatic, and military aspects; in the sphere of Jewish history, it was the intellectual and religious aspects that had been focused on since the beginnings of German Wissenschaft a century before.

In emphasizing that his work would relate to both social and religious factors, Baron both advocated and limited the role of social considerations, including economic ones. Baron frequently indicated that one did not have to be a Marxist historian to appreciate the significance of the economic perspective—economic and other social factors received first billing in the Baronian order. But at the same time, Baron clarified that the social perspective alone would be insufficient for a proper understanding of Jewish history. Baron quickly became identified with the social approach in part because earlier Jewish historians, especially Graetz, had concentrated their attention on religious and intellectual materials.[95] However, both in the SRH and in The Jewish Community, Baron frequently and consistently argued the relevance of the religious factor in his understanding of Jewish history.

At the very outset of the SRH, Baron set the stage by arguing that although there may not be a direct correlation between the fate of Jews and that of Judaism, the two are nevertheless dependent on each other. "The unity of Jews and Judaism thus has a deep meaning and the interrelation between the two, the interplay of the social and religious forces throughout the entire course of Jewish history, appears to be of controlling significance."[96] In asserting the legitimacy of the religious factor in history, Baron was joining forces with Max Weber and in a sense with Werner Sombart as well. In Baron's view, economic determinism had overplayed its hand, and a synthetic view was more strongly desired.

But there is another and nonhistoriographic way to understand the title of Baron's work. In later years, Baron referred to his social-religious approach to the writing of history in such a way that the term did not seem to have meaning beyond the historiographic sense. But there is considerable evidence that Baron originally had at least one other meaning in mind. Let us first recall that the original title was *Jews and Judaism*. The opening pages of the work make clear that Baron was postulating an organic mutually dependent connection between the people and their religion.

His position in this context is not purely historiographic, but very much polemical as well. Later in the introductory chapter, Baron wrote, "The intrinsic unity of Jews and Judaism has been somewhat obscured in recent generations." He referred first to the Reform movement, which "at least in the earliest formulations, tried to emphasize more and more strongly the universal element in the Jewish religion. In consequence, the Jewish people as a whole lost its essential standing within the Jewish creed." Meanwhile, "Zionism and other Jewish national movements laid increasing stress upon the secular aspects of the Jewish people, often trying to detach the national being of the Jews from their religion." Baron made clear that he saw both extremes as inaccurate presentations of Jewish history. In the past, nationalism has proven to be an integral part of Jewish religion; and in the future, religion will have to be just as important a part of nationalism. "In the opinion of numerous observers, however, it is very likely that, just as Jewish nationality represented a vital element in the Jewish religion of former days, so the Jewish religious heritage will soon be more generally recognized, under one shape or another, as an integral part of Jewish nationalism."[97]

In both the *SRH* and *The Jewish Community*, Baron warned that a secular nationalism devoid of Judaism's religious characteristics would result in schism and a general disfunctioning of the community. Obviously, Baron was calling for a synthetic path between the classical position of Reform and that of Zionism. Indeed, he observed that the "middle course" was proving victorious in countries where Jews were a comparatively small section of the population—as in Central and Western Europe and America—and that Reform was modifying its anti-Zionist position. But in the case of Russia, Poland, and Palestine, "should secular Jewish nationalism really prevail there in the end, and for the first time in history divorce the Jewish people from its religion, the possibility of a deep schism in Jewry would become real, the ultimate effects of which cannot be foreseen" (*SRH,* 1:28).

Further evidence that Baron sought to argue against the two polar positions can be found from the beginning of his next work, *The Jewish Community*, where Baron again distinguished between the positions of Reform on one side and Zionism and Diaspora nationalism on the other. Eastern European Diaspora nationalism sought to transform the community from a religious institution into a *Volksgemeinde,* whose security would be guaranteed by a program of national minority rights. These cautions placed Baron in political conflict with Dubnow. Baron explained that "the main champions of the Volksgemeinde were recruited from among those diaspora-nationalists in Russia who, headed by the 'bourgeois' historian Simon M. Dubnow and by the 'proletarian' publicist Chaim Zhitlowsky, envisaged the future of world Jewry as that of a permanent national minority living a culturally sheltered life under constitutional safeguards of minority rights."[98] Baron argued that this position overlooked the continued vitality of the religious factor in Jewish life. In fact, Baron was adamant that even at the time of his writing, religion was far more vibrant in Western Europe and America than secular institutions such as community federations or those organizations responsible for defense activities.

In sum, when in the 1930s Baron referred to *A Social and Religious History of the Jews,* he was expressing his personal perspective not only on the nature of Jewish life in the past, but simultaneously indicating his views on what was required to best guarantee the future. In so doing, and as becomes even clearer from the opening pages of *The Jewish Community,* Baron was directly opposing Dubnow's political and historical positions.

I would now like to propose a third approach to the title of the *SRH* and its main thesis. This final line of explanation relates Baron's historiographic development to the context of his personal biography and especially to events that took place just prior to the Schermerhorn lectures. And yet, it should be emphasized that there are no contradictions between any of the three lines of interpretation that I have suggested. Each successive explanation has not delved deeper toward the truth, but rather has narrowed the context to a more specific level.

Something about the origins of the *SRH* should be said before proceeding with our discussion. When did Baron conceive of and then actually begin to work on a history of the Jews? In January 1929, Baron wrote about his work to Louis Ginzberg, then on sabbatical leave in Palestine. There was no reference to a full-length history. At that time, as we have seen, Baron was occupied with studies of several precursors in the discipline, and he was producing some of his most sweeping and original ideas in the framework of his essays. Both enterprises laid an important basis for undertaking the history, but as of early 1929, that was not yet his preoccupation.[99]

In the spring of 1931, Baron delivered the Schermerhorn lectures that became the basis for the *SRH*. The title and the notion of calling the work a history of the Jews came much later, actually as late as 1936. Yet the fundamental thesis of the *SRH* was put forth quite clearly at the time of the lectures: "the interrelation of social and religious forces, as exemplified in the long historic evolution of the Jewish people."[100] When submitting the idea of the book to a commercial publisher in 1935, Baron described the work in similar terms as "showing the mutual influences of Jewish social (including economic and political) and religious history from their earliest beginnings to the present."[101] Both of these references emphasize

145

the balanced interaction between the social and religious forces in Jewish history. I would now claim that it was not totally a historiographic question that raised the matter in the first place, but that Baron was also preoccupied with balancing the relationship between social and religious forces in part because of the question of his departmental affiliation at Columbia.

Two letters from that time highlight the intellectual unrest that was fermenting new thoughts. We have already quoted each of these letters, but they take on a new meaning in the present context. In an unmailed letter to the academic secretary, Frank Fackenthal, Baron argued against his joining the Department of History: "After all Judaism is primarily a religion and culture. The political, economic and social history of the Jews, although doubtlessly of supreme importance, is only one part, and perhaps not even the most essential in the subjects included under the heading of Jewish History, Literature, and Institutions."[102] Yet, some six weeks later, after the affiliation with the history department, which was part of the faculty of political science, had been settled, Baron wrote to Frank Gavin of Central Theological Seminary in New York: "The novelty of the experiment is externally emphasized by the fact that my Chair constitutes a part of the Faculty of Political Science so that the purely historical part of Jewish culture outside of pure philology will come more to its rights."[103]

As long as Baron had taught in Jewish institutions, as in Vienna and at JIR, he naturally assumed his position as an instructor of history. But when he moved to the broad setting of a major university, he had to struggle with the question of where the study of Jewish culture and institutions should be placed. Of course, his desire to remain independent derived from reasons other than the intellectual. But once the mundane question of departmental affiliation was settled, and especially after Baron was placed in the history department somewhat against his will, the intellectual questions remained.

I suggest that when Baron turned almost immediately thereafter to the question of the mutual interaction between social and economic forces in Jewish history on the one hand and religious and cultural forces on the other, he sought to explain to the Columbia intellectual community not only how Judaism should be studied in its historical context, but also the importance of the continuing vibrancy of religious culture in a proper understanding of the essence of Judaism. In short, in a specific sense, first the preparation of the Schermerhorn lectures and then the writing of the *SRH* represented the intellectual exercise that emerged out of a new situation— where the historic study of Judaism should take its place within the university context. Baron brought to this question a synthetic view that would allow neither historiographic extreme to dominate. He approached the problem convinced that the pure political solutions of Zionists and of Dubnow alike were inaccurate for the past and inadequate for the future. These ideas would eventually have found their expression in one way or another, but the Columbia lecture series gave him the ideal opportunity.

CHAPTER 4

THE *SRH:* IMPACT AND CRITICISM

The Scholarly Response

How did the world of Jewish studies and academia in general respond to the appearance of Baron's *Social and Religious History?* Of course, by the late 1930s Jewish scholarship was, as we have noted, in a marked stage of transition, and in Europe by 1938, it was well into the process of a steep decline. Nevertheless, in areas still outside Nazi hegemony, Simon Dubnow in Russia and Cecil Roth in England wrote two of the more interesting reviews of Baron's work. In fact, Dubnow's review appeared in a Yiddish journal published in New York, graphically illustrating the changing venue of the field.

In America, the leading journals of Judaica at the time were the popular *Menorah Journal,* where Baron had published several of his early essays and where Roth's review appeared, and the *Jewish Quarterly Review.* The *SRH* was reviewed in the latter by Jacob Marcus, a medievalist at Hebrew Union College who was at that time reorienting his forces in the direction of American Jewish history, where his pioneering impact proved considerable.

Meanwhile, the institutionalization of Jewish studies in Palestine was still at an early stage. But despite the enormous difficulties facing the new settlement, important scholarly developments were taking place. After the Hebrew University opened in 1925, two significant journals were established by the late 1930s. *Kiryath Sefer,* a bibliographic periodical published jointly by the university and the Jewish National Library, commenced publication in the 1920s and *Zion,* a journal of Jewish history published by the Israeli Historical Society and edited by Yitzhak Baer and Ben Zion Dinur, was initiated in 1936. Baer, a German-born specialist in medieval Spanish Jewish history, reviewed the *SRH* in both journals.

Reviews provide only one measure of the impact of a work of scholarship. But once we have taken into account the innate critical tendency of reviews, they do provide the fullest medium of serious discussion of Baron's work, with many of the leading figures in the field of Jewish history of the time participating. Indeed, a survey of the reviews of Baron's *History* provides a virtual road map to the state of Jewish studies in the 1930s. In the course of this discussion, Baron's critics raised a number of important issues that still disturb and divide the field; and Baron himself, responding to the pressures of criticism, provided helpful statements of his own understanding of the *SRH.* In short, the review literature is well worth examining.

. . .

Across the board, the reviewers marveled at Baron's bibliography and the footnotes that provided lengthy and sophisticated discussions of research issues covering the entire gamut of Jewish history. This response to the bibliography helped justify both the author's and publisher's efforts and pains during its compilation. Still it all seems ironic considering that Baron originally had not intended to include a bibliography at all. Cecil Roth summed up its significance this way:

The third volume is the key to the whole. There are notes on the entire work, some of them veritable excursuses, all replete with further guidance for the student and with that ripe, extraordinarily extensive knowledge which makes the reviewer stand in amazement. There are 128 pages of bibliography—largely of articles and of recondite works which have escaped the knowledge of most of our scholars. An index is, of course, a *sine qua non* in any work of scholarship; but an index such as this, extending to 100 pages, is an unusual treasure. Indeed, it is this that provides the key to the work, which suffers (as it seems to the present reviewer) from a certain lack of cohesion.[1]

Most reviewers would have agreed on Roth's last point as well, because they almost unanimously criticized Baron's arrangement of the material. Both Roth and Jacob Marcus expressed their preference for the title of the original lectures on which the *SRH* was based. "Jewish Society and Religion in their Historical Interrelation" may have been cumbersome, but it avoided the claim to represent an inclusive history. Roth referred to the *SRH* as an essay, Marcus called it a series of notes, and Dubnow expressed similar objections. Marcus also emphasized that the work assumed considerable previous knowledge of the field and was actually a work for scholars.[2] But their fundamental criticism concerned the lack of a chronological arrangement of the material. Consequently, several reviewers declared that the *SRH* simply didn't represent a work of history at all.

The review prepared by Ismar Elbogen, by then living in America, appeared on the pages of the opening volume of *Jewish Social Studies,* edited by Baron himself. But despite the obvious problem raised by this connection, Elbogen was able to combine his laudatory remarks on the *SRH* with several poignant observations and questions. The general tone was set by his opening and sweeping acclamation that the work "belongs to the most notable achievements in the field of Jewish historiography that have appeared for a long time." Elbogen did not go into depth as he discussed several of the unifying principles, but he did question whether some of Baron's generalizations and descriptions did not "go far beyond what is found in the sources." In this light, he queried Baron's sharp delineation between history and territory and several of his phrases such as "ethnic Pharisaism versus nationalist Sadduceeism."[3]

When the *SRH* appeared, Simon Dubnow was still considered the reigning master of Jewish historiography. His review of the *SRH* seemed far more respectful than Baron's own references to his predecessor. As we have already seen, more than a decade earlier, Baron had lambasted the opening volume of Dubnow's *World History.* In contrast, Dubnow not only praised the work, but emphasized that the appearance of the

SRH strengthened the hope that America was emerging as a spiritual center for Jewish life. The gravity of that pronouncement can be better understood by other references in the review to a Europe heavily threatened by Hitler on one side and Stalin on the other.[4]

Dubnow welcomed Baron's socioreligious approach and saw it as a continuation of Dubnow's own sociological perspective. Among his historiographic criticisms of the work, Dubnow referred to the lack of emphasis and explanation of the transition of the Jews from an Eastern Oriental people toward the West. This was particularly important to Dubnow because of his own conception of the hegemony of centers of Jewish life. Dubnow also demurred from Baron's revisionist dating of the beginning of the modern period to the middle of the seventeenth century, with Dubnow arguing that only limited segments of the population were exposed by that time to the forces depicted by Baron. Dubnow's own position was that the later Haskalah and especially political emancipation brought by the French Revolution were the harbingers of the new period.

Whereas several reviewers hesitated to transgress into the realm of Baron's epilogue with its analysis of contemporary developments and predictions of the future, that chapter actually provoked Dubnow's harshest comments. He objected strongly to Baron's suggestions that Jews should learn to accommodate to the new systems of Hitler's Fascism and Stalin's Communism. Both represented a betrayal to the ideals of democracy, and neither bore well for the future of Jewish life.

Dubnow concluded his review with poignant, albeit mixed,

words of praise, emphasizing that the *SRH* provided a gateway for the American reader to the vast European literature on the field: "Baron's book contains a treasure of thoughts about the most important questions of Jewish history. Not all its ideas are new, and not all its new ideas are good. But in the new American Jewish scholarly literature, this book will remain a basic text and a guide through our rich historiography in all languages" (*Zukunft,* 42:768).

Two reviews in particular warrant special attention: the most critical review was that of Solomon Zeitlin, professor of rabbinics at Philadelphia's Dropsie College and editor of the *Jewish Quarterly Review;* the most substantive discussion came from Palestine in the two reviews written by Yitzhak Baer.

Zeitlin's review, one of several bitter exchanges between Zeitlin and Baron over the next few years, appeared in 1937. Zeitlin too expressed dissatisfaction with the title of Baron's work: "Far from being a social and religious history of the Jews, it is more a series of portraits of social and religious institutions of the past." Zeitlin further asserted that the work failed to communicate to the reader the significance of some of the truly fundamental institutions of the Second Temple period, the area of Zeitlin's own specialization.[5]

Zeitlin now proceeded to a more fundamental attack. Recalling that the *History* was based on a series of lectures, Zeitlin referred to the audience of novices that had been present. In revising the work for publication, Baron had failed to fathom the depths of his subject. He had also neglected to consult the relevant primary sources, but rather had contented himself with the existing secondary literature, "most of the

time following the theories of his predecessors." This procedure had resulted in a number of errors and misunder-
standings concerning the Second Temple period. Zeitlin provided several examples and then harnessed these errors to
demonstrate his concluding point that no single individual is
capable of writing firsthand an entire history of Judaism. He
believed this kind of project required a team of collaborators.
One author can only resort to secondary literature, which in
Baron's case resulted in numerous errors and could easily
mislead the nonspecialist.

Baron responded to Zeitlin's review, explaining that although he usually did not reply to reviews, he was making an
exception in this case. Actually Baron did occasionally answer
critical reviews, and when he did so, it was always with the
disclaimer that this was an exception.[6] Baron's stated motive
for replying in this case was that Zeitlin's review was likely to
be the lone discussion of his *History* in a French journal, and
he, therefore did not wish the critique to go unanswered.
There would seem to be an additional and significant factor at
work here, for the *Revue Des Études Juives* (originally founded
in 1880) was one of the best established journals in the field
and Zeitlin represented a significant force in Jewish studies at
the time. Furthermore, Zeitlin's attack presented fundamental
questions about Baron's undertaking, and whereas other reviewers were citing disagreements within their own special-
ties, Zeitlin more than any other scholar had questioned the
entire enterprise.

Baron contended in his reply that Zeitlin had failed to
provide the reader with a clear understanding of what Baron
had attempted to accomplish in his work, which was to

demonstrate the effects of social, economic, and political developments on the Jewish religion, and the reciprocal influence of the Jewish religion on the secular aspects of Jewish society. If Zeitlin had explained these intentions, it would have been clear why Baron had resorted to a sweeping review of the entire Jewish historical experience, rather than a study of a particular period. The significance of the social and religious institutions in Jewish history stands out more boldly as a result of the panoramic view of dynamic evolution than in the case of ordinary works of history. Presumably, Baron was referring to works of traditional, chronological structure.

In his response, Baron highlighted the importance of the index volume to the coherence of the entire work by claiming the reader could find entries on any subject by using the index. Baron added that perhaps it would have been easier to write six volumes instead of three based on the accumulated material. Presumably, he meant to imply that he would then be able to supply sufficient details to accompany his theories so that his critics would be satisfied. Interestingly, Jacob Marcus emphasized in his review how such a compact publication had resulted in excessive brevity on a number of points. Marcus also suggested that a true history, written to support Baron's basic claims on the interrelation of Jewish society and religion would have required at least ten volumes.

Baron took seriously Zeitlin's accusation that his extensive use of secondary rather than primary materials, resulted in numerous misreadings of the sources. Baron responded by discussing each of the examples brought by Zeitlin. Having answered Zeitlin point by point to his own satisfaction, Baron concluded that he had countered the fundamental attack on the feasibility of a single author writing such a work. True, collective works of history, such as the Cambridge histories, had their advantages, but they also suffered from a lack of unity and perspective. And if the objective is to provide a new historical interpretation—such as, for example, concerning the interrelationship between society and religion—then the work requires the unity provided by a single author. Pointedly, Baron ended with the comment that anyone would prefer reading a chapter in the histories of Graetz or Dubnow than in a collective history despite its scientific standards. Ironically, his reviewers could easily have rejoined that the same could be said of Baron's history as well: it was still easier to read a chapter in Graetz or Dubnow than to follow the difficult structure of Baron's history.

Yitzhak Baer reviewed Baron's *History* in two different Israeli journals. In *Kiryath Sefer,* Baer discussed the bibliographic value of the work, indicating that even though there was considerable room for disagreements, Baron's innovative thinking forced the reader to rethink his positions.[7] Concerning the third volume, Baer saw significant value in Baron's summaries of research problems and the existing literature dealing with them. But here Baer touched on the problem raised by Zeitlin and that has in one variation or another concerned the field of Jewish studies all the more since the work first appeared: can an individual scholar master the entire breadth of Jewish history sufficiently to present such a summation single-handedly?

Actually, Baer's doubts did not really derive from the

enormity of the task, as much as they did from his sense that Baron had addressed these bibliographic issues from his own personal perspective:

In general, my argument regarding this section corresponds to what I have to say concerning the entire work. Baron cites some of the most recent scholarly works, but even in the third volume, the author shuts his eyes against their conclusions and against the direction and general spirit that direct the steps of progress in scientific scholarship.

Yet pointedly, Baer was not prepared to concur with the opinion expressed by Zeitlin that an undertaking of this kind required a team approach. Baer countered that as necessary as a collective work might be, "it was also necessary to have a unified survey of all the paths of development." A single and unified viewpoint will always be accompanied by the danger of subjective judgments, but these can be largely avoided by open discussion not only of the details of research, but of the broader principles and fundamentals involved in the work. It was such a critical discussion that Baer undertook in his second and much more extensive review of Baron's *History,* which appeared in the historical journal *Zion.*

Baer's review essay in *Zion* presented the longest and most comprehensive review of the first edition of the *SRH.* Baer's somewhat sympathetic yet generally critical discussion was written from a distinctly Zionist perspective. Indicating at the outset that there was little point in quibbling over details, Baer wrote that "the author had not intended to write a detailed history, precise in all its details, but rather to illumi-nate the mutual relationships between the social and religious forces at work in Jewish history." Baer was quite critical of the significance attributed by Baron to the Diaspora. He complained that Baron tended to exaggerate its importance, frequently overstating its population during different periods. And he criticized Baron for favoring the rationalist and elitist elements in Jewish history, a serious criticism coming from the leading expert in medieval Spanish Jewry, but also one of its sharpest critics. Actually, according to Baer, it was from the impoverished classes that significant connections could be found between religion and society, "at least as long as their faces were directed toward the land of Israel."

Baer's historiographic complaints were less precise. Repeatedly, he complained that Baron's analysis was unhistorical, but because of Baer's expansive style, the exact nature of his discontent remained evasive. Baer did protest that Baron's organization was too mechanical because materials were categorized according to given formulas, which often caused Baron to miss the true significance of the phenomena he was describing.

Baer also emphasized the importance of the internal factors in Jewish history and complained that Baron was overly indulgent of factors that derived from outside. This emphasis made it impossible to truly appreciate the significance of the inner spirit of the Jewish historical experience.

The author explained well . . . the social-religious teachings of the Levites and Prophets. We should have paused especially on these teachings, if Baron had seen it obligatory to demonstrate that the religious-ethical life of that time continued and functioned as a living force continually from then until recent periods in Jewish history, and they are fully capable of acting still today. However, this living force was quickly transformed by the author into a program of wood and stone.

It would seem from this reference that, according to Baer, emotionalism and relevance were among the missing elements in Baron's historiography. Yet, paradoxically, whereas Baer criticized Baron for failing to reveal the inner forces of the biblical period that continued to find vitality later on, he simultaneously complained that the historian should not be guided by later implications of the phenomena he was describing. He also criticized Baron for finding the same historical structure in the early periods of Jewish history that would govern later periods and thus "closed the way from an organic understanding."[8]

Two of Baer's observations struck close to the heart of Baron's historical approach. Baer noted several times that Baron had emphasized the social and religious aspects of Jewish history, but that he had failed to properly describe or appreciate the significance of the political developments taking place. Thus, for example, Baer cited the lack of attention given to the Hasmonean revolt, leaving the impression that this was but a marginal incident (*Zion,* 3:280). Elsewhere, Baer suggested that, conceptually, by emphasizing only the social and religious aspects of Jewish history, Baron was missing the essential importance of the political sphere (p. 289).

On Baron's critique of the lachrymose conception of Jewish history, Baer elaborated:

At first came the antisemites who claimed that the Jews should not complain so much about their bitter fate. Later, there arose people from among us who concluded that we tend too much toward self-pity and that ultimately the exile isn't so terrible. Historical research has laid a basis for this view. We have learned that there existed a realistic political view that acted for the benefit of the Jews. Despite the persecutions, Jewish-Christian relations had a legal basis. Social connections did not totally halt. . . . Furthermore, they commented on the cruel torment of the peasants and on the persecutions and slaughter of Christian sectarian groups. However, despite all of this, there remains the fact that medieval Jewish history represented one unending line of persecutions and that the lack of self-confidence regarding the foundations of survival were felt even in Spain.[9]

Baer was particularly harsh on Baron's discussion of rabbinic social philosophy, arguing that the section was full of unfounded generalizations that paid little attention to variations over time and place. On the specific question of the close sympathy between Judaism and capitalism, Baer argued that Baron and the other scholars claiming such a connection had overlooked the literature of the very period in which capitalism was emerging. Such an examination would reveal the basic conservative tendencies of the Jewish community that would in fact have obstructed the development of a capitalist spirit.

Finally, Baer claimed that Zionism had not been properly appreciated by Baron. Indeed, Baron had warned that Zionism represented a resurgence of the forces of land and nature against the forces of history, of independence from the land, that had successfully defended Judaism's survival through the centuries. Such a perspective represented for Baer the consequences of Baron's partiality toward external forces in history—for those "have no magnetic power to attract the specifics of history until they unite into a whole" (*Zion,* 3:297). It also reflected Baron's rationalism, which paid no attention to the popular outcries of the people. In his conclusion, however, Baer once again congratulated Baron for going beyond the usual professional limits of the historian and for forcing a reevaluation of the opinions—even of those who are in disagreement with his views.

Baer sent Baron copies of these reviews expressing further appreciation of his work and assuring him that this is a debate "for the sake of heaven." Baron in turn expressed his gratitude for Baer's reviews, indicating room for disagreement, but also claiming that some distortion of Baron's views had naturally taken place in providing a brief rendition of his theories in another language. The result, Baron claimed, came out quite different from the original. Baron also mentioned that he had considered preparing an article for *Zion* on external and internal factors in Jewish history, presumably in response to Baer, but that he currently lacked the time.[10]

Because several of the reviewers in the general journals were in fact Judaic scholars (e.g., Solomon Gandz, Solomon Grayzel, and Guido Kisch) it is in some ways superficial to draw a distinction between the journals, and yet some of the questions and emphases were indeed different. Reviewers in general journals were less interested in questions related to internal politics and paid more attention to such questions as Baron's place in general historiographic trends, the chances of continued Jewish survival, and the prognosis concerning the current wave of Nazi-inspired antisemitism. Both Gandz and the review in the *American Sociological Review* placed Baron's emphasis on social and religious interactions within the historic stream of Max Weber and Werner Sombart. Baron was congratulated for his use of ancient Greek and Roman sources, and with some significance, Fritz Heichelheim of Cambridge, writing in *Classical Weekly,* called for greater reciprocal scholarship: "It is a matter of regret that classical scholars do not, as a rule, use to the same extent the highly important Jewish sources."[11]

The recurring comment that Baron's work did not really represent a full history was perhaps best described in the pages of the *Catholic Historical Review.* Observing that the work was originally prepared as a series of lectures, the reviewer continued:

Collectively, they are a series of monographs loosely following one another in a semi-chronological order, without the slightest attempt at linking them together formally. This of course does not detract from the value of the book; indeed, in one respect it has its advantages. *Nevertheless, it might well have been considered a sufficient reason not to decorate the book with a title generally reserved for writings strictly governed by the law of unity of composition.* (my emphasis)[12]

The reviewer concluded that although "this book in itself is not a social and religious history of the Jews, it is, however, an excellent contribution to such a history. . . . May Dr. Baron live to write that history!"

Several more popular journals related the work to the contemporary antisemitic atmosphere. W. E. Garrison, writing in *Christian Century,* commented: "He has made clear the reasons why the problem of their present position in the world is so difficult both for themselves and for those who wish them well." For David Krinkin, writing in *The Nation,* Baron's work was of "great importance for every person who is interested in the study of modern sociological problems in general, and the Jewish problem in particular. Anti-Semite and pro-Semite alike will find an authoritative and abundant source of information which should prove equally valuable to both."[13]

Interestingly, the Jewish journals seemed to gloss over the hovering presence of an international antisemitic atmosphere, but these reviewers were essentially correct that Baron himself had not been so oblivious. After all, the epilogue itself had dealt at length with questions of Jewish survival. In the words of H. H. Hyvernat, "This is truly a book of poignant actuality. . . . Non-Jews often wonder whether and how our present social order is going to endure. . . . The Jews, painfully conscious of passing through one of the greatest, if not the very greatest, crises of their tri-millennial history, more and more frequently ask whether they will survive it."[14]

The scholarly response to Baron's work acknowledged a significant contribution to the writing of Jewish history. Here was a history written in the jargon and with the methods used throughout the profession. Signs of increased acceptance were apparent. A major university press had undertaken its publication; a classicist had called for increased attention to Jewish sources. But ironically, many scholars objected to the claim that Baron's work was a new history of the Jews. After all, that was certainly what Baron had intended to write—a successor to the earlier works of Jost, Graetz, and Dubnow. That recurring assessment, occasionally accompanied by an estimate that a minimum of six or ten volumes were needed to fulfill the objective, presumably planted itself in Baron's mind when, a decade later, he set out to issue a second edition.

Response to His Critics

Baron responded to his critics in the opening issue of *Jewish Social Studies.* In "Emphases in Jewish History," Baron took the opportunity to explain some of the basic principles of the *SRH* that had been called into question by the reviewers.[15] Some of what had been only implicit in the work itself now became explicit, but under the challenge of criticism, Baron also offered new explanations and perspectives on his work. Although many of the methodological observations made in 1939 subsequently appeared elsewhere, "Emphases in Jewish history" remained Baron's fullest statement on the subject of methodology for half a century.[16]

Most reviewers had questioned the lack of a chronological arrangement, even raising the question of whether the *SRH* should be considered a history. So Baron naturally tackled that problem first. He maintained that a strictly chronological structure blurred the underlying principles that could make the study of history relevant for each generation. He also argued that in contrast with the "annalist" approach that described events of a particular year, the increased tendency away from diplomatic and military history and toward social perspectives necessitated a focus on longer periods of time. "When the emphasis was shifted, however, to underlying social events, it was easily recognized that certain basic movements took decades, if not centuries, to generate, grow, and decay."[17] These changes in historical writing were effecting the writing of Jewish history as well. The annals of earlier writers had been succeeded by the chronologically structured works of Jost and Graetz, who were followed by Dubnow's "more extended epochs of the successive hegemonies of distinctive Jewish centers."

Dubnow had argued that it was confusing to mix political, socioeconomic, and literary developments within the same chapter. Others, like Israel Abrahams, adopted a topical arrangement, but in so doing, neglected the necessary chronological and geographic variations. Thus, Baron determined to follow a variation of the topical arrangement, which would provide increased opportunity for a fine-tuning of his material.[18]

But his defense of larger time spans—justified by the significance of slow-moving, almost imperceptible, social changes—evaded the thrust of the criticism that the *SRH* presented material out of chronological sequence. Baron argued that whereas a chronological framework could be maintained during the ancient period, that was not possible during the later medieval and modern periods when, for example, there were geographic factors to consider as well:

After that time [the ancient period] the chronological sequence became less and less important and, for example, the history of the Jews under Islam, medieval as well as modern, had to be separately treated from medieval and early modern Christendom. The story of the rise and development of Hasidism had to be told in conjunction with the evolution of the Kabbalah and popular ethics within the general make-up of the medieval and early modern ghetto. At the same time the chronologically preceding influences of the Protestant Reformation upon Jewish history had to be treated in a subsequent chapter as an integral factor in the transformation of modern Europe and in the ensuing emancipation of the Jews.[19]

Baron admitted that he himself had entertained doubts about calling his book a history, but in the end he felt justified to do so because of the changing nature of the historical discipline at large.[20]

Baron then engaged in a discussion of three approaches to historiography—the geographic, economic, and idealistic—before turning to the sociological approach with which he identified himself. Both the geographic and economic approaches fascinated Baron, providing a method that would extract Jewish history from its inner confines and its emphasis on uniqueness and place it instead within the broader context of historical patterns. In Baron's view, both of these approaches also broke down when used exclusively.

Geography probably appealed to Baron because of its presumed scientific methods, and indeed he harnessed the massive geographic literature on Palestine as he found it relevant to his writing. "It can definitely be shown . . . that the geography of Palestine played a very decisive role in the shaping of the destinies of the Jews in antiquity and thus also influenced profoundly the succeeding generations." Geographic considerations would be conducive for the Palestinocentric view that meaningful Jewish history only occurred there and that Diaspora Jewry had little chance of survival. Obviously, a history of the Jews that was concerned with the significance of the Diaspora experience would face a complex task in considering geographic factors for the wide-spread communities of Jewish history. "A thorough investigation of the Jewish settlements in various periods and of the forces emanating from their respective natural environments would undoubtedly help elucidate a number of otherwise unexplainable phenomena in the history of many Jewish communities" ("Emphases," pp. 70–71). But individual studies of that kind were available in only a few instances.

Under the present circumstances, an exclusively geographic approach was more conducive to a school of history that negated the historical importance of the Diaspora, but this was far removed from Baron's own outlook. "Most scholars and teachers will undoubtedly take the middle position that a clear analysis of every facet of physical life affecting both Palestinian and Diaspora Jewry is of supreme significance for the understanding of Jewish history in its entirety." Indeed, this tension between an Israeli-centered perspective and one that takes the Diaspora experience into account as well, stood at the basis of Baron's interpretation of the Jewish experience as a continuous struggle between history and nature.

These remarks are not to be construed as an advocacy of the extremist Bucklean views on the influence of the geographic factor in Jewish history. On the contrary, in the present author's opinion, the history of the Jewish people offers a supreme example of a group attempting (and to a certain extent succeeding) to live on despite nature; of a nationality gradually divorced from state and territory, which has consequently become somewhat immune from the influences emanating from the soil and its derivatives. . . . Nevertheless, a better understanding of the influences emanating from the physical factors, which have consistently threatened to submerge the people's conscious endeavor to emancipate itself from the forces of nature, will greatly help to clarify the successive relapses of various groups of Jews into a state of acquiescence with the dictates of nature, and the serious handicaps encountered by the people as a whole in its main historic procession.[21]

In sum, this short discussion indicates two factors at play in Baron's construction of Jewish history as a conflict between the forces of history and those of nature. One factor was his ideological conflict with an exclusive Zionist perspective; the other was his deep attraction for the scientific potentials of geographic historiography.

Considering how important the place of economic history was in the *SRH,* it is strange how brief and ineffective was the relevant discussion in the "Emphases" essay; it was placed within a two-and-one-half-page section that was shorter than his discussion on geography. The influence of both Marx and Werner Sombart was duly noted, as were monographic researches on specific periods. But, according to Baron, there was still no synthetic view of the influence of economic factors in Jewish life, and even more lacking was a history of changing economic attitudes within Judaism. Baron had attempted such a description in his discussion on "Rabbinic Social Philosophy," a section that had been singled out by the critics both for weak substance and questionable methodology. Baron explained in his defense that in writing that section he had been "at a loss to indicate any scholarly literature on the subject," and in a footnote, he responded that, despite the paucity of material and the criticism that had been directed by Baer, a beginning must be made in order to stimulate more research.[22]

Baron's agenda for Jewish economic history did not become particularly clarified in the course of this discussion. Under the rubric "Rabbinic Social Philosophy," he had sought in the *SRH* to study economic realities in contrast with the prescriptions of rabbinic law: "Such studies, dealing with the normative, with what ought to be, cannot satisfactorily answer the main economic inquiry of what is or what was." That attitude was characteristic of Baron's general skepticism toward law as a source of social history, but use of the term *Philosophy* in the heading nevertheless seems a blatant misnomer.

Having failed to adequately explain his position, at the end of this section Baron virtually teased the reader by hinting at an important argument of broader historical implications; he wrote that "we feel, however, no less strongly that among the histories of the different human groups, that of the Jews will most stubbornly resist any full explanation which may be advanced for it exclusively on the basis of the progressive changes in the means of production or of any other economic transformations" ("Emphases," pp. 74–75).

Far more cogent was Baron's dismissal of what he called the idealistic type of historiography, with its emphasis on the inner spirit of Judaism that determined the direction of Jewish history. In ancient and medieval times this spirit was identified with Divine will and responded directly to the moral-religious behavior of the Jews. In modern historiography, such a theocratic view was replaced by a secularized conception of the national will, such as that found in the writings of Ahad Ha'am and Dubnow. "They set up a sort of autonomous national will which was the driving force in shaping the destinies of the people and which, in the supreme interest of national self-preservation, made all the necessary adjustments required in the different periods and regions."[23]

For Baron, this approach, so deeply embedded in Jewish historical tradition, postulated a uniqueness in the historical experience of the Jews that was no longer acceptable. "The historical explanations of the Jewish past must not fundamentally deviate from the general patterns of history which we accept for mankind at large or for any other particular national group." Here Baron was expressing the views with which he was becoming strongly identified—to subject the study of Jewish history to the same rules, the same methods, the same modes of explanation that would be used in the historical study of any social group. Of course, there was still room for peculiar characteristics, but this was also true of other national groups as well.[24]

I would call Baron's prescription described here as the "normalization of Jewish history." It provides the second half of the basic coin of Baron's historiography, complementing his dictum to Jewish historians to go beyond the lachrymose conception and to approach Jewish history as a rich and complex historical experience. As we shall see, social history represented Baron's euphemism for the kind of historical writing he was prescribing, and it was consciously meant to indicate the polar opposite of lachrymose writing.

But Baron left his understanding of the sociological approach basically undefined, suggesting instead a number of its components. These included what he called the "biological approach," which would usually be called demographic analysis. Baron indicated his oft-repeated hope to undertake a study of Jewish history "in the light of numbers," which would analyze the processes of population growth and decay, birth and mortality rates, urban and rural distribution, the frequency of intermarriage, and the effects of these phenomena on economic, cultural, and religious history.[25]

Also under the broader rubric of the sociological approach, Baron included the communal study of Jewish history, which would seek "an analysis of the changing aspects of Jewish communal co-existence in different environments and of their influence upon the daily life of the masses as well as upon the conscious formulations of the leaders."[26] By this time Baron was already occupied with his next major work, the three-volume study of the Jewish community.

Still within the parameters of his understanding of the sociological approach, Baron also referred to a rather cumbersome nomenclature of a normative-factual approach. Baron was referring to his frequent contrast between the normative prescriptions of Jewish law with the social realities of Jewish life. Presenting this point in an abstract formulation was not particularly useful, but it did emphasize that a social study of Jewish history cannot make the a priori assumption that, even in traditional society, normative behavior was identified with Jewish law. The true objective of the social historian was the study of actual behavior patterns.[27]

Finally, Baron sought to elucidate his understanding of the socioreligious approach. Warning against generalizations, he argued that in the case of Judaism, "religion could generally be classified as just another social force," that is, that a proper sociological approach to the study of Judaism would have to emphasize the importance of religion.

There is no doubt that among the various social factors, population, economics, community, secular culture, and religion, the latter has held the most conspicuous place at least in the consciousness of the Jews throughout the three and a half millennia of their existence. In no other people's history has the impact of religion been so strong, continuous, and comprehensive as in the history of the Jews, especially in post-biblical times. ("Emphases," p. 86)

Obviously, as we have already seen, the relationship between social and religious forces stands at the crux of a proper understanding of the *Social and Religious History,* and Baron's adherence to both perspectives may help explain the popular as well as the critical success that greeted the work.

Popular Response

Sales of the *SRH* exceeded anything predicted by the press or the people it consulted, although they did not meet Baron's more optimistic estimates. A new printing, separate publication of the last chapters, and even a new edition quickly became the issues at hand. One rabbi wrote to Baron to explain the more popular significance of the work:

It helps one to think through along the lines of the important movements and tendencies. It has helped to illuminate for me many a point of view which was clouded by doubt and uncertainty. Of course you already have the judgment of scholars, but from the standpoint of preachers it is also an invaluable piece of work.[28]

Elisha M. Friedman, a New York businessperson and writer on Jewish subjects, wrote to Baron in January 1938: "I enjoyed keenly the exact scholarship, the broad historical background and the effective style." Friedman criticized Baron for ignoring "the interpretation that a biologist or sociologist would make. . . . You devote somewhat too much attention to the historiographical and theological aspects." Friedman also proposed a separate edition of the chapter on nationalism and the epilogue. He suggested the volume be published separately at a price of $1 to reach a wider audience and that the Jewish Publication Society would be ideal for such a venture. Baron forwarded this suggestion to Columbia's press. When Proffitt asked Geddes for his opinion, the reply was enthusiastic.

They are the cream—no doubt about it. They stand perfectly well by themselves. About next fall, I should think it would be a good idea to do just what Friedman suggests. I don't agree that the Jewish Publication Society should do it, though. For a dollar, we could certainly sell a thousand easy—maybe 2,500. It makes a *very good* semi-trade book. Friedman is to be thanked.[29]

Obviously, the press's attitudes toward potential sales of a book on Jewish history had changed radically as a result of the *SRH*'s success. But Proffitt put the matter off for a few months—and this was in 1938. By the time the press got back to the question, too much had happened to publish the work in its present condition. An office memo written in May 1939—still four months before the actual outbreak of war— put it this way: "These chapters were presumably written in 1936 and the book published in the Spring of 1937. A year ago the material was still quite up to date, but so much has happened in the past year that several passages I looked up now sound almost pathetic."[30]

If Baron's observations on the contemporary situation became outdated so rapidly that they sounded "almost pathetic" to an observer, then this raises questions about his understanding of what was happening in Europe at that very time. This is dealt with later on. But almost to strengthen that point, Baron did not let the idea of reprinting the epilogue drop even after the press had concluded that the material was too dated. Proffitt wrote to Baron that "so much has happened, however, that we are now inclined to feel that your ideas would reach their biggest audience and would be most effective if you could condense them into an authoritative article for some scholarly periodical." Baron answered Proffitt that he had in fact already written several such articles, but he returned to the question at hand. Would those chapters "revised and brought up to date . . . not prove to be a well-marketable volume. The 200 large pages of the present edition, could, with some minor amplifications in detail be easily reprinted in a volume of 300 ordinary pages or more."[31]

Obviously, Baron did not envision considerable changes in light of the new circumstances of Nazi aggression, and the people at the press simply could not understand his position. On 22 August 1939, Geddes wrote to Wiggins, the managing editor:

Originally we had an idea that the Epilogue as such could be reprinted without change. . . . Then it developed that the Epilogue would require revision and after that it appeared that the Epilogue would require *extensive revision,* and then enlargement, until finally we don't know just what it is that the Epilogue now requires. It seems to me that Baron is talking about the possibility of writing a new book on the framework of the old Epilogue. I don't know just what kind of a new book it would be.

In the end, Geddes suggested that the press encourage Baron "to bring all of his manuscripts to Columbia University Press, to prepare as many manuscripts as possible, and by all means to do a manuscript on the skeleton of the Epilogue, and to assure him that we look forward to the pleasure of examining it."[32]

The press's heightened interest in Baron's writings reflected, of course, the greater-than-expected sales of the *SRH.* At least one commercial publisher as well was considerably more inclined toward Judaica manuscripts. An editor at Alfred Knopf wrote to Baron in 1937, expressing interest in books dealing with Jewish history and affairs and asking if Baron had something for them.[33]

Meanwhile, even during the discussions concerning separate publication of the epilogue, Columbia's press began to consider reprinting the entire work. In fact, only a year after its publication, the press was already contemplating a new edition—although it was expected that this would not be needed until somewhat later. These questions were discussed in a letter from Proffitt to Herbert Schneider, written in June 1938. The press had printed 1,100 copies of the first two volumes, but only 800 copies of the third volume, anticipating lesser sales for that volume. But on the whole their predictions had proven incorrect. As of that time, the press had sold 830 copies of the first volume, 840 of the second, and 780 of the third. A new printing of the third volume was required immediately and one of the first two volumes would be needed by early 1940.

Explaining that absolutely no changes could be allowed in the text or bibliography at this time, Proffitt asked Schneider if he thought the work could be "revised about five years after publication, limiting most of the changes to the latter part of Volume II, and of course to the bibliography and index in Volume III." Proffitt was interested in a new edition appearing around 1942 or 1943, by which time he thought sales could be substantial. If Schneider concurred with this analysis, the press might well decide to hold the type on the first edition. Thus, as early as 1938, Columbia University Press had set the basis for the second edition of the *SRH.*

Schneider's response included some interesting points. Instead of Proffitt's proposal of a new edition within five years, Schneider wrote, "I should estimate that a period of ten years would be better. . . . It takes many libraries and professors five years to get around to ordering the first edition. Furthermore, unless extraordinary developments take place, the book will be substantially up-to-date for 10 years."

But when revisions are made, Proffitt had, according to Schneider, misjudged what would be required. "Possibly the most significant revisions will need to be made in *Chapter I* of Volume I, as a result of the recent archeological discoveries in and about Palestine. These are just [as] necessary as the revisions in contemporary Zionism."[34]

One thousand additional copies of the third volume were ordered in August 1938. Again sooner than expected, a reprinting of the first two volumes was required by May 1939. Apparently, eight hundred copies of the two volumes were printed at that time. Sales continued throughout the war years, and in 1946, low stocks required another reprint.[35] A third printing of one thousand sets was originally ordered that year, but plans were soon changed in favor of a second and revised edition.[36]

CHAPTER 5

SCHOLARSHIP AND COMMUNITY

Family, House, and Work

FOR THE NEXT fifty years after the publication of the *Social and Religious History*, Baron remained remarkably productive. When *The Jewish Community* appeared in 1942, Cecil Roth reviewed the three-volume work in the *Menorah Journal*, where a few years earlier he had praised the *SRH*. This time he was more critical. And one paragraph, intended to cast doubts on the accuracy of Baron's work, captures marvelously the mystique around his accomplishments.

"And still they gaz'd, and still the wonder grew, That one small head could carry all he knew." But does it? Personally, I am filled with admiration for Dr. Baron's remarkable learning; I have stated more than once that he is in my opinion the most gifted Jewish historian of our day (there is certainly no one other than Fritz Baer, of

Jerusalem, who can be compared with him); and I have informed spiteful critics that they are more actuated by jealousy of the author than jealousy in the cause of learning. *Nevertheless, it is difficult to understand how a single busy person, after having produced in 1937 the Social and Religious History—the work of a lifetime—should be able to produce the work of another lifetime in 1942.* (Closing emphasis is mine)[1]

Adjectives like "genius" or "disciplined" fail to explain adequately the Baron phenomenon, for they do not reveal the spark of his personality or the constellation of his life-style that contributed and ultimately made that continuous productivity possible.

Baron was consumed by his work. Tobey Gitelle recalled her father walking around waving cards in his hands, composing and dictating while her mother typed. Lloyd Gartner recalled watching Baron at the New York Public Library with a stack of books in front of him. For an hour and a half, Baron checked notes, going from one book to another without even raising his head from the table. Stories abound of Baron's workaholic behavior from people who saw him in unusual circumstances. Once when Baron was in his mid-eighties, he visited his niece, Shoshanna Eytan in London. Coming into London from the airport, Baron walked across the city directly to the British Museum Library to begin work. But the real secret of his productivity lay not with the unusual, but with the established routine of his daily work and life-style.

In 1933, Salo Baron adopted the middle-name of Wittmayer. He explained the change in a note to Henry Hurwitz. "P.S. Don't be astonished at the increment in my name. It is supposed to be a commemoration of my deceased grandfather, H. Wittmayer."[2] That year, he also met his future wife.

Jeannette Meisel, a graduate student at Columbia in economics working on a subject related to Jewish bankers, was referred by her adviser to consult with the professor in the history department who dealt with Jewish history. Oral testimony describes an almost-typical student interview with Baron, emphasizing such questions as whether she knew the languages that would enable her to conduct the research. However well or poorly that first meeting went, subsequent encounters in the library stacks led to marriage and a working partnership of over 50 years.

Jeannette was born and raised in New York. Her father had a prosperous business in Harlem, and the family was rather wealthy during her childhood years. An only child and somewhat protected by her parents, Jeannette was chauffeured to school daily. Her father's death in 1928—when she was seventeen—followed by the crash of 1929, left the family in less fortunate, though still comfortable circumstances.

According to one daughter's description, their wedding in June 1934 was a "planned elopement." The couple did not have the full blessing of Jeannette's mother because she did not want to be left alone. Also, seeking to avoid the considerable expense of a party, Salo and Jeannette decided on a small ceremony; they did inform Jeannette's mother when it would take place. After the ceremony, the following engraved announcement was sent out to family and friends: "Mrs. Joseph Meisel announces the marriage of her daughter Jeannette Gladys to Doctor Salo Wittmayer Baron on Tuesday, the twelfth of June nineteen hundred and thirty-four, New York City."[3]

In 1934 the Barons acquired a large house in Canaan, Connecticut, situated on a piece of property covering over a hundred acres. Baron's daughter Tobey referred to the house as an engagement present for her mother: they were living there within a month of their wedding. Canaan was chosen to meet a list of specific criteria: located near water; not too close to New York City in order to avoid frequent interruptions, but not too far and on a railroad line in order to remain accessible.[4] Baron had written to a real estate agency: "I am interested in purchasing a farm with a house, modern improvements, good location—in radius of seventy miles from New York. Preferably Connecticut."[5]

The property in Canaan was given the name—Yifat Shalom, combining the couple's respective Hebrew names and translated by them as meaning "Beauty of Peace." Not accidentally, the inscription *Yifat Shalom* marks the conclusion of many of the prefaces to Baron's writings, for the house—as Baron emphasized in our sessions—played a major role in facilitating his productivity.

At first, the house served as a summer home, although this is a loose definition. Baron managed to be free for unusually long summer breaks, extending that period by giving only oral examinations at the conclusion of his courses. This left him free from around late April until late September. The Barons were registered to vote in Connecticut, and so the family continued to spend weekends at the house until election day in November.

Shoshanna was born in 1935, and Tobey, in 1938. Shoshanna recalls that her maternal grandmother was an important figure in her childhood experiences. She would visit the family daily in New York and spent the entire summer with them in Canaan. When Baron and Jeannette traveled abroad for the first nine months of 1937, Shoshanna stayed with her grandmother.[6]

In 1941 or 1942, Canaan became the family's permanent home until around 1946. Jeannette's mother had moved in with the family in 1940 but died the following March. Jeannette apparently did not want to remain in the same apartment. But because the navy had established a considerable presence on the Columbia campus during the war years, faculty housing was not available. The family moved to Canaan around Pesach time.[7]

During those years, Baron traveled into New York City for teaching and meetings, and stayed there for two days each week. Baron described his routine in a 1944 letter to Henry Hurwitz:

I shall be delighted to attend the Menorah Dinner if it will take place on an evening when I am in the city. You probably know that I live permanently in Canaan, Conn., more than 120 miles away, and come only to meet my classes, etc., on Wednesday morning, usually leaving Friday afternoon. I am, therefore generally available on Wednesday and Thursday nights unless I have some meeting or other.[8]

In an interview for the *New York Times* on the occasion of his eightieth birthday, Baron explained the difference between work and retirement: I "used to work from 7 A.M. to 11

P.M., and since retirement from 6 A.M. to midnight."⁹ His
daughters described his working arrangements in Canaan. He
would rise early, prepare breakfast for the children, and send
them off to school. Although his wife didn't get up until
quite late, once she did, she devoted herself totally to his
needs.

Baron worked at a boat house by the lake, a wooden room
with a closed-in porch, located about half a mile from the
main house. After breakfast, he walked down, taking a scythe
to clear the paths. Exercise was always important to him, and
in Canaan he walked, cut down trees, and cleared paths.
During the winter, he would shovel snow in order to clear a
path out of the house. When he returned to the house around
1:00, he ate a hearty lunch, read mail and newspapers, and
returned to work in his upstairs study. Jeannette assisted him
in answering his mail. Around 4:30, he would break to play
games like ping-pong and badminton with the children. At
6:00, he would listen to the news on the radio, and at 6:30,
at Baron's insistence, the whole family ate dinner together.
Around 7:30, the couple went back to his study and worked
until the family had tea and cake together around 10:30.
After the children went to bed, the parents continued working. Tobey estimates that altogether he worked at least fifteen
hours a day. Jeannette, who had some difficulties sleeping,
would read until quite late, which explains why she slept late
in the morning.

At the beginning of the summer, Baron took an old Un-
derwood typewriter with him down to the boat house to type
his first drafts. When he hit an impasse, he sometimes
jumped into the river and went swimming. Both daughters

thought there was a definite difference between the work done at the boat house and that in the study. He probably did his first draft by the lake in the mornings. He devoted afternoons to bibliographies, correspondence, reviews, and editing obligations. At night, the couple would check page proofs and galleys. The daughters could not go into the study at all or play nearby when Baron was working there. In general, the home atmosphere was controlled to facilitate Baron's working.

Around 1946, the family decided to move back to New York where Baron's daughters would enjoy better educational facilities. In 1948, they moved into the apartment on Claremont Avenue near Columbia where Baron lived until his death. Shoshanna was enrolled in the Bronx School of Science, and Tobey went first to Hunter College Jr. High School on the East Side and later to Bronx Science.

The routine in New York followed the same principles, but differed in its details. Baron sent the girls off to school, which in New York included walking them to the 125th Street subway station. He next walked down to 96th Street and Riverside Drive every morning and then returned to the Columbia library. Lloyd Gartner recalled that in his student days at Columbia (around 1950) the students were not supposed to know the location of his study in Butler Library. Baron was generally quite accessible to his students, but primarily at given times and places.

Tobey Gitelle recalled the scenes at home when Baron and Jeannette worked together. "Mother was his right hand." They read galleys together. As time went on, he dictated first drafts to her; this was the case by the early 1950s. By the time Tobey was in college, her mother was totally involved in his work.[10] He dictated; she typed triple-spaced; he would go over it, and then his secretary would retype it. "Mother did a terrific job juggling household responsibilities. Her life was secondary." In the public eye, the couple was known as working partners. Even artist illustrations were made of the two working together.

At times, Jeannette assisted in checking notes. Baron was emphatic that no one other than she was to be involved. Repeatedly, he declared that there were no research assistants involved in his work. In 1969, he wrote about bibliographic entries in the preface to volume 13 of the *SRH:*

In this connection I believe I ought to deny rumors, which have extended as far as Australia, that bibliographical material has been assembled for me by a staff of coworkers. I must emphatically state that throughout the preparation of this *History* I have operated without any research assistance except that offered to me—in a truly invaluable fashion—by my wife, in so far as she could spare the time from her numerous family and communal obligations.[11]

This insistence that his writings were the products of his own endeavors alone—accomplished only with the assistance of his wife—probably derives both from Baron's keen sense of independence, as well as the carefully nurtured image that he was a master of the entire breadth of Jewish history. It was that total scope that continually amazed his readers and led to questions about the staff and procedure that could accomplish such an undertaking. The emphatic tone of Baron's response on this point may have derived from his impression that stories of his research staff were being distributed by jealous colleagues.[12]

Both his sense of independence and the self-confidence in his mastery of the breadth of materials were key points in Baron's personality. Baron related to me an incident that occurred when he was head of a Jewish student group in Vienna and a guest speaker had failed to appear. Baron told the group that if they informed him of the topic they wished to hear about, he would take a few minutes to prepare and then deliver the talk. I was reminded of this story when examining the documents of Baron's appointment to the Miller chair. As I indicated earlier, Baron seemed to resist affiliation with any particular department, and I wondered if he saw himself as transcending departmental boundaries.

Baron's tendency to dominate situations came partially from his banking genes. Stories abound of his mastery of small details concerning financial matters and of his arguments over compensation. Some of these episodes appear in this study. It is insufficient to describe Baron as being stingy or frugal. Baron was a banker's son and had been designated to succeed his father. At times he acted out that role. But even more important, he absorbed the image that bankers are entrusted with grave responsibilities and become accustomed to controlling situations. At a meeting of the American Academy for Jewish Research shortly after Jeannette's death, Baron was obviously shaken by his loss. But he nevertheless reported in detail on the academy's financial holdings, including the interest rates being received for deposits and ways in which those returns could be improved. [13]

Similar stories are told within the family framework. Shoshanna Eytan, Baron's niece living in Jerusalem, told me how her mother had once entrusted Baron with some money. Years later, Baron presented the family with a detailed record of how he had invested that deposit and dispensed the funds. Baron viewed himself as head of the family, including the Jerusalem branch where neither parent was alive. Eytan once neglected to immediately inform Baron of a certain development within the family. She explained that she simply had not had the opportunity. Baron responded when he heard of the news: "I should have been told!" [14]

Baron's obsession with walking represented another crucial element in his life-style and self-image. As a youth, mountain climbing was one of his hobbies. As an adult in America, walking became a fixed part of his daily routine. In Canaan, he hiked down to the shack by the lake; in New York, he walked his children to the subway station and then hiked from 125th Street to Riverside Park and 96th Street and back up to 116th Street. David Rosenstein, head of the Ideal Toy Company and long-time treasurer of the Conference on Jewish Social Studies, was Baron's main walking partner. Baron and Rosenstein walked for hours regularly on Sunday mornings, far exceeding the usual distance of his daily walks. [15]

His daughter Tobey felt that walking was the secret of his longevity, because Baron was, for most of his life, a stout man who loved food and ate heartily. He saw exercise and walking in particular as central to his working habits. A few years before his death, Baron had fallen and hurt his hip. Very much concerned with the effects of this injury, he requested Lloyd Gartner to watch him walk back and forth a number of times and to see if his walking looked proper. Gartner under-

187

stood that somehow Baron was convinced there was an integral connection between his capacity to walk and his ability to keep writing and to function in general.

How did Baron manage to write as much as he did? Asked to sum up his personality, family and those former students close to him describe Baron as a determined workaholic who spent long hours in isolation day after day at his research and writing. The daily routine described was followed seven days a week for the entire year. Yom Kippur is the only day about which there is some question concerning whether Baron worked at his writing. Baron traveled considerably, but he often combined his travels with the need to consult special collections in the libraries around the world.

Longevity also provides part of the answer to Baron's accomplishments. His first books in English were the three-volume *History* that appeared when he was already forty-two. Of course, a history of the Jews over four thousand years is a rather ambitious first work. And by that time he had earned three doctorates, written two books in German as dissertations for those doctorates, and published several essays that contained the basis of his revisionist approach to Jewish history. He had also moved from Galicia to Vienna and from Vienna to New York. Obviously, even by 1937, Baron had proven that he was capable of accomplishing a great deal.

And yet, the corpus with which scholars of Jewish studies are most familiar all appeared from the age of forty-two on. This includes close to thirty original volumes and three collections of Baron's essays organized by themes. Thus, part of the explanation lies with his long life and continued productivity—until around the age of ninety, at the time of Jeannette's death. History's one loss was that he waited too long before he sat down to write his memoirs. It was a life story well worth telling.

The Immigrant Experience

With work his highest priority, Baron maintained few close friendships. He was a solitary man, independent and private. Neither he nor Jeannette discussed personal relationships with others, including their family. His daughter Shoshanna commented that only in his last years did Baron even talk about his own family and childhood in Europe. In our interviews, I found myself continually prompting Baron about acquaintances, because he repeatedly strayed from the question. [16]

A few names emerged from consultation with his daughters. Heschel Bernstein, a physician who had also come from Vienna, was a close friend. David Rosenstein, head of Ideal Toys and active in the Conference on Jewish Social Studies, was his main walking partner. In the 1930s and early 1940s, before the family moved to Canaan, Alexander Marx, Louis Ginzberg, and later Saul Lieberman (all faculty members at the Jewish Theological Seminary) were friends for intellectual exchange. Shabbat afternoons were frequently spent visiting either at the Marxes or Ginzbergs.

Letters between Baron and Marx during this same period reveal some of the contours of this personal and intellectual bond. In the mid-1930s, they wrote their personal letters in German; Baron's letters began with "Lieber Freund." These letters were about family, about life in the country, and about their work.

A few weeks ago, I spent a couple of days in New York. It was very hot and uncomfortable. My wife and I had a number of errands to do and especially we had much to take care of in the libraries. Here in the country, everything is in contrast much better. The young one is developing very nicely. She is now over 13 pounds and daily demonstrates more and more intelligence. Hopefully, on your way back you will be able to stop off and observe Shoshanna in her natural setting.[17]

In 1936, Marx carefully read the galleys of Baron's history, providing corrections and suggestions. Later they discussed *The Jewish Community,* and, as chairperson of JPS's publication committee, Marx facilitated its publication.[18]

Thus, during the 1930s, Baron found in Marx an older friend who provided guidance, support, and intellectual companionship. But, when the family moved to Canaan in the early 1940s, Baron's New York relationships must have suffered, and in any event, his personal habits and working schedule now reflected a more pronounced inclination toward isolation that was further nurtured by seclusion in the country.

In the later 1940s, after the return to New York, Baron and Hannah Arendt became intellectual companions. Baron assisted Arendt with some of her early publications and placed her as director of the postwar Commission for Jewish Cultural Reconstruction. The two walked in Riverside Park and discussed contemporary American and Jewish problems. On a number of occasions, Arendt came to the Barons residence for

Passover Seder, and she invited the Barons to dinner to celebrate the liberation of France from the Nazis. Gradually they drew apart, but close contacts were still maintained between Arendt and Jeannette. In 1975, the Barons were having dinner at Arendt's home when she suffered a heart attack and died. [19]

On the occasion of Baron's sixtieth and seventieth birthdays, Arendt joined with others in sending letters of congratulations. At the earlier event, Baron thanked her for remembering his birthday and continued: "I grew up in a family which did not observe birthdays, and I actually often forgot my own birthday." Ten years later, Arendt joined a collective effort organized by Gerson Cohen, Baron's immediate successor at Columbia. Arendt's stirring letter was quoted at length in the introduction to this study. [20]

What was Baron's immigrant experience like? [21] Baron first came to New York in the spring of 1926 for a single semester of teaching. A year later, he decided to remain in America. Roughly speaking, the decade between 1926 and the beginning of 1937 — when Baron and Jeannette left for a sabbatical trip to Europe and Palestine — represents the immediate period of Baron's immigrant experience. Thus, his arrival in America preceded the intellectual migration from Central Europe of the thirties. And, indeed, he was sufficiently established by that time to serve as a contact for numerous newcomers who were referred to him by friends and colleagues.

The faculty minute books at JIR show that at first Baron rarely participated in their discussions, but gradually became considerably more active and was entrusted with an increasing number of responsibilities. By the time of his appointment to Columbia at the end of 1929, he was in charge of JIR's history program, director of the library, and responsible for the program in advanced studies. Wise also frequently appointed Baron to ad hoc committees to deal with problems that arose during faculty discussions. His closest friend during this period was George Kohut.

From the outset, Baron's relation to Europe reveals two contrasting tendencies during this period. On the one hand, he maintained close contact with family and colleagues in Europe; yet, he almost immediately undertook to prepare publications in his newly adopted language. Baron frequently spent his summer vacations visiting his family and working in libraries in various parts of Europe. Although Berlin and Vienna were his favorite destinations, he also spent time with his parents in Tarnow. Apparently, he still preferred the rich libraries of Europe to which he was accustomed over the developing collections in New York. Indeed, he devoted some of his time during these trips to expanding the JIR library. When "Ghetto and Emancipation" appeared in 1928, he was equally concerned over responses in America and in Europe.[22]

It was precisely at the time that the "Ghetto" essay was in preparation that the Jewish Theological Seminary in Breslau offered Baron a position in Jewish history. As indicated earlier, Baron was quite proud at the invitation, but he seems to have been more flattered than actually tempted. Yet, even at that stage, he yearned for his annual summer return to Europe. In December 1929, right at the time of his appointment to Columbia, he wrote to Emil Damask, "I have been back here for three months now, and my thoughts are turning once again to Europe."[23]

Baron and Jeannette spent the summer of 1934 honey-mooning in Europe; but they also purchased the house in Canaan around that time. With that stroke, Baron cemented his roots in America. The establishment of a summer residence in Connecticut obviously indicated an end to his almost annual summer travels to Europe. Such trips were now reserved primarily for sabbaticals, like the one he took in 1937, one year before the Nazis seized Austria.

In January 1937, Baron and Jeannette set out on a nine-month trip to Europe and Palestine. In June, he wrote to Alexander Marx from Moscow describing their experiences.[24] He mentioned his visits with Agnon during their stay in Palestine and that he had spent Passover in Jerusalem with his newly married niece, Shoshanna Eytan, and her mother (Baron's eldest sister) Gisela Sussman, who was also visiting. Concluding with a reference to having spent the Shavuot holiday with his parents, Baron indicated that altogether "I have no reason for complaint."

But interestingly, Baron did complain about the progress of his work. "From the point of view of research, my journey has thus far been moderately successful." To his surprise, Baron was unable to locate "an important volume" of the *Allgemeine Zeitung des Judenthums* in Paris. In addition, he wrote: "I have found some interesting material in Paris, less so in Palestine and still less in Vilna." He then complained that he was unable to enter the Moscow archives despite previously being given permission to do so. Baron was frustrated by the quality and availability of material in these centers, which may indicate that the process of making New York his primary work center was complete.

Baron wrote this basically personal letter to Marx in English. Only two years earlier, their personal correspondence had been written in German with English reserved for more official correspondence. But Baron had switched his language of publication almost immediately after his arrival in America. From the first items listed in his bibliography, written at the age of seventeen, through the nine entries for 1926, the primary languages of publication had been first Hebrew and later German. Baron's debut in English came in 1927 with the first of his essays on the Renaissance historian Azariah de' Rossi. The following year "Ghetto and Emancipation" appeared in the *Menorah Journal,* and two essays on the study of Jewish history appeared in the JIR student journal. The *Menorah Journal* gave Baron access to a wider English-reading audience, and he returned to its pages in 1929 with "Nationalism and Intolerance."[25]

Baron continued to write some reviews and other peripheral pieces in German; but as early as 1930, all five entries in his bibliography appeared in English. Even more important, these articles provide an excellent measure of his adjustment to America and his acceptance both in academic and more public circles. In addition to the publication of scholarly articles, Baron had been commissioned by the American Jewish Congress to prepare a report on the current situation of Romanian Jews. This report drew attention in the Jewish press, and a separate interview with Baron on the teaching of

Jewish history indicates that his prominence was indeed growing.

Of course, Baron's usage of the English language revealed the continued entrapments encountered by an immigrant. It is obvious from the excerpts from his letters of this period that there were idiomatic difficulties. Elliot Cohen had explained that the delays in editing "Ghetto and Emancipation" resulted from the considerable effort required to clarify Baron's English style.[26] As we have seen, Baron was later engaged in ongoing conflict with the copy editor of the *SRH*. The quality of his English, however, was not the cause of these hostilities; publishers were rapidly becoming accustomed to the "Teutonic English" of the current migration, but Baron was adamant about the correct usage of various terms, which became a subject of debate.[27]

But the more important point was that early on Baron committed himself to adapting to publication in English. In his study on the intellectual migration from Europe to America, H. Stuart Hughes emphasized what must seem obvious — that migrant scholars who failed to make the language adjustment remained obscure entities in their new countries. Yet Hughes observed that numerous scholars, often belonging to certain disciplinary groups, clung to the languages from across the Atlantic and failed to impact upon the American cultural scene. Whether the result of cause or effect, some of these refugees eventually returned to Europe, frustrated with their experiences and content to be back home.[28]

Language was, of course, only part of the issue. The state of the particular field in America was of more fundamental significance, especially the strength or weakness of the bonds between the scholarly approach of the migrant and that of the new hosts. Hughes explained how these relationships affected the success or failure of the integration process, and in particular, that "those branches of American activity that were on the verge of making a great leap forward could profit to the full from the arrival of the refugees from Europe."[29] This is important for understanding Baron's successful adaptation because it provides an accurate description of the state of Jewish studies at the time of his migration. The seeds of growth were just beginning to blossom.

By the time of the rise of Nazism and the accompanying flight of many more scholars, Baron was well known enough to become a contact for refugee scholars and sufficiently established to assist them. In the process, he found new friends and associates with whom he shared a common Central European background. Hannah Arendt was the most prominent, but Baron specifically indicated in an interview that he had a number of acquaintances, both Gentiles and Jews, at the New School—a haven for academic refugees, primarily from Germany and Austria. His own immigrant experience was transformed as he became patron and guide to some of the newcomers. We will turn to this later role in our discussion of the Nazi period.

The Columbia Community

When Baron passed away in November 1989, it had been over twenty-six years since his retirement in 1963 from Columbia's active faculty. Altogether Baron had been a fixture on its campus for almost sixty years. During much of that time, Columbia had been the primary university center in America for the training of Jewish scholars.

It seems almost remarkable that the significant bond between Columbia and Judaica is rarely mentioned in the many discussions about Columbia's attitudes toward Jews. Nevertheless, Nicholas Murray Butler, the same man who headed Columbia for almost all of the first half of the twentieth century and who is known as the primary force behind the establishment of admission quotas on Jewish students in America, also provided the necessary administrative support for the development of Columbia's renown and pioneering program in Jewish studies. Surely, a discussion on Columbia and the Jews, especially on the question of Jewish faculty at Columbia, as in the oft-discussed case of Lionel Trilling, cannot be complete without considering the experience of the one faculty member at Columbia who, though hired at approximately the same time, was actually designated to be immersed in Judaic scholarship, and was simultaneously so completely involved in Jewish affairs.[30]

The Miller chair was established at Columbia when Jewish faculty appointments at major universities were still quite restricted. At Yale, the few Jews appointed before 1930 were usually connected with one of the science departments or professional schools. "Jews who received tenure before 1930 numbered well under a dozen—and none were tenured in Yale College before 1940." But even a prestigious faculty appointment did not guarantee social acceptance. In 1920, the Graduate Club Association sought to exclude the dean of the medical school from admission, succumbing only to pressure from Yale's president.[31]

At Columbia, early controversies centered around the question of Jewish trustees. When in 1900 Jacob Schiff protested the lack of Jews on Columbia's board, President Seth Low answered that Columbia did have four Jewish faculty members. Yet, Low's attempts to appoint a Jewish trustee were rebuffed by the board. Prospects of a large endowment renewed the issue in 1913, but the trustees again opposed the move. As one outspoken opponent wrote to the board chairperson: "We can both of us recall many times when free discussion in the Board would have been very seriously handicapped by the presence of one of this people." The reference apparently was at least in part to discussions on restricting the admission of Jewish students. But by the late 1920s the trustees were satisfied that the question of such restrictions had been resolved, and in 1928, Benjamin Cardozo, then chief justice of the New York State Court of Appeals, was appointed to the board. Still, no other Jews were made trustees until 1944, when Arthur H. Sulzberger was appointed.[32]

Columbia Economics professor Eli Ginzberg offered this comment on Butler's policies:

President Nicholas Murray Butler . . . had taken pains not to become indebted to Jewish benefactors. In the late 1920s there was no building on the campus that was named for a Jewish donor. Butler had attracted a small, select group of benefactors, which, incidentally, did not even include the Rockefeller family.[33]

As to Jewish faculty members, Ginzberg recalled the situation during his own undergraduate days of the late twenties: "The tenured faculty at that time was not *Juden-rein,* but one could quickly count those who were of Jewish extraction, and even more quickly those who had any Jewish affiliation." Ginzberg referred to anthropologist Franz Boas, economist Edwin Seligman, and Robert Loeb, the head of the Department of Medicine. "There were a few others scattered through the departments of mathematics, law, and Semitic languages."

It was also Columbia, and especially Butler, who in the early decades of the century perpetrated the quota system restricting the number of Jewish students.[34] Between 1905 and 1910, the issue of the number of entering Jewish students became important at Columbia. Frederick Keppel, dean of Columbia College from 1910 to 1918, openly discussed his views on these matters. Keppel and many of Columbia's trustees were concerned that a large influx of Jewish students, especially from the ranks of recent immigrants from Eastern Europe, would alienate and even drive away Columbia's "natural" constituency "who come from homes of refinement." But Keppel also reasoned that many Jewish parents sought to send their children away from home; that in any case the numbers involved were not as large as commonly thought; that many Jews were in fact desirable students; and that those who were less desirable as companions, but qualified for admission, should nevertheless be accepted as "every reputable institution aspiring to public service must stand ready to give those of probity and good moral character the benefits which they are making great sacrifices to obtain."[35]

Harold Wechsler's study of the history of selective admissions in American universities focused on Columbia's role in the emergence of the quota system, and Wechsler explained why the issue became so important at Columbia and why it did so earlier than at other parallel institutions.

> Social anti-Semitism was not peculiar to Columbia. . . . And yet, there was something special about Columbia's social anti-Semitism. Located in New York City, Columbia was the first university with elitist pretensions to be confronted with a large influx of Jews. Its admissions policies had been designed to facilitate the entrance of New York City high school graduates to the College, a situation that hastened the influx. Finally, the men who became Columbia trustees during these years displayed an intense social anti-Semitism. In fact, the trustees' attitude probably made Columbia's "Jewish problem" among the most significant issues that university faced during the teens.[36]

Looking back on Columbia's policies to screen candidates for admissions, Eli Ginzberg found justification for the restrictions that emerged: "With the large heterogeneous population of New York City and environs, it would have taken only a few years of a blind-admissions policy to turn Columbia into a predominantly regional college."[37]

The combination of the depression and World War II brought about a transformation in the attitudes toward Jews at major universities. Seymour Martin Lipset wrote that "the dike broke" at Harvard with the end of World War II and the university "hired Jews in significant numbers." Marcia Synnot commented in general that "although World War II was itself a catalyst, because it led to a reaffirmation of democratic values and a decline in anti-Semitic feeling, the way had been paved by the higher standards of scholarship established for faculty recruitment during the depression years."[38] Eli Ginzberg also explained that it was the combination of the depression and the war that brought about a transformation in the attitudes toward Jews at Columbia. With the vast expansion in the demand for new faculty at the end of the war, the disproportionate number of Jewish graduates finally found their way into academic positions.

The combination of fifteen years of restricted faculty appointments and promotions from the start of the Great Depression through the end of World War II, the large stream of students who flooded the campus, aided by the GI Bill, and the explosion of new career opportunities . . . created a demand for qualified faculty that could be met only if discriminatory barriers were lowered and removed.[39]

When Baron arrived at Columbia in 1930, these processes of change were just beginning. With the quota system in place, Butler provided the establishment of the Miller chair, primarily an academic matter emphasizing research and graduate study, with his full support. This too must be seen as part of his attitude toward Jews and Judaism at Columbia.

The history department at that time was still part of the faculty of political science. Robert Livingston Schuyler, Gouverneur Morris Professor of History, wrote that Columbia's was "the first graduate faculty of the political and social sciences in the United States. The founding of the Faculty of Political Science also marks Columbia's beginning of graduate instruction, and it is a milestone in the transformation of the College into the University."[40]

The political science faculty had been founded in 1880

under the leadership of John Burgess, who had been especially brought to Columbia for that purpose from Amherst. In his memoirs, Burgess described his plan as follows.

A faculty of Political Science should be created, composed of all professors . . . already giving instruction in history, economics, public law, and political science . . . in the School of Arts and the classes of the School of Law and of such others . . . as might be called to chairs in the new faculty. The plan provided a program of studies in history, economics, public law, and political philosophy, extending over a period of three years, and for a . . . Ph.D. to be conferred upon students completing successfully the curricula of the three years and presenting an approved thesis.[41]

Some trustees and faculty members were becoming increasingly convinced that the time had come for a program of graduate instruction in America that would curtail the European draw of American students. For Burgess, the question of establishing a graduate program in political science would determine the future of Columbia's rank in the academic world. But stiff opposition split the faculty and delayed a positive decision. Opponents were sincerely concerned over the future of the undergraduate college; others preferred, in the words of R. Gordon Hoxie, the "status-quo as against change, the old classical college as opposed to the new scientific university."[42]

It was Burgess himself, appointed in 1876 as professor of history and political science, who laid the modern basis for instruction in history at Columbia. A few years later, Burgess explained his understanding of the historical discipline:

Through (history) we seek to find the origin, follow the growth and learn the meaning of our legal, political, and economic principles and institutions. We class it therefore no longer with fiction or rhetoric or belles-lettres, but with logic, philosophy, ethics. We value it, therefore, not by its brilliancy, but by its productiveness.[43]

Burgess's emphasis on political subjects fit the historiographic consensus both in America and Europe at the time, but in the early twentieth century, it was also Columbia that led the way in America toward a fundamental revision of historical concerns.

In 1912, James Harvey Robinson published *The New History*, in which he criticized an exclusively political focus as "a sadly inadequate and misleading review of the past."[44] Robinson had come to Columbia in 1895 in a move to strengthen instruction in European history. His own effective teaching and the widespread impact of his popular textbooks on European history gave him considerable influence.

With the appointment of Robinson and that of William Sloane as Seth Low Professor, the way was set for the formal establishment of a Department of History in 1896. Sloane and Robinson differed greatly in their approaches, thus supporting Richard Hofstadter's contention that no single perspective totally dominated the instruction of history at Columbia. Sloane chaired the department from 1896 to 1916, and in 1915, just prior to his own retirement, Sloane wrote to Butler complaining that Robinson and James Shotwell had strayed considerably from traditional instruction at Columbia in extent amounting almost to a secession and to the creation of a new department; to wit, the establishment of elaborate courses in the history of thought and culture. In these courses they teach didactically and from a modernist point of view . . . everything except history, as their colleagues understand it. Neither is expert in any one of the subjects as discursively treated, and the departments of economics and sociology have been disturbed by the trespass.[45]

But Sloane's opponents were also of considerable influence, and contrary to Sloane's desires, William Dunning filled the chair until his death in 1922, at which time it was assumed by Carlton Hayes, a leading spokesperson of the New History school.

There were several fundamental effects of the New History on teaching at Columbia, including breaking down large lecture classes into smaller instructional sections in order to better challenge the students and to convey a sense of historical method. In James Shotwell's words, emphasis was placed on "those things of the past which in some obvious way play upon the present." Hayes justified the presentism involved in this approach: "We emphasize present-day affairs and look backward. It is illuminating how much nineteenth century history can be treated by this method." Instructional methods were further enhanced by the establishment of a historical laboratory, equipped with maps, important American and foreign newspapers, and major reference works. The press provided the primary laboratory experience, as students regularly clipped articles related to assigned themes and prepared seminar papers based on these sources.[46]

. . .

Given the emphasis within the department on interdisciplinary history involving sociology and economics, as well as the significance attributed in course instruction to firsthand experience with primary sources—and even considering the model exemplified by Hayes himself of the historian as an active participant in current affairs—there would have been plenty of reason to expect that the selection of Salo Baron for the position in Jewish history would be welcomed by the department. Indeed, the event would seem to have been well "overdetermined." This might be all the more so in light of Hayes's own active involvement in the formation of a Catholic Historical Association in 1919.[47]

And yet, it didn't happen that way. Even if Baron's rendition of what transpired during the 1930 discussions on departmental affiliation was not accurate, we should probably assume there had been some basis for his sense that the history department was reluctant to grant him a place within its ranks. In fact, until the end of his life, Baron was bitter at what he described as the poor reception he initially received from the department. There are no surviving colleagues to provide additional information.

As the years passed, Baron felt a thaw in that reception, but he numbered only a few department members as close colleagues. These included the ancient historian William Westerman and the American historian Richard Morris, who was also involved in the Conference on Jewish Social Studies.[48] By 1937, Baron's acceptance in the department seems to have been established. The *SRH* appeared during his sabbatical leave of that year, and upon his return from his travels in Israel and Europe, Baron spoke to the history department seminar on contemporary developments in Russia.[49] Gradually, Baron rose to an honored position at Columbia and was appointed to some of the highest positions held by faculty members, including chairperson of the Committee of Instruction, responsible for curricula matters.[50]

University seminars played a significant role in Columbia's intellectual life, giving the faculty the opportunity for interdisciplinary discourse on a number of topics. Having heard for years of his active role in several of these seminars, I was surprised when a volume describing the development of the program offered no reference to Baron at all.[51] Fortunately, Aaron Warner, Buttenwieser Professor Emeritus and director of the university seminar program, recalled Baron's participation and was able to find the relevant records.

The seminar on Israel and Jewish studies was founded in 1968, and Baron generally served as its chairperson or co-chairperson until 1981. He was also a member of Ancient Mediterranean Studies founded in 1966 and the Middle East Seminar formed in 1971. However, much earlier, he was a member of the Religion and Culture Seminar, and indeed even served at times as its chairperson. Thus, when a series of papers on religion and democracy was published in the *Review of Religion* in 1948, Baron wrote the preface as chairperson of the seminar that had sponsored the series.[52]

Despite the overall image of Baron as a solitary and private man, he also could express personal and touching feelings. In 1953, when Baron spoke at the funeral of a friend, Irwin Edman wrote him a note saying: "Dear Baron, I cannot refrain from writing you to tell you how eloquently and appropriately and enlighteningly you spoke at the funeral services for Jerry Michael the other day. It was fine to have you say so well just the things you did and to have you say them."[53] Later that same year, Baron wrote a very touching letter to Arthur Hertzberg to tell him that Louis Ginzberg had indicated just a few hours before his death how satisfied he was with Hertzberg's translation of his Hebrew essays.[54]

Baron was a serious and respected teacher. A former student specializing in American history during the early 1930s described his teaching style:

He . . . took his place at the desk. He had no notes, no props, only himself, his enormous mental capacities, and a quiet style! He sat there, his hands clasped and placed on the desk. He then spoke, lectured, taught, revealed—all without notes, without hesitation! Each lecture was a perfect entity. And he never raised his voice, never changed his seated posture, never unclasped his hands.[55]

Lloyd Gartner came to Columbia as a graduate student in 1949 and took courses until 1951. According to Gartner, Baron always came into the room a few minutes late and sat down at the desk. He never stood up, not even to write on the board. He would be holding an envelope, and from time to time, he would take out a small card to read a quotation. Otherwise, he lectured without notes. He had a stupendous memory and tremendous power of organization. He would welcome questions and stop at any time. The larger courses were open to both graduate and undergraduate students.

Baron remained polite and generally accessible to his students. Gartner added that, in general, Columbia's style at that time was somewhat aloof and reserved. Baron was known to be very demanding on doctoral students. He was also very proud of the dissertations that were done under his supervision. Gartner reported that he had been warned that Baron was very tough and wouldn't let a thesis be finished; but Gartner didn't find that to be the case. Gartner related that a student once asked Baron in seminar, "Do you really tell students that they shouldn't continue, that they should drop out?" "No, I don't do that," Baron answered, "but the right ones fall by the wayside."[56]

Others had a different tale to tell, and there were, as in the case of almost any teacher, those who found Baron a difficult and even obstinate supervisor. When one of Baron's students argued bitterly about the order of chapters in his dissertation, he was finally forced to concede that "if you insist, I have no choice but to follow your plan of rearrangement." Subsequent correspondence between the two, however, reflects a respectful relationship.[57]

Another student, serving as a teaching assistant, wrote a scathing rebuke to Baron on his teaching patterns, which he claimed affected the quality of Baron's scholarship as well.[58]

Both your vast erudition and the superiority of your German training are such that you are apt to be over-generous in estimating the capacities of others. . . . Now I know that you have little respect for our great Americans—Cardozo, Santayana, Dewey, Adler, et. al. But after all you are teaching American students in American schools, and it seems to me, if I may presume to say it, that you might profitably strain to acquire an insight into their attitude, shallow though it may be. . . . At Columbia it has probably already come to your attention that your scholarly presuppositions are such as to repel many students—undergraduates, Gentiles, poorly trained Jews. This makes of your department a kind of ghetto which, whatever may be said for it in general, certainly has no place on the Columbia campus.

The student was assisting Baron at the time at the Jewish Training School and apparently had wandered off from the assignments in Margolis and Marx's *History of the Jews* to offer some of his own interpretations. He suggested that a different point of view could only be to the benefit of the students, admitting that the choice lay with Baron.

It is your course. And I need the job. But I should be sorry to think that you are so much the bachelor as to be unable or unwilling to enter into a fruitful collaboration or cooperation. You know I already feel that your book [the *SRH*] suffers from that circumstance.

But for scholars like Moshe Davis and Herbert Bloom, Baron had been their mentor, greatly influencing the course of their careers. Davis, one of the pioneering figures in the writing of American Jewish history, spoke of his years under Baron's tutelage as the "most exciting experience in my life from the point of view of training." They didn't meet very often. Baron approved his outline and told Davis to write a chapter to the point where it could be published. Davis did this for three years and in fact did publish the articles. Davis explained that the significant point was that Baron had taught him not to wait until the material was accumulated, but to get immediately into the writing. They met each time an essay was ready.[59]

For years after Bloom had completed his dissertation on the economic activities of the seventeenth-century Jews of

Amsterdam, he continued to write to Baron on personal and professional matters. Baron took a great interest in Bloom's life and rabbinical career and even traveled to upstate Newburgh, New York, to install Bloom as rabbi of the congregation there.[60]

In 1947, Baron's friend Rabbi Joseph Baron (not a relative) of Milwaukee requested information, based on Baron's experience, that would support a local effort to establish a chair in Jewish studies at the University of Wisconsin. Baron's response provides a sweeping commentary on the course of Jewish studies in America and especially at Columbia and justifies quotation at length.

I am delighted to hear that a movement is afoot to establish another Jewish chair. . . . This evolution so auspiciously started in the 1920's was, unfortunately, interrupted by the depression. Let us hope that American Jewry can resume its work and establish a few more scholarly centers of this kind. My own experience at Columbia University for the last seventeen years has been extremely encouraging. . . . I am sending you announcements . . . which will give you a more detailed idea of the framework into which the chair of Jewish history, Literature and Institutions has been placed. My primary association is with the Graduate Faculty of Political Science where . . . Jewish history is considered a field of primary interest along with various other branches of social science. The courses in this field are fully recognized for credit in all related fields and students qualifying for a Master's or a Ph.D. degree are treated fully on a par with such students in other fields.

My lecture courses have from the beginning been attended by a large number of graduate students as well as some undergraduates. . . . These students were of all denominations and a variety of interests . . . and considered a course in Jewish history as rounding out their training. . . . Others have attended the course merely out of general cultural interest; still others have specialized in it.

Among the Doctors of Philosophy in this field there are several prominent younger rabbis and ministers who have already made a mark in their profession. Others went into teaching. . . . It may be mentioned that one Jewish dissertation was honored by the Dunning Prize as the "best dissertation" written at Columbia in any field of European history in three years.

Indirectly, too, the existence of such a chair at Columbia has contributed to the diffusion of interest in Jewish subjects among a variety of students. For instance, Columbia and Union Theological Seminary have recently embarked on a joint project . . . in the field of Religion. . . . It was but natural to ask the professor of Jewish history to join that committee. . . . Similarly, . . . [in a] course in the History of Spanish Civilization, . . . sessions were set aside for a discussion of the position of the Jews in medieval Spain. . . . In short, both faculty and students became far more aware of the importance of the Jewish factor in world civilization than they had been before.

If one believes that real, substantial knowledge is going to foster good-will between the Jews and their neighbors, if one believes that a recognition of the Jewish contribution to civilization is a matter of great scholarly, as well as public, concern and if one, finally, believes in the need of Jewish cultural achievements and cultivation of interest in their own past by the Jewish people itself, then there is probably no better means for achieving all these purposes than the establishment of Jewish studies at various universities.[61]

How shall we sum up the question of Baron's involvement with the Columbia community? On the one hand, there is certainly evidence that Baron faced no special problem as a professor of Jewish history. Butler had proven to be extremely receptive to the idea of the chair; and indeed the search committee would have had a strong excuse for appointing a totally different kind of personality, because the benefactress would have preferred a Reform Jew considerably less involved in Jewish national affairs. Over the years, Baron also enjoyed continual support for his research, approved by Butler as part of the endowment. Finally, with the exception of the early period, Baron himself claimed that he had not encountered any antisemitism at Columbia.

And yet, there are also signs that all was not well. First, Baron was thick-skinned and self-confident; he was a loner who didn't seem to need or want a great deal of contact with others or to have intellectual exchanges with colleagues. Moreover, during the 1940s when the family lived in Canaan, Baron's presence on the Columbia campus was down to no more than two days a week, often Wednesday through Friday; and during that limited time, he had to fill his considerable organizational commitments as well.

Even in earlier years, Baron's involvements were primarily within the sphere of the Jewish community, and only later— after the return to New York—and only to some extent, did he become involved in the Columbia community. The letter to Joseph Baron with its positive perspective on Baron's integration into Columbia dates precisely from that time period.

In sum, Baron might not have sensed any real antisemitism because he was basically satisfied with the world he had constructed for himself. He wasn't rebuffed by the Columbia community because he didn't totally try to join it—and this wasn't true of Lionel Trilling. Baron's primary community was full of considerable involvement in the contemporary affairs of Jewish life and in the organizations that encouraged and sponsored Jewish scholarship.

Communal Leader

One of the more enigmatic subjects in describing Baron's life-style concerns the question of religious observance. Of course, the idea of raising a family in Canaan, Connecticut, particularly chosen for its relative isolation, underscores the question of Baron's religious outlook and practices. When I raised these questions with close friends and family members, they were astonished both at how little they had to say about the topic and that they did not really understand Baron's actions.[62] As we have seen, Baron wrote frequently on the importance of religion for the survival of Jewish life.[63] And yet, for virtually all of his adult life, Baron paid minimal attention to matters of religious practice.

Both daughters, Shoshanna and Tobey, received a Jewish education. Shoshanna was tutored for several years and then went on to Herzlia High School; Tobey went to a nearby Hebrew school. Although Jewish observance was not emphasized in the home, Shoshanna recalled the lighting of Friday night candles and reciting the Shema prayer before going to bed. Passover seders were conducted, and one report indicated that Baron conducted the traditional search for *hametz* before the Passover holiday. The home in New York was kept kosher specifically so that colleagues, for example, from the Jewish Theological Seminary, would be able to eat there. On the other hand, Baron never went to synagogue to worship, and Tobey reported that she herself was never taken to a synagogue.

As a youth Baron was more observant than his parents, and he was still religious when he moved to Vienna in 1914 just before the outbreak of war. In fact, as an indication of his continued religiosity, he maintained some private fast days during the war: in one example, he prayed and fasted that Allenby at the head of the English forces would conquer Jerusalem. Baron recalled that his religious attitudes changed around 1918 when he was twenty-three. He was unable, however, to explain the change. Baron joined the echelons of American Jewish leadership that combined a personal indifference to religious practices with a deep sense of Jewish identity. Of course, within that category Baron possessed a remarkable combination of qualifications that allowed him to make a truly significant contribution to American Jewish life.

Baron's attitudes toward Zionism and Israel present another one of the enigmas that friends and family found rather difficult to penetrate. Baron visited Palestine and then Israel frequently. His sister Gisela's children had settled there, and this was one of his motivations. At several junctures, he considered settling in Israel permanently. At one time, apparently in the 1950s, he was actively considered as a candidate to become president of the Hebrew University.

Ankory related that he had always assumed it was Jeannette who opposed settling in Israel. He was surprised, therefore, when at a late stage in their lives, Jeannette revealed that it was Baron who did not want to move. In Ankory's interview with Baron, Baron explained that the question came up regularly since his first visit in 1937, and that for most of his life, he considered this matter to be a serious problem. He explained that he would not have been able to write his history the way he wanted to if he had gone to Israel.[64]

Yet, Baron's attitude toward Israel and Zionism was extremely positive. When asked to describe that attitude, Arthur Hertzberg employed the terms of cultural Zionism best represented by Ahad Ha'am.[65] Israel was understood by Baron to stand at the center of Jewish life. It was characteristic of his approach that he should actively support the Hebrew University, one of the original gems of cultural Zionist accomplishment.

His position toward Zionism was, nevertheless, a difficult position to understand, primarily because he balanced it with a deep appreciation of the potentials of Diaspora Jewish life. In one interview, the contradictions became explicit. Responding to Zvi Ankory's questions about Zionism, Baron replied that at the time of the destruction of the Second Temple, two-thirds of world Jewry lived outside the land of Israel. But, he explained, Israel alone made Jewish history, and Israel must carry the burden of Jewish history. This response, offered in 1987 to an Israeli interviewer on behalf of the Diaspora Museum, was not characteristic of Baron's historical outlook, and indeed, contradicted it. We have already seen the extent to which Baron firmly believed that the Diaspora must take initiatives in safeguarding Jewish survival.

Baron's position toward these questions represented his own synthesis of the positions maintained earlier by Ahad Ha'am on the one hand and Simon Dubnow on the other. Hertzberg put it this way: Baron essentially accepted Dubnow's thesis that every five hundred years or so a new Jewish center arises, and this time America was that new center. Baron was a Zionist, not an anti-Zionist, or a non-Zionist. Israel was the single most importance place in the Jewish world, but the most important Diaspora center was America.

In addition to scholar and teacher, Salo Baron was an enormously active man of Jewish affairs. Many, but not all, of his involvements were academically oriented. During American Jewry's noteworthy tercentenary celebrations, he served as president of the American Jewish Historical Society. For decades, he and Talmudist Saul Lieberman were the pivotal leaders of the American Academy for Jewish Research, and during the 1940s he headed the American academic committee of Hebrew University. He was involved with various activities of the Jewish Welfare Board, and B'nai B'rith turned to him frequently over the years as a consultant or lecturer. In our talks together, Baron estimated that he spent about twenty hours a week on organizational work.[66]

Something else about those interviews should be reported in this context: Baron continually focused on his organizational activities, and at times it was actually difficult to prod him on toward other spheres of interest. Eventually, it became clear to me that Baron felt that his organizational work had played a crucial role in his life, and he was concerned that these activities might be overshadowed by his academic accomplishments. Later in my work, I reread a certain passage in Baron's writings, and I realized that what Baron had written in his 1939 essay "Emphases in Jewish History" presented a revealing statement about his own perception of the professional task of the historian.

Others, however, have maintained that the main purpose of history is not to restate facts and correlate them into a consecutive narrative, but to serve as a magistra vitae, as a teacher and guide in meeting contemporary situations. It is this elasticity of history which makes it so easily applicable to new situations and establishes its position not only in the realm of theoretical studies intended for the satisfaction of intellectual curiosity or amusement, but as an applied social science which is of practical significance to statesmen, men of affairs, and the intelligent public at large.[67]

In these few lines, Baron lay bare a revealing perspective on his own image of the historian as professional. Baron—whose father had intended for him to enter the banking profession; who himself was not just a doctor of history, but a doctor of jurisprudence as well; who had in Vienna been both a history instructor and a legal representative of Jewish institutions— balanced throughout his professional life his academic career with an unusually active leadership role in communal affairs. Baron not only saw himself as a man of affairs—many academics do—but he *was* a spokesperson of the community. And, in this passage, Baron suggests that to ignore that aspect of his life would preclude a proper understanding of his historical work as well. What Baron intimated in this passage was his own self-image of the historian as man of affairs.

Baron's entry into such intense communal activity came gradually, beginning with JIR itself and then the Menorah Society. His appointment to Columbia strengthened his position, but it was in the late 1930s that the wide spectrum of involvements took hold. He became editor of *Jewish Social Studies* precisely with the appearance of the *SRH*, but communal involvement did not precipitate a decline in his writing output. Although publication of his *History* increased his stature still further, I suspect that the chronological framework for his burst of activity can be better explained by the coincidence of his increasing comfort as an American combined with the crises precipitated by the rise of Nazism and the outbreak of war. As we shall see, the sense of patriotism increasing within him applied both to the country and to its Jews. Taken together, his new understanding of both the place of American Jewry in the world community and American patriotism provide the best explanations for his expanded horizons of activity.

For a scholar, Baron was unusually well-accepted by the leaders of organized American Jewry as a consultant and even as a spokesman. The intellectually oriented Menorah Society, certainly not typical of American Jewish organizations, was one of the first organizations to recognize and utilize Baron's public talents. Despite the difficulties that accompanied the publication of "Ghetto and Emancipation," both Baron and the Journal editors were pleased with the impact of its publication. Baron's reputation in America had been established; and, as we shall see, Henry Hurwitz had found a spokesman whose message fit with much of his own thinking. Within a year, Baron published in the Journal a two-part article on "Nationalism and Intolerance." Baron also began to play an active role recommending and evaluating articles for the editors, and the Society turned to Baron regularly to participate in its own public affairs.[68]

His own willingness and even desire to fill such public roles provides part of the explanation of how this came about. Needless to say, not all scholars were so willing. Thus, for example, Harvard's Harry Wolfson, the only other leading university professor of Judaica at the time, had over the years become more and more of a recluse into his study at Widener Library. In earlier years, Wolfson had played a role in the Menorah Society not only at Harvard, but nationally as well. By the 1930s, he was less involved, and in 1944, Henry Hurwitz, long-time head of the Society, wrote to Wolfson: "I don't know how serious you were the other day in saying you had given up your civic conscience."[69]

Also important was Baron's accessibility to the leading Jewish institutions and his proximity to the dominant community of New York. But this too was insufficient, because not all New York personalities were acceptable for general communal leadership. When in need of a speaker or consultant, secular institutions were often reluctant to turn to rabbinical school faculties identified with the different religious movements. In commenting on an article on Solomon Schechter that Louis Finkelstein, president of the Jewish Theological Seminary, had submitted to the *Menorah Journal*, Hurwitz wrote in reply: "I really think that this paper as it stands, sounds more like a Memorial Address to the Seminary's own public rather than a reappraisal of Schechter for the general public."[70] In contrast, Baron transcended the particularism that was perceived within the different movements, making him still more attractive as a spokesperson for the broader community.

Baron's lecturing skills further increased his popularity. Both the Jewish Welfare Board and B'nai B'rith frequently turned to Baron or recommended him. His personal files are full of lecture requests. Probably his most rememberable lecture trip was to South Africa in 1946. Packed halls awaited him and the Jewish press reported in detail on the substance of his delivery. From those reports and others of Baron's lectures, it is possible to understand that the most important single factor behind Baron's public popularity was the social significance of his message.[71]

Baron emerged in a major public role in the Jewish community with the outbreak of World War II. From that time on, Baron appeared regularly in public forums, in more popular Jewish periodicals, and as one of the main features of the Jewish lecture circuit. The themes of his talks, not surprisingly, corresponded to the subjects of his research and writing. But Baron had a clear talent for harnessing his scholarship and presenting his interpretations and conclusions in such a way that his message was laden with relevancy for the contemporary audience. I purposely avoid the no less obvious possibility that the themes of his scholarship were framed from the outset by their immediate significance; whether true or not, that formulation strikes me as not particularly helpful in this context. Many an obtuse scholar has chosen subjects consciously or otherwise that echo the contemporary situation. Baron, however, could reproduce his scholarship with a popular vibrancy that, along with the other factors we have mentioned, explains his unusual position as spokesperson and consultant for the Jewish community in America. The substance of his message will better concern us when we examine the years during and just after the war.

Of all Baron's organizational involvements, the one with which he was most closely identified, and, which, therefore, warrants a more extensive examination, was the Conference on Jewish Relations and its journal *Jewish Social Studies.*

An Intelligence Service for the Jewish People

In June 1933, under the leadership of City College philosophy professor Morris Raphael Cohen, a group was formed to discuss the consequences of the rise of Nazi Germany and, most especially, its potential implications for American Jewry.[72] The Conference on Jewish Relations, formally established in 1936 and known from 1955 as the Conference on Jewish Social Studies, set out to combat these developments through scholarship. Cohen explained in his memoirs that he had been "profoundly disturbed by the rising tide of antisemitism in the United States, which seemed to me to be part of a general decline of liberalism," reinforced still further by the bitter opposition to Roosevelt exhibited during the 1936 election campaign.[73]

Special attention was given to the implications of these developments for academicians and professionals.

The news from Germany has bared to the world the helpless plight of the intellectual Jew in that country. But it has also served to make us acutely aware that that plight is not limited to Germany, and that it is not a passing phenomenon. Discrimination against Jews in the professions and academic life, if less dramatically, is yet no less actually present in other parts of the civilized world, not excluding America.[74]

Baron became especially involved in the Conference in 1937, when he was appointed editor of its journal, *Jewish Social Studies*. After Cohen, Baron served as president for many years and continued to be intimately involved virtually until his death. His wife Jeannette also served as president for most of the 1970s and early eighties. Of all the organizations that Baron was active in, I have chosen to emphasize the conference because it was the organization most exclusively identified with Baron personally. Others, like the American Jewish Historical Society or the American Academy for Jewish Research—both of which Baron served as president—had an independent existence; the conference did not, at least not once he took over in 1941. Nevertheless, it did not start that way.[75]

Born in Russia around 1880, Morris Cohen moved to America with his family at the age of twelve. Cohen attended public schools in Brooklyn. His experience as a lone Jewish youth facing doubts from his teachers and hostility on the way to and from school was strongly echoed in his memoirs. Influenced by teachers and associates at the Educational Alliance School on the Lower East Side, Cohen was encouraged to study at City College and then did his graduate work in philosophy at Harvard. At first, discrimination prevented his teaching in his own discipline. So he taught mathematics in various settings instead. But, in 1912, he secured an appointment in City College's Department of Philosophy and remained there until his early retirement in 1938.[76]

Cohen specialized in the philosophies of science and law. Oliver Wendell Holmes was one of his idols and Felix Frankfurter, one of his closest friends. Cohen wrote frequently on political matters, emphasizing his firm beliefs in the liberal perspective, but his most active foray into applied scholarship was the establishment of the Conference on Jewish Relations. Indeed, in his memoirs and letters of the time, Cohen referred to his increased involvement in conference activities as the reason behind his early retirement, although his chronic ill health and his no less chronic bad relations with the college president seemed to have played a primary role.

Cohen's daughter, Leonora Cohen Rosenfield, described his role in the early years:

Not until 1937 was there an office other than the Cohen apartment. . . . He carried on like a juggler keeping a good many balls in play. He became not only the Conference's chief planner but also its principle money raiser. He helped to guide research and to obtain sponsorship of research projects from universities, foundations, communities, and individuals of wealth. He organized meetings on crucial topics, tried to build up membership, sponsored publication of the research, . . . [and] wrote annual reports, . . . Beginning in 1939, there was considerably more.[77]

Cohen himself captured the early spirit of the conference in this description from his memoirs:

There were many agencies of good will . . . to disseminate and utilize generally accepted facts—and sometimes generally accepted myths—in all sorts of Jewish affairs, from vocational guidance to the defense of civil rights. But it was dismaying to see what poor, makeshift data most of these agencies had to use as the factual starting point of their work. And no one of them was devoting its primary efforts to the task of operating an effective intelligence service for the Jewish people in their fight against the forces which would degrade them and deprive them of their human rights.[78]

There was a spirit of elitism about the organization; businesspersons were approached for donations, but policies were to be set primarily by intellectuals. In fact, the conference represented a kind of academic revolution against the current leadership of American Jewry. Morris Cohen explained the academic protest in a 1937 address:

We Jews of this country suffer from insufficient respect for knowledge and understanding as values in themselves. This is a defect which we have recently acquired. For two thousand years the Jews have admired scholarship and have looked up to the Talmud chochim as a leader in the community. But in this country . . . it has been the practical man who has been most admired. . . . [We Jews] have made no room at all for the scholar in our communal affairs, leaving leadership to gifted orators, journalists, or to men of affairs whose philanthropies give them deserved distinction. . . . [A] man may be a persuasive orator or well informed and wise in business affairs and yet not have the requisite insight into issues that require long historical and other study. . . . Generally in the past we have relied upon our scholars or rabbis, and I think in the main quite wisely so.[79]

More generally, the conference represented an American Jewish response to the rise of Nazi Germany, concerned primarily with possible repercussions in America to widespread Nazi propaganda and the complications of mass Jewish immigration. Conference chronicles also related its early history to the effects of the depression, as reports frequently spoke of the difficulties encountered by Jewish professionals and how these problems were being compounded by the real and potential influx of refugee counterparts.

Baron put it this way, "The world-wide Nazi propaganda had also begun affecting the United States, and it was found that many faulty or inaccurate Nazi assertions could not be contradicted with solid facts." Baron also quoted Cohen as saying around the time of the formation of the conference: "With the growing complexity and urgency of these problems in the United States as well as in the world at large, accurate and verifiable information in this field has become a matter of vital necessity."[80] Thus, formation of the conference represented the response of a group of scholars, with the support of a limited number of businesspersons, to an increased threat of American antisemitism aggravated by worldwide developments.

Paradoxically, Morris Cohen, and for that matter Baron as well, were doubtful of the efficacy of investing significant resources and energy in a struggle against antisemitic forces. Cohen explained in his autobiography that he considered antisemitism to be a function of world stress and that "Jews cannot expect to receive justice in an unjust and sick world." The actual purpose of the conference was to study and strengthen the resources of Jews and especially to combat the economic problems that derived from antisemitism.[81] This internal emphasis of conference activities differed, for example, from those of the American Jewish Committee, which emphasized legal, political, and educational endeavors to combat antisemitic forces themselves. The committee dealt with diplomatic efforts to the outside; the conference represented a group manifestation of Jewish introversion.[82]

The conference underwent a period of incubation between 1933 and the spring of 1936 when it became incorporated as a public institution. For the first three years, the organization functioned informally, but subcommittees concerning the medical and legal professions were formed almost at the beginning. In December 1934, the medical committee submitted a report concerned with the deteriorating situation of Jewish doctors in Germany and the limited prospects and difficulties effecting their emigration.[83] The report effectively described the plight of both younger and older Jewish doctors in Nazi Germany and of the minority that by 1934 had managed to leave, but it was unable to point to concrete action. "No solution is apparent. . . . The outcome depends of course on world events which no one can forsee {sic}. But the problem deserves and is receiving the sympathetic attention of Jews and of generous minded persons of other races everywhere."

The conference emphasized the need for accurate information to benefit long-term policy planning. "The greatest need today is for facts and carefully matured, long-ranged plans based on these facts."[84] Still, concrete results enhanced the value of public appeals. But, when fifty years later Baron searched the conference's history for instances of practical consequence, there were few examples. A noteworthy exception dated from the early period.[85]

In July 1935, the conference together with the American Jewish Committee sent two scholars to assist James G. McDonald, the high commissioner for refugees at the League of Nations. Oscar Janowsky, a professor of history at City College, and Melvin Fagen, a lawyer and later the executive secretary of the conference, were to assist in the preparation of a petition by McDonald to the league for international intervention on behalf of Jews and others being persecuted in Nazi Germany.

Initiative for the project was begun by James Rosenberg, a lawyer, artist, and philanthropist who was involved in both the conference and the American Jewish Committee. The purpose was to research the legal possibilities of international action against Nazi policies. But after two years in the position and in light of the Nuremberg laws, McDonald resigned at the end of 1935. Janowsky and Fagen prepared historical and legal material that accompanied the letter of resignation and a petition sent in support of McDonald's position. Their research resulted in a volume published in 1937, *International Aspects of German Racial Policies* with an introduction written jointly by Rosenberg and Morris Cohen.[86]

In 1936, the decision was made to incorporate the organization in order to secure more extensive financial support. In perhaps the conference's most publicized moment, the cooperation of Albert Einstein was drawn upon to invite a select group to a founding dinner and to preside over the occasion. Morris Cohen, British political thinker Harold Laski, and Baron addressed the gathering, and Henry Morgenthau delivered an appeal for support. Chronicles of conference history highlight this event, which provided necessary financial resources to maintain its program of research.[87]

In an address to the membership delivered in early 1937, Cohen outlined the more significant conference undertakings to date. The place of the Jew in American higher education was considered the most important area of inquiry.

The attitudes to racial and religious differences developed during the formative years of college life is {sic} apt to have important, if not decisive, influence. . . . This committee is trying to get at the basic facts in regard to the status of Jewish students and instructors in American universities.

The committee sought information on attitudes toward Jews on college campuses, the extent to which Jewish students received scholarships and fellowships, and hiring practices concerning Jewish applicants for academic positions.[88]

The medical committee of the conference sought to compile a listing of Jewish doctors in the country, to gather information on opportunities for medical practice outside of New York, and on the placement of Jewish doctors in Jewish and non-Jewish hospitals. Cohen's remarks again reveal the Conference's orientation toward fact-finding rather than action, as well as a sense of defensiveness concerning the position of Jewish doctors.

We hope to get a great deal more information in regard to what may be done to bring about better conditions of admission, safer distribution after graduation, and what may be done to safeguard their conformity to the accepted standards of proper practice. . . . [It] is certain that we have a relatively greater proportion of doctors to our population than the rest of the community. Under such conditions there is always the temptation to practice on a lower level, and that creates very serious difficulties. The conference cannot undertake the practical remedial measures, but we can get the information and put it at the disposal of those who can make proper use of it.

Soon after its incorporation, the Conference made Jewish population studies a matter of high priority. An announcement from late 1937 explained that the motivations for such studies were a matter of both local and national interest. Individual communities required not only general population information, but also more detailed demographic statistics in order to plan their programs—for example, for both the young and the elderly. In addition, national planning required more precise information on geographic, economic, and vocational distribution. These topics were recurrent themes in conference thinking and related very much to concerns about antisemitism, as well as the capacity to absorb European refugees.

In order to encourage local research, the conference undertook to subsidize and assist such endeavors. Sophia Robison, a professional sociologist and demographer, was engaged to supervise the project. Beginning in the summer of 1936, a series of census studies was undertaken in a number of communities including Minneapolis; Trenton; Passaic; Buffalo; Pittsburgh; New London and Norwich, Connecticut; Detroit; Chicago; and San Francisco.[89] Conference files show considerable interest during that period by local communities large and small. Several communities reported studies already in progress, and several of the conference studies continued work begun previously. In part, this enthusiastic response may have derived from the considerable sociological interest in communal research in general. This was the period of the famous work of Robert and Helen Lynd on Middletown and then of W. Lloyd Warner on Yankee City.[90] When the results of these studies were published in 1943, Robison alluded to demographic and economic implications deriving from the research.

South America and its Jewish population were areas of ongoing interest to the conference during the 1930s and 1940s. In 1937, a specialist in Latin American affairs was engaged to convey reports on the condition of Jews in those countries. At this juncture, the conference was apparently concerned primarily over the effects of increased German influence in both the South American economy and public opinion.[91] Later, in the 1940s, the region was again being observed as a potential destination for refugees. In June 1943, the conference met with representatives of the American Jewish Committee to discuss plans for a feasibility study on various aspects of Jewish immigration. In 1944, it announced that its legal committee was studying the legal aspects of such a project.[92] Cooperation between the conference and the committee was high at that point, partly because Morris Cohen had become influential in both organizations.

In 1937, the conference decided to undertake publication of a journal. This is when Baron, though already a vice-president, first took an active role in conference affairs. In becoming editor, Baron demanded independence from the conference in performing his duties and sufficient funding to guarantee the journal's future. He also disagreed with the name selected,

Jewish Social Studies, preferring the more inclusive title *Journal of Jewish Studies.*[93]

Baron had been contemplating this kind of undertaking for some time. Starting in 1928, Baron and George Kohut had pressured Stephen Wise to establish a "Journal of Jewish Studies" under the auspices of JIR. At that time, Kohut wrote to Wise:

I know of nothing which will more powerfully spread our influence abroad, especially in the world of scholarship, than the publication of a learned periodical issued [under] our auspices. It will definitely put us on the map not only as a Rabbinical Seminary, but as a Research Institute dedicated to Jewish scholarship.

Baron and Kohut were to serve as co-editors. Wise, however, was reluctant to make the financial commitment to such a journal. This idea was revived a decade later under the auspices of the conference.[94]

During the spring and summer of 1937, when Baron and Jeannette were traveling in Israel and Europe, active preparations were begun for the journal's first issue. The steps taken during his absence caused considerable friction and threatened his willingness to remain as editor.

On 24 June, the JTA, a Jewish news service, reported the Conference's announcement of the journal "devoted to contemporary and historical aspects of Jewish life." Perhaps as a premonition of future patterns, the report indicated that the first issue was due in July; this was unlikely since none of the articles had yet been completed.[95] Baron was also troubled by the decisions reached in his absence.[96] Moreover, the very name had been changed, to which Baron responded: "I do not like the name *Jewish Social Studies* and still less the arguments advanced in its support." However, the appointment of Hans Kohn as coeditor seems to have been the main issue. Baron wrote to Cohen:

While I have profound respect for Professor Kohn and I think that we ought to get along nicely together, I cannot visualize the exact division of labor between us. . . . When I consented to cooperate with you as coeditor, it was because you were to "represent the outlook of the Conference"—whatever that may mean—and because the gains accruing to the journal from the fine prestige of your name would outweigh the disadvantages of divided management and possible divergence of views and methods.

Finally, Baron objected to the way such important decisions had been reached in his absence. As a result of these objections, Baron tendered his resignation "at least for the time being."

During July, Baron received a letter from Koppel Pinson, managing editor of the journal, enclosing a copy of a prospectus describing several significant changes and actions that had been taken.[97]

I have, as you no doubt know, already assumed my duties as Managing Editor of *Jewish Social Studies.* I have delayed writing to you all this time because I wished to wait until I had more to report. We have done quite a number of things already and I am now in a position to give you such a report.

Given Baron's inclinations toward control of situations, including small details, it is not difficult to imagine his response to the news that much had already been done. Baron wrote to Pinson within "half an hour" of receiving his letter. He repeated that he wished his name withdrawn from any active connection with the journal.[98] "I have also explained the reasons [in the letter to Cohen] which induced me to give up this long-cherished and deeply thought-out idea. . . . The election of a co-editor . . . and an editorial council and the publication of a Prospectus under my name, without previous consultation with me is an innovation in journalistic history."

Baron was also quite critical concerning the prospectus itself. Specifically, he considered it apologetic regarding the role history would play within the journal's contents. "You and I know that History in its wider sense is the very essence of Jewish culture, and any apology for its treatment in a Journal of this sort is little short of *dilettante*."

In a conciliating response, Pinson answered the questions regarding the role of history in the new journal.[99] Pinson explained that the choice of Kohn was made as "a concession to you and your view of the Journal. . . . The choice fell upon Hans Kohn because he approximated your own historical standpoint and therefore would work for more harmonious functioning of the Journal. . . . To me it seems that the effect will be only to make the Journal more like what you want it to be." Pinson somewhat clarified what was at issue. "I, as a historian myself, can hardly be accused of being apologetic for history. But we do have people like Karpf and Lurie and Cohen and others to deal with whose feelings regarding history are not like yours or mine. Apropos of this, I must say that I am amazed at the concessions which Morris Cohen has made and is making to the historical viewpoint."

Baron continued the discussion in a subsequent letter:

233

It was clearly understood that this was not to be a house organ of the Conference, representing merely its program and ideals, but a central organ for Jewish scholarship, uniting in itself the interests of the Conference, the various seminaries, and academies, the Graduate School, the Yivo, the Hebrew University, etc. . . . Please do not misunderstand my insistence on *history*. A glance at my recent "History" ought to convince everyone that I am personally as much interested in economic and sociological as in strictly historical studies. But my primary stress is on *quality*. We simply have no *first-rate* Jewish economists devoting their whole undivided attention to *Jewish* economy. The *Journal* may stimulate research in this field and, in the course of time, develop younger talents. But as long as we shall insist upon a certain content in the Journal rather than upon its level, we shall at best add another second-rate organ to those hitherto issued.[100]

Jewish Social Studies did attain the position of quality that Baron sought and for several decades was known as one of the finest journals in the world of Jewish studies. Its pages continued to balance historical and contemporary research, unified by an emphasis on the social aspects of Jewish life. The identification of Baron with the journal continued to forge his image as primarily a social historian. But, as we have seen, the question is more complicated, and Baron was also a dominant force in the more intellectually oriented American Academy for Jewish Research. Indeed, even for this journal, he had preferred a name that would not emphasize social and economic aspects.

In 1938, in the midst of strong disagreements with its president, Morris Cohen retired from City University and left New

York City.[101] In March of that year, Cohen sent a letter to members of the conference board in which he assessed past accomplishments and setbacks.[102] The most pressing problems had always derived from the lack of financial resources. Those entrusted with that responsibility had been lax in their duty, but Cohen accepted part of the blame: "As president, I should have pressed them more to live up to their undertaking, but that is, unfortunately, a task beyond my temperament as well as competence." Among the implications of the constant shortage of funds was the direction of research: "there is the basic need of securing greater continuous attention to the advancement or development of the general scope, purpose, and plan of our organization. Because of our very limited funds, the choice of our various research projects has hitherto been somewhat opportunistic, though I am confident that the future will show them to be of basic importance."

Leaving New York City meant that Cohen would be devoting less time to conference activities.

Without any false modesty or ignoring the fact that some have joined the Conference because of personal devotion to me, or because of my reputation in an altogether different field of human endeavor, it is still true that it is not good for any society to be too much of a one-man organization, especially if that man cannot possibly give all of his thought and time to it. I have not been able to abandon my interest in theoretic philosophy or give up my effort to complete some writings long overdue. . . . I am more persuaded than ever of its [the conference's] indispensability, but I think that I can do a great service to it by insisting that the burden be more widely distributed and that there be a more general recognition of the fact that my value to the Conference is much more that of a critic of ideas, rather than as an organizer or director of practical activities.

In 1941, Cohen stepped down as president and was replaced by Baron.[103]

With the exception of the journal, Cohen had dominated all aspects of the conference's activities for eight years. Even in the area of population studies, a sphere close to Baron's heart, it was Cohen who provided the guiding hand in the early years. The significance of this is hardly to belittle Baron's contributions; once he took over the conference, he threw himself into its activities. But it seems to me that an analysis of conference activities provides us with a reading of some of the concerns, thoughts, and plans of a group of active and socially conscious Jews during the troubled years just before and during World War II. The picture we have presented here differs from the on-going debates over petitions, boycotts, and immigration quotas.

The conference never hid its intentions to relate primarily to the implications of current European developments on the American Jewish community. Nor did it camouflage its primary concern with problems relating to Jewish professionals and intellectuals. Increased occupational variation and demographic distribution were recurring themes in the reports of the legal, medical, and education committees. The conference was quite concerned with where Jews lived, hoping to avoid concentrations of Jewish population. In 1939, the board engaged quite seriously in the so-called Alaska Project as a haven for refugees, and Cohen traveled to Washington to gain support.[104] The conference set out on the whole to prove that Nazi and other antisemitic accusations were fundamentally incorrect and to help guarantee that they remained untrue.

Baron took over the conference leadership just a short time before America entered the war. Within a month of Pearl Harbor the conference initiated discussions to formulate programs for the postwar period. By January 1942, the conference had planned a meeting to be held on "Organization for Post-War Reconstruction." A trace of Morris Cohen's shadow could still be seen in this program: Cohen appeared on that panel in his capacity as chairperson of the American Jewish Committee's Research Institute on Peace and Post-War Problems. [105]

Cohen had been appointed chairperson of a preparatory committee in the spring of 1940. That September, Cohen's group recommended "a program for a sustained and intensive study not only of the actual situation of Jews abroad and at home, and of the possible effects of the various plans and proposals for post-war reconstruction, but also of the problems which are likely to confront the Jewish people after the war." The report indicated that despite the considerable accumulation of information in recent years—presumably a reference to conference efforts—"there was an urgent need for additional knowledge as well as for better integration of existing data." The research institute was established by the American Jewish Committee in January 1941 with Cohen as chairperson and Max Gottschalk as director. Ambitious programming and convoluted structures seemed to be Cohen's style, and the institute's activities were divided into three divisions dealing with political, economic, and social status; migration and colonization; and relief and reconstruction.[106]

Given the vastly greater resources of the Committee, it seems likely that Cohen left the conference confident that he would find in the committee the support for the research he felt was necessary.[107] Meanwhile, the conference began to move in very parallel lines. A 1943 memo describing current projects began as follows: "With the possibility emphasized by many allied spokesmen that the war may end in 1944, the task of preparing adequately for the readjustment and stabilization of Jewish life in this country, and for the reconstruction of Jewish communities abroad, becomes particularly pressing."[108] The conference proceeded to organize a series of discussions on the theme "Jewish Problems of the Post-War World." The individual sessions were on the reeducation of Axis countries concerning Jews; the resuscitation of Jewish cultural life in Europe; the utilization of Jewish refugees in post-war reconstruction; and the future role of American Jewry.[109]

By the end of 1944, the conference presented a list of postwar projects. In a letter sent to prominent Jews requesting support, Baron indicated the various components of the program. A commission for the cultural reconstruction of European Jewry had been established to serve as an advisory body to the United Nations in the rehabilitation of European Jewish cultural institutions.[110] This body would later be officially recognized to represent world Jewry before the Allied authorities. In addition, committees continued to study the distribution of Jewish physicians and the possible migration of Jewish refugees to Latin America.[111]

. . .

The work on Jewish cultural reconstruction became one of the most significant and lasting of the conference's activities. The previous references to lectures and symposia indicate that the term *reconstruction* was widely used even during the early war years, primarily in the context of rebuilding the European Jewish communities themselves. Morris Cohen, as we have just seen, used it frequently during this period in a broad context of meanings. Later, during the war and especially immediately after its conclusion, usage of the term *reconstruction* was transformed into a more specific undertaking.

The conference initiated plans to establish a Commission on Jewish Cultural Reconstruction that would focus on the distribution of Jewish cultural treasures that had been confiscated or otherwise lost during the war. Baron later recalled that with the end of the war and full disclosures of the extent of the Holocaust, the orientation of these activities was fully changed. It was now understood that the treasures would be extensively redistributed to America and Palestine.[112]

Near the end of 1945, Baron headed a delegation together with Alexander Marx and Aaron Freimann that met with General Lucius Clay, who was the American military governor in Germany. They expressed their concern that American soldiers were reportedly removing Jewish cultural objects and convinced Clay that these materials must be dealt with systematically. The commission received authorization as trustee on behalf of world Jewry. Clay also established a special depot for storing the objects in Offenbach. Other organizations now joined in the effort, and a more extensive organizational structure was established. Baron served as chairperson and Hannah Arendt was named as executive secretary.

Jewish Cultural Reconstruction became an independent organization, and Arendt headed its activities with intensive efforts during the late 1940s and early fifties. She was responsible for negotiations both with occupying forces and with the new European Jewish communities then emerging. Ceremonial objects and books were distributed if their rightful owners could not be identified or located. Thousands of objects and an estimated half a million books were distributed—approximately forty percent were transferred to America and Israel, with the rest remaining in Europe or going to smaller communities like South Africa.

The story of Jewish Cultural Reconstruction provides a touching footnote to the passing of the scepter of Jewish life. Baron was deeply involved in its activities and continued to preside over the organizational structure until its demise in the late sixties. In Baron's mind, Arendt's contribution to these efforts was so significant that it counterbalanced the negative impact of some of her later writings—a reference to the controversy stirred by her *Eichmann in Jerusalem*. [113]

Finances were always a problem for the conference. Of course, the conference was at a clear disadvantage in its pursuit of funding. First, its activities were oriented toward professionals and academicians usually of limited financial capabilities and who constantly complained of lack of time. Second, its program emphasized research and not activity. Even public events were publicized as an opportunity to study the implications of different policies.

Yet, conference projects often found a receptive response. The call for community population studies in the late 1930s and early 1940s coincided with the classic sociological work of the Lynds in Middletown and others. Prominent medical personalities seemed to share the conference's concern over future placement of Jewish medical students and interns, but often these people lacked the time to devote to the studies and committees that were called for. This was especially true during the war years when hospitals were all the more short-handed.

Of course there was discord as well. One rabbi wrote the conference in 1939 that he could not support its activities or its new journal because "you do not reckon with the religious element that is so essential in Jewry." Lucius Littauer wrote to Baron in 1942 concerning the work of the medical and legal committees that he was not in sympathy with their work, nor did he think that such research would correct the situation. Only victory in the war would eradicate intolerance, and all efforts should be extended in that direction.[114]

From the outset, the Conference on Jewish Relations primarily encouraged scholarly research. When it undertook to oppose specific forms of discrimination against professional sectors of the Jewish population, the emphasis again was usually on fact-finding. Under Baron's leadership, a gradual and subtle change of orientation took place. Almost ironically, the priorities of Cohen the philosopher had been with occupational distribution, whereas Baron, the social and economic historian, was very much more concerned with the cultural and the spiritual. Under his leadership, the leading project of the 1940s was the Commission for Jewish Cultural Reconstruction. By the 1950s, Baron was enthralled with American Jewish history, and the conference joined in supporting the tercentenary celebration.

As the conference became increasingly identified with Baron, it seems to me that it also provided the framework for his own personal identification with the Jewish community. It became the medium for his self-expression of Jewish concerns, and through it he related to what he saw as the pressing needs of the contemporary community: first Reconstruction, then the celebration of America. In his older years, the conference reduced its sphere of activity primarily to the journal. Baron and the conference alike became more exclusively concerned with the pursuit of scholarship.

CHAPTER 6

THE JEWISH COMMUNITY

IN 1942, THE JEWISH Publication Society issued Baron's study *The Jewish Community*. The three-volume work with two volumes of text and one volume of notes and bibliography became and still remains a ready reference for describing Jewish communal life. This study and the *SRH* are Baron's most cited works.

Baron had already emphasized the concept of Jewish community in the *SRH,* especially in his opening theoretical statements. With the beginning of dispersion, the communal structure assumed new importance. "We shall see how throughout the ages the Jewish community partly replaced the missing state, how the Jewish quarters of ancient Alexandria or under the caliphate, in North Africa or in medieval and modern Europe, were a surrogate, however poor, for Israel's territory." [1] Thus, the interrelationship between the Jews and their community played a pivotal role in Jewish history.

By the mid-thirties, Baron was giving considerable attention to the phenomenon of the Jewish Community. During the same period that he was revising and editing the *SRH,* Baron also wrote several short pieces on the significance of the community in history. In "An Historical Critique of the Jewish Community" (1935), Baron revealed that he was already thinking of a more extensive work on the subject and put forth a number of major conclusions in more succinct form than they would appear later in the three-volume monograph.[2]

The essay opened with reference to the idea of Jewish autonomy, commenting that previous discussions had been based on biased views. "The term 'autonomy' itself unfortunately lends a predominantly political note to largely nonpolitical developments." Thus, he presented the Jewish Community as a multifaceted phenomenon, while simultaneously hinting that his own conceptions were quite different from those of historians who advocated a program of Jewish autonomy.

Characteristic of Baron's popular style, he structured his presentation as a revision of popular misconceptions, including the notion that the Jewish Community in medieval and early modern times was a democratic institution. Aside from the anachronistic difficulties in using this modern term to describe an ancient institution, such a description also failed to consider that under Islamic rule there were pronounced monarchical and oligarchic tendencies within the community. In Christian Europe as well, leaders often emerged because of wealth, political connections, or other such external reasons not necessarily in accordance with democratic principles,

244

but that served rather to concentrate power into the hands of a limited number of families. Baron's reasons for negating the democratic description became clearer only at the end of this essay, where he commented on the efficacy of the pre-Emancipation community despite its nondemocratic nature.[3]

Baron also confronted the notion that the Jewish community was the creation of a mystical inner urge of self-persistence. Baron countered that although persistence was one factor in its preservation, the community was reinforced by legal compulsion—from both internal and external sources, such as rabbinic law on the one hand and the state on the other. Indeed, the interests of state and community often coincided. Frequently, the state, for fiscal reasons, demonstrated greater interest in strengthening the community than did the Jews themselves. This combination of religious traditions and legal coercion resulted in a community with "greater influence over the lives and destinies of its members than many an absolute state."

In contrast, the postemancipation community has been reduced to but a shadow of its former effectiveness. Religious divisions resulting at times in secession from the community had weakened the institution from within, and the separation of state and community in most emancipation countries had removed the coercive factor in communal power.

In those countries where community and government maintained a connection in the realm of tax collection, the communities enjoyed greater financial resources. But the membership had become rather indifferent and, at times, Jews resigned from the communities in order to save the corresponding tax expenses. Thus, the compulsory institution offered greater effectiveness, whereas the voluntary association, as in the American congregation, maintained a higher level of interest among its members.

Baron indicated that the challenge facing contemporary Jewry was to form a new communal structure within contemporary social conditions. He also expanded on the importance of studying communal formation in ancient times. Because the contemporary crisis marks the greatest since the first exile, it would be important to study the methods of the leaders of that earlier period to construct a community that preserved the ethnic identity of a minority people within an alien environment.

Significantly, Baron cautioned that the future community need not be democratic in nature. "With all its shortcomings the pre-emancipation Jewish community was one of the most successful and most enduring social experiments in history, perhaps primarily because it so well blended the principle of authority with that of freedom." Judaism represented "a basically non-political religion and culture"; the Jewish Community, he argued, was its organizational counterpart ("Historical Critique of the Jewish Community," p. 49).

In a 1938 essay Baron returned to the tension between freedom and authority. He prefaced his discussion with these general remarks, already somewhat more favorable to the cause of democracy than what he had written three years earlier.

The problem of individual liberty versus social control in Jewish communal life has become of crucial significance in the life of

modern Jewry. The Emancipation having undermined the foundations of the traditional, overwhelmingly powerful, community,
ever new organizational forms have been sought and tried to recon-
cile the often conflicting interests of the free Jewish citizen of a
modern state and of the Jewish community as a whole.[4]

In 1938, Baron also delivered a lecture on "Democracy
and Judaism" at the Hadassah convention, which was later
published in the organization's newsletter. Once again, Baron
provided through the public medium an incisive summary of
his thinking. Much of this essay's message concerns us in a
different context, but he did deal in part with the challenges
facing the contemporary community.[5]

With the end of the compulsory Jewish community, "there
is a real danger that, if that organizational dissolution is
allowed to go on, the Jews would lose one of their mainstays,
one of the basic forces of their preservation, their age-old
communal organization." But this time, Baron struck a more
hopeful chord, explaining that whereas a democracy could not
enforce communal affiliation, Jews within a democratic society were free to build communal institutions. Baron's attitudes toward democracy were clearly changing; accordingly,
his optimism toward the future of the Jewish Community,
especially in America, was increasing as well. By the time
these essays appeared, the *SRH* was already being acclaimed,
and Baron was busy writing his study on the Jewish Community.

In 1938, Baron wrote to Alexander Marx concerning refugees
from Germany and Austria, mentioning incidentally, "I have
made some progress on my book and hope to tell you more

about it when I next see you."[6] Two years later, in April 1940, he wrote to Marx about his work:

I should like briefly to outline for you the scope of my book on the Jewish Community on which I have been working for more than two years. It is now approaching completion.

The tentative title is: "The Ghetto Community: A History of the Jewish Community from the Babylonian Exile to the Emancipation." This title is of course subject to change.

Baron also explained that he was placing the notes at the end of the work in order "to make the reading of the text less cumbersome to the general reader—to whom this book addresses itself as much as to the scholar."[7]

Baron was a master of popular presentation. In his lectures and essays, he reduced the massive detail into a schematic format that combined scholarly accuracy with penetrating generalizations. In 1928 Baron told the *Menorah Journal* that he cared little about what the public thought or how easily it could read his material, but twelve years later Baron wrote to Marx that he intended the work on the community for the layperson as much as the scholar. This tells us something about how Baron viewed the new work. But he was less successful in adapting the full-length study to that purpose, which made it more difficult to publish as well.

In 1937, a well-known and distinguished publishing house expressed interest in books dealing with Jewish history and affairs. It was specifically interested in a book based on Baron's course on the Jewish community. Baron submitted a proposal and received a contract, which stipulated that it was to be written for a wide audience, and that the length had to be manageable. But Baron's manuscript was rejected in 1940— rather rudely in fact—as far too cumbersome and scholarly for the audience envisioned by the publishers.[8]

Baron then turned to Marx on behalf of the Jewish Publication Society. When pressed by Baron, Marx informed him that a decision could not be reached until the end of the summer: "we have to have reports by three readers. . . . It is a very bulky book and the reading will take some time. I trust the final decision will be favorable."[9]

In *The Jewish Community,* Baron reiterated his concerns with the increasing divergence of religious and secularist approaches to Jews and Judaism. Again, Baron cautioned explicitly that a secularist formulation without religious content would falter. Specifically, he observed that even in America and Western Europe, religious institutions were far more vibrant than secular organizations like community federations or defense organizations. Ostensibly, Baron's critique fell equally on both camps; but both by nuance and emphasis, the secularist perspective bore the main thrust of his attack and his specific target was, in fact, Simon Dubnow, the leading historian of the previous generation. In his work on the Jewish community, Baron expanded his historical and ideological critique of Dubnow.

Thus, in the opening pages of *The Jewish Community,* Baron explained the dangers of turning the community from a religious institution into a *Volksgemeinde.* He then elaborated in a footnote:

The main champions of the Volksgemeinde were recruited from among those diaspora-nationalists in Russia who, headed by the "bourgeois" historian Simon M. Dubnow and by the "proletarian" publicist Chaim Zhitlowsky, envisaged the future of world Jewry as that of a permanent national minority living a culturally sheltered life under constitutional safeguards of minority rights.[10]

The critique of Dubnow was two-pronged, adding historiographic shortcomings to political ineptitude. Further on, Baron explained the fallacy of an overly dominant political emphasis in the writing of Jewish history.

This is but one example of the inapplicability of general political categories to Jewish communal history. Long before the full evolution of its diaspora community the Jewish people had become a basically nonpolitical entity. Indeed, in its long diaspora career it had demonstrated the independence of the essential ethnic and religious factors from the political principle. Through a concatenation of unique historical circumstances, it early learned to discard the general acceptance of state supremacy and to proclaim in theory, as well as to live in reality, the supremacy of religious, ethical and ethnic values. That is why a purely political interpretation, even of the constitutional life of the Jewish community, will do less than justice to the non-political core of the problem. This circumstance has often been overlooked by historians and publicists writing on the Jewish community, especially those who have preached its reorganization along the political lines of a people's community.[11]

The closing sentence identifies Dubnow as his primary target. Elsewhere Baron concluded that the temptation to describe the ever-changing communal structure in terms borrowed from the host environment would be erroneous. "No strictly political form can correspond to the essentially non-political type of organization" of the Jewish community.[12]

In addition to his critique of Dubnow, *The Jewish Community* was built on a second cornerstone, stipulating an ongoing cohesion to Jewish communal structure. Baron emphasized the vertical continuity of communal forms; he argued in the preface that the roots of the development of the Jewish community began in the ancient world.

In fact, while trying to detect the hidden springs of this phenomenally tenacious evolution, the writer found himself delving deeper and deeper not only into the obscure realms of the First Exile and the Persian and Hellenistic dispersion, but also into the early manifestations of ancient Palestinian municipal life. Many rather unexpected relationships have laid bare some of the most autochthonous roots of the diaspora community securely ensconced in the ever fertile soil of ancient Israel.[13]

Of particular importance to Baron was the deuteronomic revolution enacted in Josiah's reign. This established a mechanism for decentralized worship and thus, argued Baron, also a basis for patterns developed by Diaspora communities of the future. "In short, the life of the average Israelite was far more determined by the events and institutions in his place of residence than by what happened in the central agencies of state or religion. . . . On the whole, it resembled a loosely-knit federation of tribes and townships more than a unified centralized state."[14] Later, during the Babylonian exile, building on this tradition of decentralized worship, the synagogue was established as a substitute for the Temple.

This was a truly epochal revolution. Building upon precedents forcibly established in the Judean provinces after the Deuteronomic Reformation, the exilic community thus completely shifted the emphasis from the place of worship, the sanctuary, to the gathering of worshipers, the congregation, assembled at any time and any place in God's wide world.[15]

This continuous development later strengthened the possibilities of Jewish survival even when deprived of state or territory.[16]

Yet, subsequently, communal forms were primarily informed by the Diaspora experience, and it was during Roman times that the community attained rights of self-government.[17] "The influence of the Palestinian center, enormously significant in religion, culture and political status, was at first hardly noticeable in organizational matters, wherein the diaspora had its unique problems."[18] According to Baron, the result was the emergence of clear distinctions between the Palestinian and diaspora communities, and in this regard he differed from scholars who denied distinctions between the two types of communities or the possibility of such Diaspora creativity.[19]

In Baron's scenario, it was under Islamic influence, starting in the ninth century, that centralized control began to break down in favor of stronger local autonomy.

The ancient evolution toward centralizing control by the patriarchae and exilarchate likewise reached its peak about 800 C.E. . . . From

825 on, however, the oriental communities underwent a process of steady decentralization resulting from the rise of mighty rivaling forces led by the geonim, the Egyptian-Palestinian negidim and academies, and the other regional authorities.[20]

In the Christian world, the processes of increased autonomy begun under Roman rule were continued. But it was also in the Christian world that regional cooperation emerged between local communities, forming what Baron termed *super-communities*. "The forms of such super-communal cooperation varied. Often, as in the Orient, single chiefs, Jewish or Christian, were entrusted with some or all communal responsibilities. More characteristic of European regional leadership, however, were the loosely organized synods and occasional rabbinical or lay assemblies."[21]

Uniform church policies resulted in a high degree of similarities between communities in different countries. And whereas state policies may have sought to delimit communal powers, the church in consequence of its quest to isolate Jews from Christians tended to contribute toward Jewish self-sufficiency and autonomy.[22]

The forces of modernization caused states to develop more distinctive approaches to their policies concerning the Jews. Using language reminiscent of his childhood interest in the sciences, Baron described the effects of modernization: "When the acids of Protestantism, early capitalism and modern science dissolved that unity of Christian culture, state legislation concerning Jews underwent a sharp change."[23] During this period the community faced significant challenges to its continued autonomy. In order to explain the survival of communal institutions against considerable legal obstacles, Baron abandoned his usual rational mode of explanation and resorted to a semimystical will toward survival:

> Often subjected to fierce attacks by all forces of reaction, denied legal recognition by governments and, for the most part, ignored even by benevolent rulers, the Jews proved their mettle in establishing a vigorous, though self-imposed, communal control and in founding a number of flourishing communal institutions. . . . If they were thereby aided by the existing variety of beliefs and disbeliefs and, hence, the growing necessity of mutual toleration, their main road to such noteworthy results was their adherence to age-old tradition and their undying will to survive and to retain identity in a rapidly changing world.[24]

In the second volume, Baron focused on a sociological analysis, dividing the work into chapters on membership, leadership, and communal functions. Once again seeking to reassert the religious and cultural character of Jewish life, Baron gave related functions priority over the economic tasks imposed from without and within.

> From the point of view of the state, the community's function was primarily fiscal. Only secondarily various governments were interested in communal administration of justice and control over religious, ethical and economic behavior. . . . In the consciousness of the Jews themselves, the communal promotion of their religion with all that it embraced in the way of education, judicial action and social welfare, doubtless towered above all other activities. . . . Hence a proper evaluation of the strictly religious, education and judicial functions of the community must precede the analysis of its fiscal management, . . . as well as of related phases of economic control and social legislation.[25]

Baron frequently repeated the correlation between the community's fiscal functions toward the state and the degree of autonomy granted to it. In this way he drew a dichotomy between the internal functioning of the community filling spiritual and judicial services and the external fiscal service provided to the state.[26]

In the second volume, the nature of communal leadership was a major motif in which Baron dealt with two dominant and countervailing themes. On the one hand he was concerned with the emergence of a lay oligarchy, propelled in part in the early modern period by the emergence of absolutist rule among the European countries. He also devoted considerable attention to the important leadership position maintained by scholars in the Middle Ages. Indeed, until the dawn of modernity, scholars used their influence to keep the lay oligarchy under control.

The period after the French Revolution was outside the province of this study, so only a number of passing remarks indicate his thinking on the transitions that took place at that time. Nevertheless, these references are sufficient to provide a rather clear statement of his views.

Baron maintained that modernity arose with the appearance of absolutism, capitalism, and the Enlightenment. The Protestant Reformation and the birth of modern science were also among the primary causes of change. With the new period came signs of declining communal cohesion. Baron was especially concerned with the weakening of rabbinic influence.[27] Capitalism was seen as a threatening force both because its emphasis on private initiative and competition worked against the collective mentality of the community and because its emphasis on money undermined the more traditional values of learning and piety.[28]

The end of the European community signaled a new era in communal structure with increasing emphasis on voluntary identity. This development, like those of previous eras, demonstrated in Baron's presentation a combination of the forces of millennial traditions with the impact of a new host environment, provided this time by American influences. In this work there are only passing references to the increasing significance that America offered for Jewish life. But such references were on the increase in Baron's thought and writing, and are discussed in the following chapters.

When *The Jewish Community* appeared, Baron's distinguished colleague at Columbia, Robert Schuyler wrote him that it was an important work of scholarship, a credit to Baron and to the department as well. Schuyler also marveled at Baron's command of English and his mastery of the critical idiom.[29] A lay leader with whom Baron was in regular correspondence was less enamored with the new study and especially with descriptions of the important role played in the community by scholars.

Your book on *The Jewish Community* caused me so much pain that I was unable to finish it. It is my view that rabbis in the last two decades in America have been more interested in the prerogatives of their profession than in anything else Jewish. Your emphasis on the right of rabbis and scholars to be the leaders of the community will be interpreted as the right of the rabbis to increase their prerogatives. Since they have avoided responsibilities and since very often they are not the scholars in the community, I do not look upon such a tendency with great pleasure.

Baron responded in partial agreement:

The fact that the rabbinate played a great role in the pre-Emancipation era . . . does not entitle rabbis today to claim privileges without the corresponding responsibilities and services. I hope some day to get around to writing a continuation of these volumes, namely, a history of the modern Jewish community. There I shall have to explain the reasons for the general decline of that institution.[30]

Reviewers either didn't notice or ignored the polemical aspect of *The Jewish Community,* and, in general, treated the study as a work of pure scholarship. Norman Gerstenfeld, writing in the *American Historical Review,* opened his discussion by describing the expectations for the work.

For many years the world has been awaiting a comprehensive, historical, and sociological analysis of the evolution of the Jewish community. At last a great scholar, generally acknowledged as the most learned modern historian of Jewish life, has finally presented this critical perspective of nearly four thousand years of Jewish communal history.[31]

Baron's vertical presentation involving influence from the Palestinian period on later developments in the Diaspora seems to have presented no problems for the discussants, although Baron himself expressed some surprise that his research had uncovered such strong correlations.

Yet, some reviewers felt that Baron had undertaken too

much too soon and that the work suffered in terms of accuracy and methodological precision. In two separate reviews, William Irwin of the University of Chicago discussed Baron's failure to treat more fully the implications of his analysis regarding modern political theory and the future of the Jewish community. "For here is a matter of vital importance to our present-day life. Certainly our political theory will not tolerate autonomous religious groups within our midst." Irwin also argued that the status of the Jewish community within the larger society was not altogether unique, although in his phrase the issue had been "complicated" by the rise of Zionism. Irwin expressed disappointment that Baron had not adequately discussed these issues of contemporary importance: "a full scale discussion by a Jew of Professor Baron's competence would have been a genuine service to our social thinking."[32]

Irwin also raised some questions concerning Baron's historical judgment on certain specific matters and then concluded more generally: "Unfortunately, the nature of available sources compels us to adjudge this claim about seventy-five per cent guesswork. And the passage is not unique in this regard." In a biting conclusion, Irwin commented with considerable sarcasm:

Professor Baron's knowledge of the intimate life of such communities rouses the envy of the rest of us, dependent as we are on an almost complete blank in source material. A frank admission of ignorance is still an indispensable basis of all true scholarship.[33]

The writer in the *Catholic Historical Review* raised the question of perspective. He purported that Baron made several errors in Christian history, and also maintained that in some instances Baron had not adequately presented the Christian side.[34]

And yet, all reviews praised the breadth of his undertaking and of his knowledge. Cecil Roth struck a balanced cord in his essay for the *Menorah Journal*.[35] Roth also criticized Baron for making factual errors and questionable interpretative judgments, maintaining that Baron dogmatically and without qualifications issued statements that should have been viewed only as hypotheses. "I feel that one of Professor Baron's weaknesses is a tendency to pontificate regarding theories which are only provisional, and to draw uncompromising generalizations from isolated facts." But Roth concluded that these corrections and criticisms aside, the work "has found its niche in my reference shelves, . . . and hardly a day will pass without my consulting it." He added that it represents "one of the major historical achievements of our day."

Even more, the compliments indicated a perception that the study of Jewish history had found in Baron a worthy representative within the academy. Horace Kallen, writing in the *American Journal of Sociology*, put it this way:

I know of very little writing about the Jews which has not been tendentious. . . . It has not been easy for either Jews or Gentiles to write of the Jews in the spirit and according to the methods of science—always a difficult thing in the social sciences, whatever the theme. . . . But this book . . . is the result of a conscientious and, I believe, a very largely successful effort to overcome the unconscious distorting disposition.[36]

In the course of their regular correspondence, Baron wrote to Cecil Roth concerning his review, explaining that his remarks came "not to argue with you—which would be in utterly poor taste—but of offer a few explanations which, I believe, I owe you."

Possibly I have "a tendency to pontificate." But our friend Herbert Solow, who helped me with the editing of the manuscript contended on the contrary, that I was too fond of qualifications.

Roth had specifically raised a biblical matter presented by Baron, which it may be recalled William Irwin had also raised more generally in his reviews. Baron explained that readers "may be expected to know that unfortunately almost anything one says with reference to biblical history is basically hypothetical." The alternative would be "to parade an endless array of 'perhaps' and 'apparently.' "[37]

Then Baron tackled the criticism that haste had resulted in inaccuracies.

I can assure you that if I had worked five more years, I might have rectified some of the mistakes which have crept in, but I would undoubtedly have become involved in various other problems and made new mistakes. My original manuscript still shows red pencil marks at almost every entry in the notes—a sign that I have tried to verify every statement as well as I could.

Baron then referred to another specific passage cited by Roth and concluded: "I should have immediately deleted it as I have in the case of other dubious passages. There certainly are many other mistakes and misinterpretations in the book. But which book is free of them?"

This discussion with Roth again brings us to the question of why so soon after the appearance of the SRH Baron chose to write a sweeping study of a dominant aspect of Jewish life, a history that in many ways resembled another version of a total history of Jews. My motivation in delaying this question to the end of this chapter was to take the opportunity to explain how writing and active involvement were closely related in Baron's career during these years. That was not always the case with Baron. It was only during the late 1930s that Baron became deeply involved in communal life, his entry eased by his stature as the leading American academic figure in the study of Jewish history. Again in later life, it would be more difficult to draw clear connections between writing and activity. It would perhaps be most accurate to notice an academic withdrawal during the last decades. But from the late 1930s through the 1950s, such connections did exist.

Why did Baron write *The Jewish Community* when he did? Published during the years of World War II, it would seem natural to suppose that the work was precipitated by the rise of the Nazis in Europe. Yet the work contains barely more than an echo of contemporary events. Once the reader moves beyond the opening pages, the Nazis are mentioned more for having created a totally new kind of Jewish community, a non-voluntary community based on purely racial considerations, than they are for having precipitated Baron's concern with the topic.

The reaction of reviewers that a historical and sociological study of *The Jewish Community* had long been desired may also indicate the potential significance of the important work in community studies being conducted at that same time. And yet, there is again barely a reference to the contemporary sociological fascination with community studies, such as the work of the Lynds on Middletown or W. Lloyd Warner on Yankee City.[38]

Today's academician of Jewish studies would be more likely to pay heavy tribute to this literature, while actively seeking to demonstrate not only its influence upon his writing, but also his own contribution to the broader domain of inquiry through the example of the Jews. In contrast, Baron's reference to the extensive sociological literature on community was limited to the opening footnote:

The differences of significance and function associated with the term community have been subjected to numerous analyses, as in Ferdinand Tönnies's *Gemeinschaft und Gesellschaft*; Robert M. McIver's *Community*; and E. C. Lindeman's *Community*. A fairly good review of the various approaches to the problem is given by George Simpson in his *Conflict and Community: A Study in Social Theory*, pp. 71ff.

Indeed, Baron didn't even struggle in this work with a rigorous definition of community as he planned to use it, only commenting that "it is used here in the prevailing, organizational sense which is even narrower than that of the German Gemeinde."[39]

In order to understand Baron's deep interest in both the history and the future of the subject it is important to consider his concerns, along with those of his associates in the Conference on Jewish Relations, to defend the Jewish community against growing antisemitic accusations in America and to help guide the future orientation of the Jewish community in its new environments. Thus, *The Jewish Community* was intended to provide a scientific basis for understanding the development of Jewish communal life in the past and to delineate its potential parameters in the future.

Indeed, Baron saw this study as being of considerable practical importance.

The tremendous task of communal reorganization now confronting world Jewry requires, then, a closer understanding of the fundamental lines of the earlier historical evolution. Only through a deeper penetration of the essential trends in the millennial history of the Jewish community will we be able to comprehend the chaotic variations of the contemporary community.[40]

Baron combined his image of the historian as statesperson and man of affairs with his conception of interacting religious and national historical forces. In this way he was able to shape his own construction of the parameters of Jewish community activity and authority in the past, and in the future.

Consequently, it was important for Baron to delineate the weaknesses of alternative positions on the nature of Jewish communal life—Dubnow's autonomy on the one hand and the purer religious definition of the Reformers on the other. American Jewry must realize that exclusively secular approaches to its identity at the expense of cultural or religious aspects would not lay the basis for a vibrant Jewish life.

Baron also sought to instruct American Jewry that it had developed a cogent new phase in communal history through the significance of voluntarism.

It may be true that about one half of American Jewry does not actively participate in any organized form of Jewish communal life. . . . But those who do belong to an organization do so of choice, albeit, perhaps, a choice influenced by the examples of neighbors, by pressure of public opinion, or other external factors. The amazing record of achievement of the American Jewish community, despite its innumerable obvious shortcomings and weaknesses, testified to the frequently superior vitality of such optional organizations as against those composed of largely indifferent or unwilling taxpayers.[41]

When proposals were put forth to form a European Kehilah-type structure in the American setting, Baron urged a greater appreciation of the value of what had been accomplished in America. Thus, at a 1952 conference reported in the *New York Times,* Baron differed with renown theologian Mordecai Kaplan, who urged greater communal control over diverse local activity. Baron "lauded the development of unregulated American Jewish communal organization," and called the American voluntarist community system a "revolutionary transformation" from the secular, national structures of Jewish communities in Central and Eastern Europe. On the threat of excessive freedom within the community, Baron remarked that whereas such freedom "seemed at times 'to engulf the community in total anarchy,' it had [actually] made the Jewish community more cohesive than ever before," noting in conclusion "that in all western countries, outside of Israel, 'the Jewish communities are increasingly reshaping themselves along American lines.' "[42]

In the past, Jewish communal structure had evolved in response to the interaction between historical traditions and new external conditions. Now the contemporary community had also successfully adapted to the open society that hosted the major existing Jewish community.

Baron paid little attention in this work to the developing dimensions of Jewish communal life of his own day. But at the time that *The Jewish Community* appeared, Baron was confronted by the ongoing demise of the European community from which he had come and where he thought his parents and one sister still lived. Simultaneously, he was becoming increasingly obsessed with the opportunities offered by America and the role that the American community would play in the future of Jewish life. This juxtaposition of historical changes forms the basis of the next chapter.

CHAPTER 7

DESTRUCTION AND RECONSTRUCTION

THE NAZI YEARS BROUGHT to a head many of the public and private trends in Baron's life discussed in previous chapters. Especially between 1938 and 1945, Baron reformulated his thinking on the essential dimensions of contemporary Jewish life. He emerged as the foremost academic spokesperson of American Jewry, he lived in continual anxiety over the well-being of his own family in Tarnow, and some years later at the Eichmann trial he eulogized the life, culture, and history of what had once been European Jewry.

In his 1939 essay "Emphases in Jewish History," Baron depicted the historian as man of affairs as one of his ideals. In fact, several reviewers of the *SRH* described the epilogue in that work as Baron's attempt to fill the role, not only of statesperson, but also of prophet.[1] Some of Baron's writings during the war years seem to confirm the accuracy of such a description. For example, in his 1940 essay "Reflections on the Future of the Jews of Europe," Baron set out to combat a growing pessimism among American Jews resulting from a wave of Axis victories in Western Europe.

At a time like this, it is not only the duty of Jewish leadership, as it was in the days of the Second Isaiah, to "comfort, comfort My people" but also to restore their composure and to urge them to look into all the facts and facets of the situation with calm objectivity. . . . Self-imposed and self-enforced objectivity becomes doubly necessary both for the preservation of our intellectual integrity and the understanding of any intelligent remedial action. It is in this spirit of self-enforced discipline that the writer, defying an anticipated emotional reaction of his readers . . . has felt in duty bound to submit the following reflections for further consideration.[2]

This chapter relates and assesses Baron's record as prophet, scholar, and statesperson during the Nazi years. As an analyst of contemporary developments in Europe, his record was actually quite poor; as a statesperson for American Jewry, he had an unusually great impact for a Judaic scholar on the community at large. But we start our examination closer to home, with Baron's more personal efforts in both arranging immigration and assisting new arrivals.

An Address for Refugees

Already in 1933, Baron took advantage of his annual summer trip to Europe to discuss immigration possibilities with a number of scholars on behalf of the American Academy for Jewish Research "which is planning to offer fellowships to

German-Jewish scholars in American universities."[3] As the Nazi program unfolded, Baron's activity deepened.

Whereas the American Academy for Jewish Research was concerned specifically with facilitating the immigration possibilities of Judaic scholars, from its beginnings in the thirties the Conference on Jewish Social Studies gave its attention to a broader spectrum of professionals. Its emphasis on population studies reflected in part the need to facilitate the successful absorption of European refugees. In June 1943, a joint meeting of several organizations was held to discuss the feasibility of enhanced Jewish immigration to South American countries, with the conference represented by Baron and Theodore Gaster, the American Jewish Committee by Max Gottschalk, and the Institute of Jewish Affairs by Arieh Tartakower. The combined group decided to research the various political, legal, and economic aspects of the question with each organization undertaking a different phase of inquiry. The files give no indication that this meeting resulted in any further action, although the conference's legal committee was still examining that dimension of the plan in 1944.[4]

On a personal basis, Baron was much more involved than this organizational paralysis would seem to indicate. As Baron explained to me, a professor at Columbia University in New York City was relatively easy to find, and "I was the address" for scholars from Germany and Austria. Some came with recommendations. Baron recalled that Werner Sombart had sent two or three Jewish students with letters addressed directly to him. Hannah Arendt came to him with a referral from Ismar Elbogen, and Alvin Johnson consulted with Baron about possible assistance for a number of refugees.[5]

Greater efforts were required for those who contacted Baron from Europe. In the aftermath of the Anschluss of Austria in March 1938, appeals from Vienna increased in both frequency and intensity. By July of that year, Baron was already inundated with calls for assistance: "I have been receiving as you may easily imagine scores of letters from Vienna. Among those which might be of some interest to you are several from Krauss, Aptowitzer, Kobler and Kristianpoller." Baron turned to Alexander Marx on behalf of the latter who had been librarian at the rabbinical seminary in Vienna. "Even a mere invitation without real salary enabling him to obtain a U.S.A. immigration visa would be of some help to him." In a letter written to Marx in August 1939, Baron commented rather remarkably that "there has been a slight respite in my refugeeitis however. The letters are becoming somewhat less numerous and less insistent. But they give you plenty of worry still."[6]

Baron actively sought to arrange and facilitate the immigration of family and friends. His daughters have told me that Baron signed as many as twenty guarantees for prospective immigrants.[7] Among these, he exerted special efforts on behalf of Rabbi Julius Augapfel and medieval Jewish historian Guido Kisch. In late 1938, Baron received several requests for affidavits from strangers with the last name Baron, but with no closer connection. In one case, he responded that he had already sent out five affidavits for close relatives, two of which were still awaiting decision, and that he expected to send out two more in the near future for other relatives.[8]

In some cases, Baron himself undertook to pay the passage. In September 1941, Baron wrote to Henry Hurwitz of the *Me-*

norah Journal concerning his article on modern capitalism and Jewish fate: "There is only one great difficulty: I cannot quite afford to place this article at your disposal without an honorarium. I have just paid in some $950 for three passages for relatives from Europe and I must seek some extracurricular revenue to cover such expenses." I initially assumed these tickets were intended for Baron's parents and his sister, but other documentation implies that they went to two cousins from Prague and to another relative named Joseph Rosenblatt. When informed that Rosenblatt had reached Spain, Baron wrote: "Although he is but a distant relative of mine and I have never met him, I am delighted to hear that at least one other victim of Hitler has reached some more hospitable shores."[9]

Baron was also successful in aiding his sister Tanya, her daughter, and her husband; the husband had been placed in a concentration camp in Germany in the latter part of 1938. Letters to and from Europe and to the State Department seem to have helped alleviate the situation. Tanya's husband was released and the family made its way to America.

It was probably during the eventful year of 1941 that Baron prepared the dedication of *The Jewish Community:* "To my parents, on the completion of more than half a century of tireless communal endeavor. Unfortunately, Baron did not succeed in bringing his parents and sister Gisela out of Europe to safety. After the war, he contacted the foreman of his parents' estate, located outside of Tarnow, who informed Baron of some of the details of their death. The events were related to me by Shoshanna Eytan, the eldest daughter of Baron's sister Gisela, and by Zvi Ankory, whose family played such an important role in the story.[10]

In 1939, Gisela traveled to Tarnow from Switzerland to help her parents leave the country before continuing on to Palestine to join her children. When the war broke out, however, they were all forced to remain. Baron attempted to maintain direct contact with the family, but I have seen only a vague reference that he was able to do so.[11] For a while, communications were maintained through Marcus Cohn, a family friend of Gisela in Basel. At first, during the last months of 1939, Cohn had no word at all from Tarnow. His attempts were directed through the offices of the Red Cross and the World Jewish Congress, but information was scarce and only the identity of those who had fled to Romania could be determined. Then at the end of 1939, Cohn cabled Baron that the three were alive and that he would attempt to help them emigrate; Baron's parents would come to America and Gisela would go to be with her children in Palestine.[12] Through the first half of 1940, Cohn assured Baron that the three were still alive, but reported that the parents refused to leave.

Baron was able to learn from the State Department that his parents had not yet applied for a visa, but that if they did so, they would be eligible for preferential treatment as parents of an American citizen. However, this special status would not apply to Gisela; so Baron also concluded that it would be best for her to travel to Palestine.[13] Meanwhile, as Cohn explained, his parents made no move to depart because Gisela did not yet have permission and they were physically incapable of leaving without her.

Baron for his part used his correspondence with Cohn to vent his own sense of frustration, explaining that he had attempted for years to convince his parents to register for American visas. Procedures became further complicated as American consulate offices closed down, and files were either lost or transferred. In April 1940, Baron expressed his exasperation to Cohn: "It seems that despite all attempts even before the war began, my people will never understand the situation or do not wish to do so."

There were gaps in their communications, as both Baron and Cohn indicated that they had not received replies to a number of letters between them in late 1941 and early 1942. But in July 1942, Cohn reported that he had not heard from the family in Tarnow since the middle of 1941. His last letters had been returned, and Cohn assumed the family was no longer there. Baron wrote to Cohn in October 1942 explaining that he too had not heard for some time and he would be more concerned except that he knew others who had not heard from their relatives since December, that is, since America's involvement in the war. This then was what Baron did and did not know, did and did not surmise during the war years themselves.

What actually happened in Tarnow is now well documented.[14] On the eve of the war, Tarnow (located in Southern Poland, somewhat to the east of Cracow) had some twenty-five thousand Jews who amounted to fifty-five percent of the total population of the city. With the outbreak of war, Tarnow was transformed into an urban center of mass flight. Thousands of Jewish refugees from western Poland converged on Tarnow, coming primarily from Silesia and Cracow. But within days, as the Germans advanced, many Jews fled in turn to the east. The city was occupied on 8 September, and Jews were subjected to physical beatings and theft. There followed orders for the Jewish star to be placed on stores, monetary restrictions, orders to wear a Jewish badge, and apparently on 9 November, most synagogues were burnt down. The first officials of the local Judenrat attempted to alleviate some of the Nazi decrees. Some of these were arrested and replaced by more compliant officials.

Sporadic killings during the early period were followed by intense activity in June 1942. The first Aktion started on 10 June when the weaker sectors of the population were deported, especially the elderly, sick, women, and children. Jewish police were forced to assist, and those who refused were killed. Polish and Ukrainian police units assisted in the roundup. On 11 June some thirty-five hundred Jews were deported to Belzec, and several hundred others were murdered in the streets or in the cemetery. On 15 June, another ten thousand were deported and many others murdered in the cemetery or in huge pits that had been prepared near the city. Estimates of the total killed or deported during that week range from fifteen to twenty thousand, with half sent to Belzec and half executed in the cemetery or a nearby woods. It is estimated that about twenty thousand Jews remained in Tarnow; some claimed work permits, whereas others went into hiding.

On 19 June, a ghetto was established, followed by another Selektion in September. Some Jews were allowed to remain to work; about eight thousand others were deported. After this it seems that the ghetto was used mostly for Jews from neighboring localities. Further actions and a successful blockade of supplies continually reduced the population until by November 1942, little more than a hundred Jews remained in the town.

Quite early on, the Nazis confiscated the large Baron home near the center of town.[15] Baron's father went to the Ankory house to hide; the women went elsewhere. His father remained in hiding, protected by the Ankorys. He was visited there by the foreman of his estate, who later related that at their last meeting Baron's father had been very worried, and their separation that time was very emotional. Both Baron's and Ankory's fathers were subsequently killed together on 11 June 1942 in the local cemetery during the first Aktion. Apparently, Baron's mother and sister were also shot by the cemetery.

Baron was unaware of his family's fate until after the war when a letter arrived from the foreman. This may help explain why he remained hopeful and even optimistic well into the war. Indeed, his writing and lecturing during this period often optimistically assessed the implications of the developing situation in Europe for continued Jewish life there.

Changing Perceptions of the Nazi Threat

Starting in 1935, in the aftermath of the Nuremberg laws, Baron objected vehemently and repeatedly to those who compared the status imposed on the Jews by the Nazis with that of the medieval period. "The Nazi attempt, consequently, to place the non-Aryans . . . outside of the pale of a united Germany citizenry is not a reerection of the medieval legal structure, but the establishment of a new, unprecedented

274

legal status." He emphasized that Nazi legislation was racial and compulsory, forcing the individual to be part of the communal destiny.[16]

Baron dealt again with the Nazi threat in the epilogue to the *SRH,* written in 1936. This time, his analysis spoke of positive possibilities. Thinking primarily of Italy, he explained at length that the fascist state was not inherently hostile to Jewish survival, and he maintained that this might be true of Germany as well. In fact, he envisioned several possible, if unlikely, scenarios in which Jews, although disenfranchised, might receive corporative rights equivalent or even superior to those enjoyed in the Middle Ages. Conversely, Baron also raised the possibility that fascist nationalism, with its strong commitment to ethnic homogeneity, could result in a renewed and invigorated antisemitism across Europe.[17]

Baron commented on the state of affairs during the early war years in a lecture delivered in May 1940 at the National Conference of Jewish Social Welfare.[18] Baron sought to combat a growing sense of pessimism among American Jews regarding their brethren, which was complicated all the more by a continued sense of indifference among Americans at large to what was still perceived as primarily another European squabble. Baron assured his audience that the eventual defeat of the Nazi armies was virtually guaranteed by their very ambition of world conquest, because a German invasion of Russia would result in a U.S.-Soviet alliance. In the meantime the sense of doom concerning the fate of the Jews should be mitigated. Two-thirds of world Jewry lived in America and the Soviet Union and therefore "at least for the time being" were outside the range of war; altogether three-fourths of the Jews were beyond Nazi reach.

Going even further, Baron referred to his historical law of increased toleration of Jews within multinational states. According to this principle, the increased diversity of the Third Reich as a result of its various conquests should lead to increased toleration of minority groups, including the Jews. One possible scenario would be for Germany to make itself Judenrein, but to be more tolerant of Jews in the newly acquired protected areas. Baron was not only wrong on this score, but the sequence of events actually moved in the opposite direction. A relative reticence that had dampened the pace of actions against German Jews was dismissed with the outbreak of war and the conquest of Poland's much larger Jewish population. Both Baron's predictions and his historical law were contradicted by the course of events, but despite this contrary evidence, he continued to repeat the law for decades to come. In fact, he maintained his fallacious predictions concerning the Nazis for several more years as well.

Baron did not intend to minimize the gravity of the current situation. The few rays of hope that he had offered notwithstanding, he assured his audience that in the event of a German victory in Europe, Jewish leadership would have to act courageously. One of their best possibilities for action would lie in the further development and settlement of Palestine, an objective that Baron thought might be amenable to the Nazis. Such an undertaking would secure the existing Jewish colony, as well as provide a haven for additional refugees. Baron emphasized that an accord would have to be reached with the Arab majority. The possibility of an Allied victory, while providing an obviously better set of circumstances, would still require that Jewish leadership struggle to achieve legal guarantees for the status and toleration of the European Jews. The complicated negotiations with the Arabs, and possibly with the Nazis, would require considerable imagination and courage by the Jewish leadership. But Baron concluded by comforting the leaders he was addressing. He maintained that Jews had not been mere passive objects in the shaping of their history, and American Jewish leadership was well equipped for the grave challenges it now faced.

A few months later, Baron continued his comments on the contemporary situation in "The Future of European Jewry." [19] This time he focused on the fate of Jews in the Soviet Union; this group comprised one-third of world Jews and was the largest community in Europe. It was possible that ties between Russia and Germany would be further strengthened, resulting in a softening of Germany's position. But, it was also possible that war would break out between them with the main battlefield being the territories most densely populated by Jews.

Still, prospects for Jews in those areas already occupied by the Nazis were far more gloomy. And yet, Baron countered again that there were reasons to be hopeful concerning the fate of Jews in those areas. "Moreover, I cannot help feeling that a victorious Germany might herself greatly tone down her anti-Jewish crusade." Once again he referred to his law of multinational empires with the conclusion that Nazis too should be expected to become tolerant at that point. But he could not rule out the possibility of the extermination of European Jewry. Meanwhile, Baron concluded, it becomes the task of the Jews in those countries that are still neutral such as America to confront these very great challenges.

By 1942, certain changes could be seen in Baron's outlook. These changes were not so much in his beliefs about the war and the destiny of European Jews, but more on the future role of the American Jewish community as leaders of world Jewry. In an essay published that year, Baron locked together the destinies of both America and the Jewish people:

Whatever one may think about the much-debated "complacency" of the American public, long before Pearl Harbor many Jews had been deeply awake to the great menace of Nazi world domination. There certainly are but few Jews today who fail to realize how intimately their own destiny is tied up with the victory of the United Nations, in a measure unparalleled in the long history of their people. In fact, not overconfidence and complacency, but irrational fears bordering on hysteria have for years affected large sections of American Jewry and may yet constitute the major drawback to the much-needed calm and rational appraisal of the existing dangers and to the adoption of remedial measures.[20]

It is hard to read this passage without considering that he was attempting to reassure not only the community at large, but himself as well. After all, America's entry into the war ended any chance to evacuate his own family from occupied Galicia before the war's conclusion.

Even in 1942, Baron still spoke of the need "to help reconstruct the shattered life of European Jewry along permanent lines. The rebuilding of the destroyed religious, educational and cultural institutions and the reawakening of the vast creative cultural energies of European Jewry" will essentially remain a task for American Jewry alone and will require vast efforts and resources. In fact, Baron added in a footnote that "the cultural re-awakening of East-Central European Jewry may, indeed, prove to be unexpectedly speedy and profound." He explained that his bibliography of recent scholarship demonstrated that research of both quality and considerable quantity was still being produced within these communities.[21]

Baron was hardly alone in his mistaken prophecies, and yet this shouldn't preclude an examination of the issues at hand. Deep into the war, Baron continued to predict the revival of a rich Jewish life in Europe, implying that European Jewry would be sufficiently unscathed. Even more specifically, he failed to detect the commitment to annihilation in the Nazi program and was convinced that their war effort would distract them away from the Jews.

As an experienced historian I thought I was free of employing hindsight in my judgments, especially concerning the Nazi years. But I find it nevertheless remarkable to read of Baron's continued optimism on the future possibilities of Jewish life in Europe after the war, not to speak of the error— shared by almost all Jewish leaders—in underestimating the Nazi threat to Jewish life. Of course, it may be that I expected from Baron greater insight into the events around him, but the issue should not be dismissed as inappropriate. In fact, analysis in place of judgments may lead to interesting conclusions.

Although we have surveyed Baron's main writings for most

of the Nazi period, there are three additional anecdotes that will add a great deal to our picture. In November 1940, speaking in Indianapolis under the auspices of the Jewish Welfare Board, Baron was reported in the press under the heading "Anti-Semitism Lessening" as saying that persecution of the Jews around the world seemed to be decreasing. "It is quite possible that anti-Semitism, rather than advancing, has been checked in 1939." He explained that Russia apparently was trying to absorb much of its Jewish population, Germany was too busy with war for a strong anti-Jewish campaign, and the United States was seeking a national unity precluding racial discrimination.[22] Considering that Nazi ghettos had been established in Poland already in late 1939 (for example in Warsaw) and in a number of other communities by the spring of 1940, Baron's statement demands attention.

The second anecdote dates from 1944 and deals with a talk given to a meeting of the Hebrew Immigrant Aid Society (HIAS) on "Migrations Spell Progress." Again, Baron was quite optimistic, barely referring to events in the war. He concluded his talk with this paragraph:

Because of our technological advances, we have now more and more means of transportation—probably cheaper means of transportation. Distances have shrunk. The world has become smaller. There is absolutely no chance that with the increased technological possibilities of migration, migration shall be stopped by decrees.[23]

Clearly, Baron was not privy to classified information on the final solution, but these statements still require commentary. I believe these two incidents each imply a different factor influencing Baron's thinking on the dimension of the Nazi threat. In the first anecdote, Baron publicly declared in 1940 that world antisemitism, including that being propagated by the Nazis, was diminishing. That optimism, it seems to me, derives from his deep personal commitment to counter the dimension of antisemitism in Jewish historical thinking. In other words, I am indeed suggesting that Baron's historical principle to go beyond the lachrymose conception broke down when it came face to face with the greatest tragedy of human destruction in Jewish history. After the events, Baron was able to accurately explain that he had never intended to deny the extent of persecutions in the Jewish past. His concern had been with the proportion of space devoted to the description of suffering, and, perhaps even more, with the dominant position that suffering had seized in the Jewish historical Weltanschauung. But precisely because he opposed the mentality of persecution with such ardor, he failed to detect the very real and imminent threats of the time.

The second anecdote hints at a much more personal reason for Baron's thinking. In suggesting as late as 1944 that migration could not be hampered by decrees, it seems that Baron was holding on to hope that his own parents and sister, who had been unable to escape, would still find their way to freedom and survival. To some extent, Baron's mitigating prognosis for the gravity of events must have derived from his personal hopes. In 1940, he had written to Alexander Marx of the distractions diverting him from his work: "I have worked less this summer than in other years, partly on account of the international situation with its individual repercussions."[24]

A third insight derives from the fact that even after the war Baron continued to proclaim that European Jewry still had an important role to play in Jewish life. But by that time, he certainly knew of the fate of his own family.

During the war and afterward American Zionist leaders consciously determined that Palestine represented the most effective focus for their limited manpower. Other American Jewish leaders realized that mass immigration in the midst of war provided no realistic solution to the plight of millions and so accepted Washington's argument that only a swift military victory could save the Jews of Europe. Yet Baron, although loyal to both sentiments, remained firmly attached to the historical greatness of European Jewry and to the prospects for its future.[25] Baron—who was born and educated in the cities of Europe, who had lived and worked in Vienna until the age of thirty, who had left a still flourishing Europe twenty years earlier, who had visited Europe regularly until 1937, and who in his life work had invested so much of his energy in the history of its communities—seemed to be blatantly clinging to a hope that these communities would continue to play a significant role in the future of Jewish life. In other words, even after the extent of human destruction had been clearly established, the toll of the war on the communal entity was still being denied.

It is fortunate that this denial was limited to certain contexts. Although Baron continued to write and speak about the reconstruction of European Jewry, we have already seen indications of how by the time of Pearl Harbor he had become an adamant spokesperson on the future role of America in international relations and of its Jews as leaders of the Jewish people everywhere.

Wartime Scholarship

A virtual flood of essays poured from Baron's pen during the war years, in addition to *The Jewish Community,* which was written in the late thirties and appeared in 1942, and in addition to a number of publications on contemporary Jewish affairs, some of which we have already surveyed.[26] During the early forties Baron also issued a number of medieval studies including a series dealing with leading rabbinical personalities—Rashi, Saadia Gaon, Yehudah Halevi, and Maimonides. This was also the period of his earliest writings on American Jewish history, dozens of book reviews, scattered essays on diplomatic history, and his classic article "Modern Capitalism and Jewish Fate."

In September 1941, Baron suggested to Henry Hurwitz of the *Menorah Journal* publishing a lecture he had delivered several times on capitalism and the Jews. "The subject is not the usual one of Jewish contributions to capitalism as discussed by some of the others, but what capitalism has done to the Jew and hence what its newest developments and possible disintegration may mean to the Jewish future."[27]

Baron clearly intended that the capitalism essay bring historical scholarship to the service of contemporary needs. But although prompted by the events in Europe, most immediately the breakdown of the Nazi-Soviet pact and the German invasion of Russia, this essay focused on the extent to which continued Jewish survival was tied to the fate of capitalist development. Throughout the piece, Baron referred to this as a matter of concern, especially to the young adult generation. Somehow I doubt the extent of that concern. Hurwitz's response seemed somewhat muted: "Your paper strikes me as a very valuable summary of the subject." Actually, this essay represents a rather convoluted presentation of what obviously struck Baron as a most pressing matter. Hurwitz suggested a sweeping restructuring of the piece, which Baron rejected, while concurring that considerable editing was required. "For some unexplained reason this particular article did not 'write itself' and for a while I even thought of delaying its completion until a more propitious time."

In the essay Baron explained that Hitler's attack on Russia the previous June precipitated a sharp increase in propaganda, lumping together Jews and communism and attacking them both. Ironically, Nazism had borrowed its conception of Bolshevism as a form of Jewish domination from Marxist thinking itself, which beginning with the founding namesake had urged and predicted society's liberation from Jewish control. According to these theories, an overthrow of the capitalist order signaled the elimination of Jewish wealth and eventually the demise of the Jewish group as a distinct entity.

What provoked Baron at this juncture was what he labeled a widespread prediction among communists and capitalists alike that the reigning social order was doomed. "When applied to the future of the Jews, the question has often been raised, with either glee or anxiety, as to whether the Jewish people, as such, was likely to survive the passing of the present civilization and the rise of a new, wholly unprecedented order." Thus, what concerned Baron here was not the famous debate surrounding Werner Sombart's thesis of Jewish influences on the rise of capitalism, first argued early in the century. Rather, the question was, if Jews had indeed prospered considerably from the capitalist system, then what future awaited them both collectively and individually in the event of its demise? [28]

Following Sombart's periodization into early, advanced, and late stages of capitalist development, Baron spoke of the benefits gained by Jews during the first two of those periods. The revolution in commerce that marked early capitalism precipitated an expansion in markets and in production techniques. New areas of settlement were opened, and Jews were prominent among the settlers. A process was thus engaged that eventually allowed Jews to reside in old areas previously closed to them. Geographic expansion was matched by population growth far ahead of the rate of the general population, and the increased significance of money over land enhanced the importance of the Jew in stature as well as wealth. Eventually, these processes paved the way to increased toleration in some countries. [29]

Of particular importance was the increased emphasis placed by capitalism on individualism and private enterprise. As the Jew came to be viewed as an individual and not exclusively as member of a legally defined group, communal influence declined and Jews began to distance themselves from communal identity. The essence of Jewish attachment now belonged to the "purely negative forces of anti-Jewish persecution or discrimination." Baron was sharply critical of this position: "Apart from the insecurity and superficiality of these negative loyalties, the ensuing concentration of communal efforts upon defense and relief has tended to exhaust the few remaining communal energies and, in all cases, to divert them from more constructive tasks" ("Modern Capitalism," p. 54).

Thus Baron argued that despite the image of a profitable alliance between capitalism and Judaism, what may have been true for the individual did not hold for the community: "In short, much as the Jew as an individual may have benefited by early and advanced capitalism, he undoubtedly lost a great deal qua Jew, that is, as a member of his group and faith."[30] The rise of capitalism was accompanied by an increased emphasis on materialism, which also succeeded in weakening traditional Jewish values and emphases. For example, communal leadership shifted from the pious and the learned to the wealthy.

To complete this picture, Baron added in the more frequently noted negative effects of rationalism and secularization on traditional Jewish religious life. In doing so, he seemed to be traveling somewhat afield from capitalism in order to strengthen his argument. "In any case, the combined forces of individualism, materialism, rationalism and secularism have placed so many question marks upon the future destinies of Jewry as to outweigh the benefits of early and advanced capitalism in the minds of many patriotic Jews."[31]

During the more contemporary period known as the late stage of capitalism, even some of the earlier benefits for individuals were curtailed. Improved production techniques no longer required increased sources of manpower. The sharp decline in fertility rates threatened Jewish survival on biological grounds alone. Past liberal immigration policies in Western countries had already changed, causing a particular hardship on Jews who were in dire need of migration destinations. Private banking and privatism in general were giving way to powerful corporations in which Jews played a diminished role.[32]

Thus, the widely predicted fall of capitalism—with which Baron seemed remarkably comfortable—did not imply only negative consequences for Jewish life. Walking a tightrope along antisemitic accusations of Jewish power, Baron continued that although the future course of economic development was far outside the parameters of their influence, Jewish leadership should not remain passive and ignore the new trends. Returning to his classic points, Baron reiterated that Jewish history meant more than suffering and that Jews had continually played an active role in shaping their destiny. Pointedly, he observed in 1942 that the crisis of Jewish life "did not begin in 1933, and has not automatically resolved itself by the defeat of Hitler. [sic!]" In his now familiar message for these years, he concluded that this was a time for "the creativeness and efficacy of [Jewish] leadership."[33]

The heading "Wartime Scholarship" should certainly not imply that the vast corpus of Baron's writings that appeared during the Nazi years was thoroughly permeated with references or influences deriving from the circumstances at hand. As we have already seen, the three-volume *Jewish Community* that appeared in 1942 derived no less from Baron's desire to formulate a history and a program distinct from the national autonomy concept of Simon Dubnow, than it did from the incipient breakdown of Jewish communal life in Europe.

During the early 1940s, Baron published four studies of medieval rabbinical personalities: Rashi, the leading biblical and Talmudic exegete; Saadia Gaon, the controversial philosopher and polemicist; Yehudah Halevi, poet and author of the Kuzari; and the period's leading philosopher and codifier, Maimonides. His synthetic study on "The Jewish Factor in Medieval Civilization" also appeared during this same period.[34]

Whereas the appearance of these essays within a two-year time span is hardly coincidental, of the four personality studies, only one essay directly reflects the issues of the time. "Yehudah Halevi: An Answer to a Historical Challenge" is pregnant with references — some explicit, many suggestive — to the contemporary crises. At the other end of the relevance spectrum is "Rashi and the Community of Troyes," which totally lacks an inner unity as it seeks to disprove certain accepted correlations between social circumstances and references within Rashi's writings and suggests new connections of a similar vein. The essay has virtually no beginning, and there is no conclusion. There was certainly no direct attempt at relevance to the times.

Let us begin our analysis with Yehudah Halevi and then attempt to understand the broader threads of connection between the other essays.

Delivered as a lecture in early 1941 and published later that year, the essay on Halevi refers frequently, especially at the outset and conclusion, to the time period in which it was written. Even prior to America's entry into the war, Baron contrasted between the depressing atmosphere of the times and the spiritual celebration of Halevi's accomplishments and held out the hope to his audience that Halevi's message could provide "a fruitful lesson for our own perplexed and intellectually groping generation."[35]

More interesting than these superficial trappings are the suggestive parallels that remained unexpressed but informed the nature of Baron's discussion. Halevi grew up in a prosperous environment during a temporary calm in relations between Christians and Muslims. But rumblings of renewed violence could already be heard during his childhood, and "the era of appeasement was speedily drawing to its close." With the violent hostilities of the late eleventh century, the "liberal cultivation of arts and letters gave way to increasing repression."

Baron readily employed the language of his own day to describe the earlier historical atmosphere. In his discussion of the disruption of Islamic-Jewish relations, he went further to connect the two periods by focusing on the economic and psychological problems of Jewish refugees coming to Christian regions. Despite his intellectual origins in Vienna, such a psychological line of inquiry was highly unusual for Baron.

He built his description on the example of Moses ibn Ezra, who fled from Granada to Castile and complained for the rest of his life that he lived as a "plucked rose among thorns and thistles" in a "desert of savages." Baron generalized the experience:

Such maladjusted refugees, knocking at the gates of various Jewish communities, helped to spread the culture of Muslim Spain, but demonstrated to all the insecurity of Jewish life. Where else were they to go, however? Apparently, very few Jewish Spaniards thought of proceeding north of the Pyrenees, to France, England, or

Germany. The economic opportunities . . . were decidedly limited. . . . Culturally, too, one could expect but little from these backward regions.[36]

Baron himself drew the connection immediately after this discussion: "In short, the prospect of settling in northwestern Europe must have appeared as formidable to a Spanish-Jewish refugee then as that of migrating to Paraguay or New Caledonia appeared to a German refugee in the 1930s."

Thus, the analogy was far more complete. Most German Jewish migrants moved at the time to the attractive Western outposts of Paris, London, and New York. Even in such centers, the new wave of immigrants faced serious adjustments, which Baron well understood. Indeed, in our personal discussions he pinpointed his personal relationships with the immigrant faculty that populated the New School, popularly known as the "university in exile." And, as we have already seen, he was a focal point for assisting new arrivals. His discussion of Spanish refugees was an unusual line of inquiry for him, written during a period in which he himself was immersed in difficulties facing a new generation of refugees.

A resounding echo of the Nazi period can also be heard in Baron's sweeping conclusions on the eleventh century: "The future of world Jewry looked very bleak indeed." The notion of considering such a global perspective for the scattered medieval communities and certainly the negative prognosis strike chords of similarity with contemporary affairs. Concerning the communities in the East, Baron mentioned the suffering of Palestinian Jews resulting from the violent attacks of the Crusaders. In the west, he specified the high rate of conversions and the religious divisions caused by the Karaites. In the remainder of the essay, Baron turned to the answers developed by Halevi to the challenges of his period, emphasizing what he called Halevi's Zionist ideology.

Baron concluded his analysis with the question of relevance: "What does Halevi mean to the present generation?" Despite the fact that Halevi's philosophy had never been influential and that racial aspects in his thinking might now be particularly objectionable, Baron nevertheless found considerable significance in Halevi's example.

His great perseverance in a period of world-wide crisis, his courage and undaunted spirit, which taught him to stand upright in the midst of persecution and danger . . . are in themselves examples to be followed by any threatened people. Even more so is his serene faith in history and the long-range forces of destiny high above the brute realities. . . . His exposition of powerlessness as a superior counterpart to the forces of state supremacy may also be fully appreciated by contemporary Jewry. His firm belief, finally, in the Palestinian ideal not only as part of a dim and distant messianic expectation but as an immediate goal . . . has long served and will continue to serve, as a source of inspiration . . . for countless Jews on the verge of despair.[37]

In short, Baron molded out of Halevi a paradigm for his recurring message of the courage and sober foresight that was required from the current generation of Jewish leaders.

Yet, Halevi was not portrayed by Baron as a communal leader, but as a scholar who had provided a model for those who accepted leadership responsibilities. His portrait of

Saadia Gaon was very different, beginning with the opening sentence: "Communal leadership was the great passion of Saadia's life." Adeptly tracing Saadia's rise to prominence from the uncertainty surrounding a foreigner to his becoming head of one of Babylon's two renown academies of learning, Baron described the conflicts, successes, and setbacks, the search for supporters, and the ever present opposition. Building on extensive research launched in part by the discovery of plentiful materials in the Cairo Geniza, Baron placed much of Saadia's literary activity within the dispute with the Karaites on the one hand and the conflict between the Babylonian and Palestinian communities on the other.[38]

Both the essay on Yehudah Halevi and that on Saadia emphasized the motif of scholar as communal leader or activist. If we turn briefly to the short study on Rashi, the same theme appears there too, albeit in muted tones. Half of the essay is devoted to dispensing with two accepted theories on the social context of Rashi's exegetical work: one relating a number of passages to commercial fairs held at Rashi's hometown of Troyes in the Champagne area of France; the other, to Rashi's leadership of rabbinical synods that met in conjunction with the fairs themselves. Baron challenged the notion that there were any fairs at all at Troyes during Rashi's lifetime and proceeded to cast doubts on the existence of the accompanying synods as well. Thus, Rashi's rabbinical leadership could not be easily explained by institutional considerations. Baron's conclusions are striking for our discussion:

From all we know, therefore, Rashi was the leader of a predominantly rural Jewish community, whose influence beyond the borders of the town was based partly upon its incipient commercial relations with more distant localities, partly upon the centralized power of the counts of Champagne residing in their Troyes castle, and, most of all, to Rashi's own intellectual preeminence. The community must have been very small, Rashi evidently serving as the principal spokesman by virtue of his learning, rather than by that of any recognized position.[39]

Thus, each of these leading rabbinical personalities was deeply immersed in the contemporary affairs of the times. And in all cases, their leadership model was legitimated by their scholarship.

These examples demonstrated generalities on the high status of scholars in the medieval community that Baron also introduced in his Jewish Community. Baron, like Morris Cohen a few years earlier, emphasized how in past generations, scholars had stood at the center of Jewish leadership.

Even discarding all obvious or likely exaggerations in the extant sources, the grandeur of the political as well as spiritual power wielded, without any state enforcement, by a handful of rabbis gathered around certain more or less permanent seats of learning, is really amazing. . . . In short, just as the local scholar-judge dominated the individual community, so the central academies of scholars rivaled the exilarchic authority in managing country-wide Jewish affairs.

Furthermore, these scholarly leaders were chosen primarily— as in the case of Rashi—on the basis of their intellectual acumen: "Even today we cannot help admiring the sound judgment of successive generations in recognizing the achievements of leading contemporaries and the relative scarcity of ephemeral reputations based on other than intrinsic merits."[40]

Thus, the three essays on rabbinic personalities published around the time of Pearl Harbor all substantiated a Baronian conception that, in fact, he shared with Morris Cohen, as well as the Conference on Jewish Social Studies in general. That is, the belief that scholars have always played and must continue to play a significant leadership role within the Jewish community. The appearance of these essays at this crucial time was not accidental, and in their own way these essays were not oblivious to the world events of the time.

Different issues precipitated "The Jewish Factor in Medieval Civilization," delivered in very late December 1941 and published in 1942, But here too the connection to the turn of events is significant.[41] Ostensibly, this essay, which describes economic and intellectual contributions and social relations between Jews and their neighbors in medieval times, might appear to belong to the genre of apologetic works against antisemitism. It was to avoid such an identification that Baron chose his title instead of "Jewish Contributions to Medieval Civilization."

Before turning to the major points involved, reference should be made to the implications of the discussion on cordial social relations between Jews and Gentiles in past ages. The extension of such relations to the sexual realm and the emphasis on high conversion rates at various times during the Middle Ages raised between them serious questions about current racial assumptions concerning Jews and Gentiles.

Baron was explicit on this argument and repeated it several times in the essay. Nevertheless, this hardly represents a serious objective for a lecture delivered and published under the auspices of the American Academy for Jewish Research with its relatively limited audience. This work primarily reorganized and reshaped arguments already expounded in his *SRH*. But several threads explain his motivations for delivering this discourse precisely at this time and to this particular audience.

Baron had first put forth his argument against the lachrymose conception of Jewish history in his 1928 "Ghetto and Emancipation." He later repeated his claims within the *SRH*, which was published in 1937. Then, just a few years later, his primary theories on the nature of the Jewish historical experience seemed threatened along with the very survival of the Jewish people. I would claim that what emerged in "The Jewish Factor" was a restatement of that thesis in light of the Nazi threat.

Baron was hardly concerned with disputing the gravity of the current situation, which he observed went far beyond anything the Jewish people had faced before, but rather with defending his more positive interpretations of medieval times.

Any comparison with the legislation of Nazi Germany and fascist Italy will reveal that we are maligning the Middle Ages when we call the Nuremberg laws a reversion to the medieval status. . . . I may be allowed to repeat here the paradoxical statement that medieval Jewry, much as it suffered from disabilities and contempt, still was a privileged minority in every country where it was tolerated at all.[42]

As Baron explained, his specific intention was not to question the insecurities of medieval Jewish life, but to emphasize the positive benefits of their legal and political status. As a corporate body more or less like any other, the Jewish community was also a protected body with both specific rights and obligations.

In a long footnote, Baron expanded on the development of his attack on the lachrymose conception and responded to his primary critic Yitzhak Baer.

These obviously unorthodox views were first expounded by me in . . . "Ghetto and Emancipation" [and] expanded in various other connections. . . . It was a foregone conclusion that they would not be readily accepted by the majority of Jewish scholars. However, the criticism expressed in this respect by Fritz Baer in his extensive Hebrew review of *SRH*, . . . seems entirely beside the point. His remark that it was antisemites who first contended that the Jews had no just reason for complaint and that Jewish authors merely followed them in denouncing the "lachrymose conception of Jewish history" is certainly erroneous insofar as I am concerned. I am still unable to locate any antisemitic forerunners; and, to the best of my knowledge I was the first to coin the term "lachrymose conception" . . . when my scholarly conscience (perhaps also, subconsciously, pride in the Jewish heritage) made me impatient with the eternal self-pity characteristic of Jewish historiography. . . . It is high time, in any case, to divorce the indubitable reality of the general insecurity of medieval Jewish life from an objective consideration of the Jews' political and, especially, legal status in the medieval countries where they were tolerated by law.[43]

Hand in hand with this defense of his antilachrymose conceptions, went his revisionist views on the Middle Ages in

Jewish history. Starting with "Ghetto and Emancipation," the diatribes against lachrymosity were directed toward a more positive evaluation of the medieval period. The Nazi on-slaught had precipitated comparisons between past and present sufferings, and Baron emphasized the inappropriateness of such a contrast. What remained implicit in this new essay, but was expressed more explicitly in others, was that the present dangers, rather than a reversion to previous times, actually derived from the considerable threat presented by modernity itself to Jewish life and to human society in general.

Thus, I am suggesting that Baron's scholarly focus on medieval times during the war years derived from a number of factors: in part, to elucidate the historical role played by scholars during times of crisis; to reaffirm his critique of the lachrymose conception despite contemporary developments; and to distinguish between the positive aspects of medieval Jewish life and the greater threats to Jewish survival that were integrally connected to modernity. With all this, it should not be forgotten that Baron hardly concealed himself in a medieval citadel and that much of his writing, as we have already seen in this chapter, concerned itself more directly with contemporary affairs.

In the *SRH,* Baron had undertaken to demonstrate the interaction between social and religious forces in Jewish history. One of the more criticized sections of that work dealt with "Rabbinic Social Ethics" and attempted to exemplify the broader thesis. In "The Economic Views of Maimonides," published in 1941 in a volume edited by Baron in honor of the eight hundredth anniversary of the birth of the outstanding rabbinic scholar of medieval times, Baron continued his argument of mutual influences between society and the traditional thrust of Jewish law. "These attitudes, as reflected in the mind of the greatest medieval Jewish jurist and philosopher, were clearly the result of endless compromises between a powerful tradition, changing economic realities, and, to a certain extent, the exigencies of non-Jewish society and legislation."[44]

With a number of examples on issues—such as slaves, labor relations, and attitudes toward money and property—Baron demonstrated legal modifications in Maimonides' opinions, resulting from changed social conditions. There is less emphasis in this essay on the opposite line of influence—that is, of religious tradition on economic behavior—but some examples do appear.

Thus, primarily, this work appears as a continuation of the fundamental thesis in the *SRH*, and its connection to the era in which it was written less obvious than several of the essays we have already discussed. It is possible that some of Baron's examples were selected in order to defend ethical practices by Jews in their business and economic relations, but this could hardly have been a major priority in a purely scholarly contribution to a volume with limited circulation.[45]

Two of the essays written during this period resulted in personal conflicts: one concerned financial matters, the other matters of scholarship. Each adds to our picture of Baron's personality and career.

When Baron first offered his essay on capitalism to Henry Hurwitz, he had explained that he required some extra remuneration in order to help defray the cost of three tickets from Europe. Hurwitz responded in early October 1941 that the

Menorah Journal would be glad to compensate Baron $100 for the essay. Most of his letter explained that he was busy seeking funds coast to coast for Jewish cultural institutions. "After all, American Jewry is now not only the most substantial but also about the only free Jewry left in the world. If we exhaust ourselves in foreign relief (which cannot, in any case, meet the gigantic problem), we shall be committing a kind of spiritual suicide in the bargain."[46] Baron congratulated Hurwitz on his efforts and accepted the offer. Over the next two months, correspondence concentrated on editing the manuscript. Baron also queried the cost of securing a hundred reprints.

The conflict arose soon after Pearl Harbor and America's entry into the war. Hurwitz wrote to Baron in January 1942 that the level of contributions was sinking rapidly. He asked Baron if he would accept a revised fee of $50, otherwise the journal would have to reluctantly forego publication of the article. Baron expressed his understanding of Hurwitz's position and agreed to the revised arrangement if the journal would also provide 100 reprints of the article. "The cost to you ought not to exceed $8.00 or $10.00."[47] It was at this point that these two personalities came to a full collision on what might be called the "ten buck controversy." So many interesting points emerge from their subsequent exchange that despite the pettiness of the matter, or perhaps because of it, it is worth some attention.

Hurwitz again explained the increased difficulties facing the Menorah Society, which would continue to do what it "can to pay refugee scholars, writers and artists." But "under these circumstances, it frankly seems to me that scholars fortunate enough to have secure incomes should be willing to cooperate for the benefit of other scholars without secure incomes." He also reminded Baron that the journal had published his work even before his appointment to Columbia and had provided considerable editorial assistance to improve the quality of those early essays. Hurwitz offered Baron a number of free copies of the issue that would contain his article and a reduced rate on additional copies. He added that other scholars were making their contributions available "for love."

Baron took issue with Hurwitz's claim that Menorah had published his first essay in English, although he expressed his continued appreciation for the editorial assistance. Nevertheless, "I should not like to consider the journal as a discoverer of a young talent in my case." As far as the contributions of others, Baron would prefer their "writing better articles, even though less 'for love.' " His apparent lack of empathy for scholars with insecure status was remarkable. "One could easily contend that just those people with so-called secure incomes are usually the greatest sufferers in periods such as ours."

The exchange continued with further insinuations, for example concerning which of the two earned the larger salary and how to best ensure the highest quality publication though lacking sufficient resources. Hurwitz labeled Baron's economic theories that people with secure incomes are usually those who suffer the most "extremely novel." In late January, Hurwitz returned the manuscript to Baron, but for reasons unexplained in the correspondence, Hurwitz apparently requested the essay again; Baron complied in April 1942. Their sometimes stormy relationship continued, and in 1944, Hurwitz invited

Baron to be the featured speaker at Menorah's thirtieth anniversary dinner.[48]

More embittered and longer lasting was Baron's scholarly conflict with Second Commonwealth expert Solomon Zeitlin of Philadelphia's Dropsie College, a rivalry that found its most outspoken phase during these same years. Zeitlin had issued one of the more critical attacks on the SRH in the French *Revue Des Études Juives,* which prompted Baron to publish a caustic response in the same journal.

Zeitlin was known for his bitterness and critical attitudes toward others in the field. Cyrus Adler, who doubled as president of New York's Jewish Theological Seminary and Philadelphia's Dropsie College, took Zeitlin to task on this very score. Adler wrote to Zeitlin in February 1939 concerning a manuscript Zeitlin had prepared for the *JQR:* "I think you have been particularly severe in certain phrases with regard to Doctor Büchler. . . . It has never been very clear to me why, if a man has a positive thesis to write, he has to dissect and try to destroy all his predecessors."[49]

Actually, the earliest shot I have found in Baron's rivalry with Zeitlin came not from Zeitlin, but in a devastating unpublished attack from Baron in 1928. Responding to a reprint sent by Zeitlin with a request for reactions, Baron replied at length, criticizing several crucial links in the argument and emphasizing that the main theories were actually quite old and redundant.[50]

To summarize I should say that what is true in your paper is known all around the world, and what is new is not true. Excuse me this severe judgment, but it is better that you know fully what I think of the paper since you showed an interest about it. I hope you will treat my publications with the same frankness although as much in a friendly spirit.

In July 1941, Zeitlin reviewed the Maimonides volume, focusing his scathing attack on Baron's essay on "Economic Views." Zeitlin emphasized that what Baron claimed as Maimonides' views were actually opinions deriving from the Talmud and were accepted by all later rabbinical authorities. "It would be a falsification of historical facts to ascribe such views to Maimonides, while in fact they were the views of the Talmud accepted by all the rabbis." Zeitlin was also perhaps the only reviewer to remain unimpressed by the vast bibliography usually supplied by Baron, "since a large number of [the entries] has no relation whatsoever to the Mishneh Torah nor to Maimonides."[51]

Zeitlin accused Baron of ignorance in rabbinical sources and pronounced a sweeping condemnation: "It is needless for me to say that such essays do not contribute to Jewish scholarship, nor to the understanding of Maimonides, nor to the history of the Jews in the Middle Ages." Nonspecialists could easily be misled into accepting the authenticity of Baron's presentation. Zeitlin concluded: "Such essays clearly demonstrate what folly it is to write on the history of the Jewish communities in the Middle Ages without adequate knowledge of rabbinics." The subsequent exchange between the two scholars resulted in heated criticisms, but also generalizations of broader interest.

In his response, also published in the *JQR,* Baron referred to Zeitlin's attack, "euphemistically called a 'review,' " and explained that he felt "incumbent . . . to write this reply as a matter of civic duty. It is high time that some one should sound a public warning against the recent systematic conversion of your journal, and especially of its review section, into an arena for venting private grudges and complexes." Baron, like Zeitlin in his subsequent reply, placed their disagreement in the context of events then overtaking the fate of Jewish scholarship: "Now after the enforced suspension of the *Monatsschrift* and the *REJ,* the preservation of the dignity and scholarly integrity of the *JQR,* at present the oldest organ of Jewish scholarly opinion, has become a matter of public concern, indeed." Baron belittled Zeitlin's objections with the assertion that even if correct, nothing of the essence of Baron's arguments would have to be changed: "The distinction between relevant and irrelevant matter is a rudimentary requirement of scholarly criticism, indeed the mark of a disciplined mind."[52]

In his rejoinder Zeitlin elaborated his main contentions. First, he purported that much of the material from which Baron sought to derive information concerning the life of Jews in Muslim countries actually reflected established Jewish law as found already in Mishnaic sources. "No rabbi . . . had the right to deviate from the Mishnah. . . . Hence Maimonides' statement . . . has nothing to do with life in the Muslim countries. And to inject such economic views into those of Maimonides is merely a distortion of history."[53]

Again, Zeitlin attacked Baron's scholarly competence as well. In replying to one of Zeitlin's criticisms, Baron seemed to cite the Jewish encyclopedia as his source. Zeitlin now jumped at the implication.

In my review of his work *{SRH}*, I pointed out that the author did not make use of original sources but depended only upon secondary material which was written on the subject, most of the time without due discrimination. A student in research has no right to rely on elementary articles published in the JE for historical facts . . . when the sources are available.

In his conclusion, Zeitlin answered Baron's remarks about reviews in the *JQR*. He too felt the grave responsibility that resulted from the current turn of events.

To our regret, some reviewers because of their inadequate knowledge of Rabbinics even give approval to books which are full of mistakes.

In this country Jewish scholarship is still a field of new research, as it has not the tradition of the old centers like Russia and Germany, which began to decline at the outbreak of the World War and have been utterly destroyed by Nazism. Especially in the rabbinic field, scholarship is still in a state of *tabula rasa*. Some of the books written . . . in this field are based on the use of translations . . . as they are unable to read the original, and many of the theories and hypotheses are founded upon secondary literature like the *JE* . . .. It was my duty . . . to expose such books without bias or favor. I saw in many works a danger to scholarship, since the intelligent laity and particularly our Christian colleagues are inclined to accept any books coming from Jews dealing with Rabbinics.[54]

The tension between them continued with Zeitlin's review of *The Jewish Community*. The bulk of the review continued along similar lines to the previous critiques, but at the end Zeitlin raised several piquant points as he questioned the terminus ad quem of the title with the American Revolution:

"What does the American Revolution have to do with the history of Jewish communities? . . . unless there was a purpose to appeal to the American public?" Zeitlin also queried Baron's identification on the title page as "rabbi" among his various credentials. "Dr. Baron has developed an unexpected predilection for the title rabbi."[55]

Zeitlin was not alone in raising questions about Baron's expertise in classical sources. Whatever the personal factors behind the feud, Zeitlin had presented cogent arguments against Baron's methodology of attributing medieval importance to legal decisions that actually dated from the Second Commonwealth. But the tension was aggravated by the circumstances in which it took place. With the European centers of Jewish studies under threat of destruction and their avenues of publication closed down, the leaders of American Jewish scholarship were becoming aware of their future leadership role in this regard as well.

Theirs were two styles of scholarship, although this hardly implies that "their paths were bound to conflict." While Zeitlin emphasized detailed textual contributions usually dealing with classical Judaism, Baron usually presented more sweeping formulations of social phenomena with greater interest in the medieval and modern periods.

Baron was actually quite close to Talmudists like Louis Ginzberg and Saul Lieberman, whose spheres of research differed widely from his own. But Zeitlin played no role in the American Academy for Jewish Research in which Baron, Ginzberg, and Lieberman were all active leaders and where Baron's sweeping presentations seemed at times out of place.

Perhaps, New York and Philadelphia saw themselves as conflicting centers of the rebirth of Jewish scholarship.

Ultimately, the feud provides testimony that both men were aware of the new responsibilities they were facing as leaders in the field of Jewish studies, as American Jewry was assuming the leadership of world Jewry. Zeitlin put it this way in concluding his review of *The Jewish Community:*

> There is indeed a growing need in this country to develop a sense of responsibility in Jewish scholarship. The American Jewish community is the only one left in the Diaspora, since the old centers of learning in Russia, Poland and Germany have been utterly destroyed. Authors and societies of learning must not only share the responsibility but must be the guardians of Jewish scholarship in this country.[56]

Baron was no less convinced that America's responsibilities were growing, as well as its potential for a positive Jewish existence.

Spokesperson of American Hegemony

While Baron was formulating his thinking on the history and future destiny of the Jewish community during the mid-1930s, his essays from that period indicate that he was still quite doubtful about the promise for positive Jewish life in America. In his 1935 "An Historical Critique of the Jewish Community," Baron cautioned Jews not to become overly infatuated with democratic principles. "There is a danger, too, in making a fetish of 'democratic' self-determination. With all its shortcomings the pre-emancipation Jewish community was one of the most successful and most enduring social experiments in history, perhaps primarily because it so well blended the principle of authority with that of freedom." Describing the European community with its sorely diminished powers in the aftermath of emancipation, Baron added: "Nevertheless, even such a strongly curtailed 'community' was frequently more beneficial to the furtherance of Jewish life in all its creative phases than the chaotic, because totally unorganized, American 'congregation.' " Yet, Baron admitted that the voluntary association was more effective in maintaining the interest of its members.[57]

In the *SRH,* Baron emphasized that the Jewish people was facing one of the gravest crises in its long history and that one would have to go back as far as the Babylonian exile to discern threats to Jewish survival of similar magnitude. In the wideranging epilogue, Baron discussed at length the varied nature of the threats and the prospects for a successful outcome.[58]

The breakdown of centralized communal authority ranked as the most serious element of that crisis, further complicated by growing indifference to Jewish religious life and education, and the questionable future of rabbinical leadership. Democracy on the one hand and rampant racial antisemitism on the other were the primary forces responsible for the weakening of Jewish ties and increased discomfort at being Jewish. Baron coined the term "inverted Marranos" to describe those who sought to escape their Jewish attachments, but found the exit ramps closed off by social hostility that continued to identify them as Jews.[59] His outlook for the future of Jewish survival was cautious, yet optimistic: "The Jewish people and their religion *are* going to survive the present extraordinary crisis."[60] But his vision of a positive Jewish future in America was just beginning to take shape.

More and more Jews are actually American-born and have thoroughly grown into the American atmosphere. Now begins their much more arduous task of synthesizing American (and not Americanized) culture with their own Jewish heritage. American Jewry has a great opportunity, implying also a great obligation to continue along the line of their ancestors in Hellenistic Egypt and the caliphate, in Spain, Italy and Holland and more recently in Germany, and to build on solid foundations the new and spacious edifice of American Jewish culture. It may not be too rash to hope that this new amalgam will prove more enduring, and exercise more lasting and beneficial effects, than any of the earlier attempts.[61]

In his 1938 lecture "Democracy and Judaism," Baron reiterated his concern over the future of a voluntary community. But, by this time, even if Baron could not yet wax positively about the potential for Jewish life in America, he could hardly ignore the dangers of the alternatives. "As long as the democratic state still allows the Jews to develop their own culture, their own religion in the way which they find is best for them, it is, under all present-day alternatives, the most welcome state for the Jews."[62] The following year Baron presented, in "Cultural Problems of American Jewry," a sober and balanced picture that continued to indicate his gradually changing attitudes.

Even voluntarism was now being transformed into a positive value in Baron's thinking. And, by the time *The Jewish Community* was published in 1942, Baron spoke highly of the voluntarism that he had formerly deprecated.

It may be true that about one half of American Jewry does not actively participate in any organized form of Jewish communal life. . . . But those who do belong to an organization do so of choice, albeit, perhaps, a choice influenced by the examples of neighbors, by pressure of public opinion, or other external factors. The amazing record of achievement of the American Jewish community, despite its innumerable obvious shortcomings and weaknesses, testified to the frequently superior vitality of such optional organizations as against those composed of largely indifferent or unwilling taxpayers.[63]

The process finally culminated when in a lecture, also delivered and published in 1942, Baron crowned American Jewry with the mantel of world Jewish leadership.[64] Looking backward, Baron declared that it was actually during World War I that the community had come into its own. Until then, it had been largely culturally and politically dependent on European Jewry, as ideologies and political leadership had derived from across the ocean. But during the war, with European Jewry divided and isolated, American Jews put forth new initiatives with the establishment of the Joint Distribution Committee and within the Zionist movement under Brandeis's leadership. The American Jewish Congress was also established at that time to defend Jewish rights, and the Jewish Welfare Board, first founded to serve Jewish soldiers, became involved in areas outside religious and philanthropic services. Shortly thereafter came the local federations and the first Jewish institutions of higher learning.

Baron's 1939 lecture on cultural problems was not nearly as positive in its descriptions of Jewish life in America. His commentary could only point vaguely to the hope that Jewish life would develop a cultural pluralism comparable to the American outlook in general.[65] It would seem that in the aftermath of Pearl Harbor, Baron had succeeded in constructing a historical basis for the community's new responsibilities. "If during the last war American Jewry came to maturity, the present war has placed in its hands undisputed leadership of world Jewry, with all the challenges and responsibilities which it entails."[66]

When Baron spoke again of the need to plan for postwar reconstruction, the responsibility fell almost exclusively on the shoulders of American Jewry. With most of European Jewry both economically and socially ruined and with Soviet Jewry isolated for a quarter of a century, world leadership now fell on American Jews. "Unlike the last war American Jewry now stands almost alone."[67]

In 1944, Henry Hurwitz, editor of the *Menorah Journal*, invited Baron to address a dinner in honor of the journal's thirtieth anniversary. In that lecture, later published as "At the Turning Point," Baron continued the development of his thinking on America's emerging role in Jewish history. "For many years to come, little Palestine with its great Jewish culture in the making, and the Jewish cultural centers of America, will loom largest in the hopes of the struggling remnants of European Jewry."[68] Obviously, at the time Baron was pinning more of his hopes on the centers of America than on Palestine, and he was certainly not counting on Europe. He continued:

Even more important, however, is what we shall do about making Judaism of worth for the Jews themselves. To combat a contagious disease it is not enough to kill germs; one must also try to increase the patient's physical resistance. We Jews, and we alone, can increase the Jewish people's physical as well as mental resistance to the inroads of the antisemitic virus. Our ancestors suffered more from antisemitic attacks than we do—at least, those of us living in countries outside of Hitler's reach. But antisemitism to them was an external evil, not one which attacked their inner composure or their conviction of the worth of their existence. Only as we succeed in instilling in our own people, especially in our children, the feeling of the worthiness of being Jews, only thus will antisemitism be for us something like any other external cause of suffering . . . which we shall combat with all the means at our disposal but which never impair our morale.

In a subsequent letter, Hurwitz commented on Baron's message:

It seems to me you could develop out of this . . . a cogent and much needed article on the relative futility of the Jewish fighting of antisemitism, —on the necessity of subordinating that to what is most important, a constructive policy of Jewish spiritual fortification. Especially in view of the world responsibilities now thrust on American Jewry. . . . In fact, your article, like your address, is bound to be a kind of Menorah manifesto.[69]

Others also found a moving message in Baron's presentation. A San Francisco rabbi trumpeted its significance in his congregational bulletin.

Dr. Baron has cut through the noisy emotionalism and superficial wrangling which obscures the essence of the Jewish problem, to reveal the fundamental, the crucial question before American Jewry. What shall be our status in this land? . . . Are we content to face the emerging era of reconstruction with no plan or program beyond the negative gestures of self-defense and the melancholy repetition of slogans for overseas philanthropy? . . . Or shall we raise our sights beyond the valleys of weeping and the fox-holes of apology, and summon our coreligionists to a vital and creative and dignified role in the shaping of the new world, as befits an historic people with a faith and culture that vibrates with resounding affirmations.[70]

Baron had called for self-dignity and sought to provide a clear indication of the direction that must be followed in order to bring the Jews of America out of the shock and slump of the post-Holocaust depression. His message was what his audience needed to hear, and frequently they turned to Baron to hear it.

Despite their differences and squabbles, Hurwitz continually turned to Baron. Their fundamental line of thinking was too similar for Hurwitz to ignore the academic legitimization that Baron provided. They had always agreed that antisemitism must not provide the essence of Jewish identity; now Baron had come to see the significance of America and the potential contribution of its Jewish community as well.

The *Menorah Journal* was only one American Jewish organization that honored and consulted Baron for his judgment. We have already talked at some length of his considerable involvements in organizational life. Baron's position as the leading academic spokesperson of American Jews was established by his accessibility both geographically and temperamentally, his talents as a lecturer, his secularized message that transcended conflicting ideologies, and his own self-image of the historian as man of affairs.

But another important factor was the vibrancy and timeliness of his message. When Baron lectured, he translated the results of his basic research into an applied medium that stirred his audiences and enhanced their understanding both of the contemporary situation and of their place in the broad canvas of Jewish history. Given the trauma of the World War II and the Nazi Holocaust, Jews were in dire need of both the rootedness and the hope for survival provided by Baron's long-term historical vision.

In February 1944, Baron delivered a lecture in Cincinnati on "A Post-War Religious and Cultural Program." The announcement appearing in the *American Israelite* explained the importance of the event:

Every nation in the world is wondering what is to be after this war. Governments have special committees studying the problem. To put it mildly, we Jews are particularly concerned. What will be the pattern of Jewish community life, local, national, and international? For these reasons we urge you to regard as a significant outstanding community event, the appearance of Dr. Salo W. Baron.[71]

In the period right after the war, Baron emphasized in his lectures the new responsibilities and burdens that American Jewry must bear. In a lecture delivered in 1946 at Temple Emanuel and reported in the *New York Times,* Baron stated that "Jews throughout the world look increasingly to Jews in the United States not only for relief but for spiritual and cultural guidance. . . . World Jewry is looking to America for finding the necessary new approaches and techniques needed for both a better understanding and more effective combating of that great menace of anti-Semitism."[72]

Earlier that year, Baron stated at the national convention of the Jewish Welfare Board that

the destruction of European Jewry had not only shifted the center of gravity of the entire Jewish people to the United States, but has also resulted in the dissolution of the time-honored patterns of the European Jewish community. . . . The American Jewish community center has long combined some of the best features of the traditional community with the new needs of a community integrated into a western nation.[73]

Also in 1946, Baron undertook an extensive lecture tour in South Africa. An account in the *South African Jewish News* reported the presence of a "large and enthusiastic audience" for the last of his series on "Jewish History: Its Meaning to Us." In this distant setting, Baron chose to discuss different themes and to impart an altogether different message. Analyzing the equivocal significance of Emancipation for modern Jewish life, a theme well emphasized in his scholarly writings, Baron extended his argument into more recent periods and indicated the increased awareness of the necessity for guaranteeing Jewish minority rights as a supplement to legal equality. His presentation exuded optimism about the chances for the establishment of an independent Jewish state and connected his themes with a call for exemplary rights for minorities under Jewish sovereignty.[74]

During the 1940s, much of American Jewry was moving into its third generation, and communal and religious leaders were involved in an extensive reassessment of the values and attitudes that had permeated the community in earlier years.

During the war years and even more after peace, Jews in America began to feel more secure; new economic and educational opportunities were opening up before them. Arnold Eisen demonstrated how Jewish thinkers during this period returned to more traditional Jewish positions as the third generation withdrew to an extent from the whole-hearted embrace of America accomplished by the previous generation. "Jewish intellectuals seized on the traditional vocabulary of chosenness and exile in order to articulate their distance from American middle-class culture and from the Jewish community which had adopted that culture."[75]

Perhaps, in fact, Eisen has provided a further explanation for Baron's popularity as a spokesperson for American Jewry. Eisen complained that during the 1930s, "More American Jewish leaders might have been as perceptive as Milton Steinberg or Mordecai Kaplan in discerning the gravity of the community's situation and in realizing that mere enthusiasm for America was no solution." But most leaders were not so perceptive, nor were they particularly literate in Jewish tradition. Although neither a theologian nor an ideologue, Baron suffered neither deficiency. Baron spoke with the authority of a scholar thoroughly versed in Jewish history and literature; indeed, he was a scholar who had been accepted by the secular academy as well. His analysis of the potentials for Jewish life in America bore the signs of a healthy skepticism, shaped in part by historical examples. By the 1940s, his doubts had been transformed into a positive outlook that was conducive to the community's new moods that pointed cautiously toward a significant Jewish future in the American setting.

It was in this context of growing American Jewish maturity

that Baron began his involvement with the fledgling field of American Jewish history.

From Pioneers to Tercentenary

Baron's first writings about the American Jewish community were, as we have seen, analyses of the contemporary situation with emphasis toward applied history. The purpose of these essays was to root American Jewish reactions to the Nazi conquest of Europe and to the growth in antisemitism in the long historical experience of the Jewish people.

At the beginning of 1943, JTS president Louis Finkelstein wrote to Baron: "It is good to see you turning to the field of American history, which is attracting so many of our best scholars."[76] The remark was probably prompted by Baron's lecture on "American and Jewish Destiny," delivered on 12 October 1942 and published later that year. The following year, Baron published "Palestinian Messengers in America, 1849–79," his first work of historical scholarship in the sphere of American Jewish history; it was also the only published work credited to both Baron and Jeannette.[77]

The war-related essays, as we have already seen, placed the maturation of American Jewry in historical perspective, tracing the growth of its institutions back to World War I. These essays combined with the work on Palestinian messengers represented the total of Baron's scholarly contribution to the study of American Jewish history for most of the forties. And yet Finkelstein was correct that Baron was becoming identified with the new discipline.

Perhaps, most significantly, Baron tried to encourage doctoral students to specialize in America, although he did not always find it easy to do so. "If I may be allowed to cite personal experiences, I found it very difficult thirty years ago [i.e., around 1940] to persuade graduate students to choose dissertations in this field, because they did not find it 'interesting' enough." [78] Hyman Grinstein and Moshe Davis were the earliest of his students specializing in America. Together with Reform rabbi Bertram Korn and Jacob Marcus, who taught at HUC, they were among the earliest serious researchers in the field.

By the end of the decade, Baron was identified as a leading figure in the new discipline. In 1949, he delivered a far-reaching address to the American Jewish Historical Society on problems and major desiderata facing those who wished to undertake research. In 1953, he was elected president of the society, his term coinciding with the tercentenary celebrations in which he indeed took an active role.

What fascinated Baron about American Jewish history during those early days of the forties? Having declared the American community as the new leader of world Jewry, Baron now sought to place its historical experience within the broader context of Jewish history. It was crucial to Baron's outlook that American Jewry not be perceived as an outside entity imposed on the continuum of Jewish history—both so that the community could better wear the mantel of leadership and because Baron found in its history a perfect laboratory for his conception of the total Jewish historical experience. Thus, while hardly disagreeing with Morris Schappes that "American Jewish History is always a part of American history, and cannot be scientifically investigated except in relation to it," Baron added in a 1951 review that "Jewish history on this continent is just as much a part of world Jewish history as it is of American history."[79]

In several of his essays, Baron sought to place the American experience within that broader spectrum of Jewish history. Perhaps there was some symbolic value in an essay on Palestinian messengers to America in that it served to illustrate precisely that kind of common theme. But this would be especially true of his 1956 essay, "The Emancipation Movement and American Jewry," pointedly published in Israel and in Hebrew; it emphasized the role of America in that major focus of the modern period usually identified more with France and Germany.[80]

On the other hand, American Jewish history was different in that suffering was not at all a dominant theme. Thus, in explaining the lack of interest among graduate students, Baron explained that this went against the lachrymose or Graetzian conceptions: "American Jewish history, unable to produce a succession of riots and discriminatory laws, could hardly fit into this traditional pattern."[81]

Students of Jewish history also search for cultural creativity. In Baron's view, such vitality was not dependent on the pressures of suffering. It was crucial to his argument that American Jewry was proving itself to be a vibrant and creative community that would take its place alongside its predecessors in Jewish history.

In several essays (15–19) I have tried to show that the frequent questioning of any genuine creativity by American Jews in the field of Jewish culture by skeptics of all kinds is not wholly justified. Historic evidence proves that it has taken many centuries for all the great centers of Jewish learning in the past to arise. One must, therefore, realize that American Jewry, whose real cultural history did not begin until little more than a century ago, still is in the early stages of its evolution. Yet it already has great achievements to its credit.[82]

Baron served as president of the American Jewish Historical Society from early 1953 to early 1955. This was an eventful period for the society and for American Jewry on the whole, and during these years, the society played a leading role in the community's tercentenary celebration.[83] In fact, the initiative for an extensive, public celebration came from the society's ranks several years earlier. The idea was passed on to the American Jewish Committee, which had the organization and resources to coordinate the large-scale planning that was required. Together with the tercentenary committee, the society cosponsored an office of historical information, established as part of the celebration's educational program. The society also sponsored essay contests and exhibits pertinent to the occasion. Most important were a conference on the writing of American Jewish history and a special session at the annual meeting of the American Historical Association.

The major celebrations emphasized the unity of the community as it faced its new responsibilities of leadership within world Jewry. American Jewry of the time was optimistic about its future within the larger society, whereas on the whole it was confident as well of the future of Jewish identity in the American setting. President Eisenhower's participation in the dinner marking the official opening of the celebra-

tion symbolized and confirmed the confidence of the orga-
nizers.[84]

The main themes of the tricentennial festivities attracted a
certain amount of criticism from a number of important
sources. Horace Kallen and Mordecai Kaplan, among others,
objected to what they perceived as an assimilatory emphasis
that denied the possibilities of cultural pluralism that would
place greater value on continued, affirmative Jewish identity.
Yet, Baron was strongly identified with the celebration and
actually wore two presidential hats at the time of the tercentenary because he was still head of the Conference on Jewish
Relations. He also served on the tercentenary coordinating
committee and chaired its committee on research and publication. Kallen and Kaplan may have had different perspectives
than Baron on the ideal parameters of Jewish identity in
America, but Baron certainly contributed a sober and scholarly element to the commemoration.[85]

In September 1954, the American Jewish Historical Society
organized a conference on the writing of American Jewish
history. The leading figures of the new field were joined by
several leading scholars of American history, including
Thomas Cochran and Allan Nevins, to discuss in seminar
style four main themes: local and regional history; economic
history; immigration; and biography. Baron reiterated in his
introduction to the volume of conference papers and discussions that American Jewish history provided challenges and
opportunities that were unique to the study of Jewish history.
Baron's presentation stands in sharp contrast to that of the
president of the Israeli Historical Society, Ben Zion Dinur,

who emphasized the place of American Jews in the rebirth of Israel. The importance of the American experience in its own right was baldly missing from Dinur's formulations.[86]

The Conference on Jewish Relations also played an active role in the celebrations. In November 1954 it sponsored a two-day conference in New York City on American Jewish social sciences. Press reports indicated the participation of some 250 communal leaders and professionals in discussions led by historians, psychologists, and sociologists. The major themes of discussion included the changing structure of the American Jewish community, the psychological dynamics of Jewish identification, and Jewish-Christian relations. Discussion paid attention to the new dominance of native American Jews and to the increased interest in religious aspects of Jewish life.[87]

Thus, although he never specialized in or even produced a major work of research in American Jewish history, Baron provided the foresight and much of the impetus necessary for the development of the new field. Through his sweeping essays, he offered vast constructions of America in the spectrum of Jewish history; he encouraged doctoral dissertations at Columbia; he involved some of his colleagues from the history department; and he espoused on the significant role the American community would have to play in the future of Jewish life. In short, through his academic stature, his position as organizational leader, and his students, Baron left his mark as a major contributor to its growth and legitimization.

Witness in Jerusalem

In 1961, Baron attained widespread attention when he was called as an opening witness in the war crimes trial of Adolf Eichmann in Jerusalem. In late December 1960, Israel's minister of justice, Pinchas Rosen, instructed the consul general in New York to invite Baron to testify on behalf of the prosecution at the trial. Baron was to provide the primary historical evidence on the effects of the Holocaust on Jewish life in Europe.[88]

The decision to invite Baron was reached in consultation with the prime minister, David Ben Gurion; then foreign minister Golda Meir; the legal adviser to the government, Gideon Hausner; senior officials from the prime minister's office and the foreign office; and historian Jacob Robinson, who served as general adviser to the prosecution. Baron was asked to prepare a general description of European Jewry on the eve of the Holocaust, emphasizing its national and cultural significance, in contrast with the remnants of human and cultural life after the war.

The prosecution, headed by the Israeli attorney general, Gideon Hausner, urged secrecy regarding Baron's testimony until two days prior to his appearance, at which time they were required by practice to inform the defense. Because the testimony was scheduled during Columbia's academic year, Baron invented a camouflage to cover his absence. His sudden appearance in Jerusalem also had to be explained, and when he met acquaintances on the streets, he recalled that twenty-five years earlier he and his wife visited Israel for the first time and spent the Passover holiday with his newly married niece.

This trip was to celebrate the silver anniversary of that occasion—the arithmetic of his alibi, however, was off by a year.[89]

Arthur Hertzberg indicated that he had never seen Baron as anxious as he was when preparing for his trip to Jerusalem and his testimony at the trial. He added that Baron came back "absolutely drained," as if to say, "I have done what I needed to do." Needless to say, he was very proud that he had been chosen to testify.[90] Indeed, Baron's testimony at the trial received front-page coverage both in Israel and abroad.

Although he testified in response to questions put to him by chief prosecutor Gideon Hausner, Baron had prepared his delivery in advance. He presented a masterly summation of the course of European Jewish history during the nineteenth and twentieth centuries. The presentation was subsequently published in essay form.[91]

Baron described a vigorous and resourceful European Jewish community that had demonstrated considerable ingenuity in combating the critical conditions presented by the interwar period. Political instability accompanied the emergence of new states and the enforced peace terms, and the depression resulted in global economic hardships.

Such far-reaching transformations called for great ingenuity and a pioneering spirit. With courage and perseverance the Jewish people tried to adjust to the new situation not merely passively, but independently and creatively. Accustomed through the long history of their dispersion to such creative readjustments, they were able to develop during the interwar period certain new forms of communal and cultural living which fructified Jewish life throughout the world, contributed significantly to human civilization, and held out great promise for the future. All this was cut short by the Nazi attack, unprecedented in scope, geographic extension, and murderous intensity.[92]

Obviously couched in apologetic terminology, Baron's testimony nevertheless brought forth the full thrust of his historical thinking in order to depict the dimension of the later tragedy.

Baron opened his account with a summary of demographic trends in the modern periods. He then reaffirmed at the end of his testimony the estimate that six million Jews had been killed by the Nazis. He added that given the trends of population growth, the world Jewish population at the time of the trial would have reached twenty million instead of twelve million Jews — the actual number.[93]

In a wide-ranging discourse on modern trends in economic life, Baron emphasized the postemancipation concentration of Jews in the free professions, but also attempts to enter the industrial and agricultural sectors. Yet with technological advancements, society in general was reallocating its occupational distributions. By the time of the Holocaust, Jewish divergence from general vocational trends was narrowing "not so much because the Jews have changed as because the Western world has become increasingly 'Jewish' in its economic structure."

In a brief six pages, Baron then outlined the main contours of his understanding of the significance of the emancipation process and its failings.[94] Objecting to dating emancipation to the period of the American and French Revolutions, Baron preferred to suggest that these trends are "both older and newer" than those events. On the one hand, legal developments should not be separated from their earlier intellectual and economic foundations, which dated back to at least a century earlier than the revolutionary period. Yet, the vast majority of world Jewry lived in Czarist Russia and at best attained emancipation along with the other Jewish populations of Eastern Europe and the Ottoman Empire only with the October Revolution and the end of World War I. Jewish diplomacy at Versailles exerted considerable efforts to advance safeguards for continued Jewish identity and security.

Even with the setbacks of violent pogroms and reinvigorated antisemitic propaganda in the form of the Protocols, the advance of Jewish emancipation at the beginning of this century seemed inevitable. But from the early nineteenth century on, Germany was the center of continued debate and controversy. Baron described primarily the literary component of the opposition, although by Bismarck's time anti-emancipation movements had attained parliamentary representation as well. Yet, claimed Baron, the march toward Jewish equality was seriously threatened only with the rise of the Nazis to power and their "far-reaching example for all anti-emancipatory forces."

Although Jews sought to combat the antisemitic threats starting in the last century, Baron emphasized that such attempts could in fact be of only limited value. "Anti-Semitism has long been recognized as being essentially a disease of Gentile nations, generated by a disequilibrium of social forces wholly beyond the control of the Jewish communities." The public outcry at the time of the Dreyfus Affair demonstrated a rare example of what could be accomplished by a non-Jewish initiative against antisemitism. In the case of the Nazis as well, Jews tried but failed to warn their neighbors of the impending dangers. "Many liberals, Jews and non-Jews, failed to realize the demonic strength of the irrational forces which were about to set Europe on fire."

Baron then described Jewish efforts to provide alternative solutions for the antisemitic threats. He discussed Zionism, although he immediately denied that Zionism had arisen as a result of the influence of antisemitism alone. He mentioned briefly the movement led by Simon Dubnow and others to attain Jewish minority rights guaranteed by law and the rise of the Jewish Bund socialist movement in Russia. He closed his discussion of emancipation with reference to the role played by individual Jews in the political life of various countries.

Again traveling across the map of Europe, Baron then surveyed the changing parameters of government support and communal autonomy. He described the varied functions of communal institutions, especially in the fields of education and social welfare and compared the status of communal authority in Western and Eastern Europe.[95] This section was concluded with a description of synagogue buildings ranging from elaborate structures in Leghorn and Amsterdam to more simple constructions in Worms and Prague. Commenting that "from time immemorial these sacred structures stood under the protection of public life," Baron contrasted that status with the fate of German synagogues during Kristallnacht in 1938.

A special section was devoted to the Jewish emphasis on

education, in which Baron surveyed the large percentages of children enrolled in an impressive choice of educational institutions, primarily in Eastern Europe.[96] His discussion of conditions in Soviet Russia was again more critical of the regime and its tendencies toward indoctrination. In Western countries, the opportunities were more limited than in the East. And in Central Europe, Baron emphasized the leading rabbinical seminaries as well as the day schools that still functioned.

His description of archival collections, libraries, and museums was particularly detailed, benefiting from the study and lists compiled by Hannah Arendt in the immediate aftermath of the war. At least 430 Jewish institutions had housed cultural treasures, and there were in addition at least 274 important general repositories containing Judaica. Indeed, the number of Jewish periodicals appearing in Europe was, in Baron's words, "astonishing." Even the relatively small community in France had some 96 Jewish journals, including dailies and weeklies in French, Yiddish, and Russian. The total number in the countries occupied by the Nazis and their allies reached 854 periodicals.

Baron found particular significance in the continued scholarly output deriving from Europe and long before the trial had frequently referred to the five thousand publications he had listed in his *Bibliography of Jewish Social Studies, 1938– 1939*. Some of these in fact represented antisemitic polemics. But most, Baron explained, were the results of scholarship and primarily reflected the continued vitality of traditional Jewish life.

In each section of his testimony, Baron concluded with a

discussion of the impact of Jews on the societies in which they lived. He had spoken of Jews in political life and on Jews who were actively involved in educational institutions, and now he spoke at length on significant contributions "to the science, literature, and art of the nations." Baron constructed a rich and varied list that included Einstein, Freud, a number of composers, artists, philosophers, and social scientists, as well as reference to seventeen Jewish Nobel Prize winners.

Then Baron suddenly turned his testimony into a more personal mode as he hinted elliptically at his own contact with some "of these extraordinary minds." He was referring specifically to Hebrew poet Chaim Nachmann Bialik, Zionist statesperson and Israel's founding president Chaim Weizmann, and Albert Einstein. Baron briefly described the power of these men's minds and personalities as viewed especially from up close. It was a paragraph out of place in his presentation, for several reasons. Coming in the midst of a description of contributions to general society, the example of Bialik was a non sequitur and even that of Weizmann was questionable because Baron made no reference to his scientific contributions. Interviews with those close to Baron indicate that he rarely, if ever, bragged of close acquaintanceships with renown personalities, which was certainly what he was doing on the witness stand. Finally, I do think that Baron somewhat exaggerated the extent of his relationship with Einstein, for example.

The thrust of his testimony had been to outline the brilliant and the noble in European Jewish society. "Of course, the Jewish people also had its sinners and idiots, thieves and lunatics. But on balance, future historians are likely to call the first third of the twentieth century the golden age of

Ashkenazi Jewry in Europe, just as they will see in it the beginning of a modern Sephardi renaissance." I personally know of no historian who would speak in such hyperbole of the community on the eve of destruction, nor do I know if Baron truly believed his own statement, for it is possible that the circumstances and the spotlight had their effect. And yet the statement reflected, I suspect, the culmination of considerable inner turmoil. Throughout his more than thirty-five years in America, I think the thought of what had been in Europe, what had been destroyed, and what and whom he personally had left behind colored his judgment on the past glory. The personal direction that had begun in his talk about his personal contacts with the great minds had continued with his judgment on the greatness of the community in which he was born, raised, and matured.

Baron next set out to explain how these notable achievements had come about, expressing caution that the accomplishments of such Jews had provoked considerable envy and resentment. But the explanation lay not with racial genes, but with historical circumstances.

As a permanent minority for some two thousand years, Jews were forced to seek the kinds of openings that were available to newcomers. . . . When they found and used such opportunities, they were working for both their own benefit and that of society as a whole. I have long believed that much of Jewish history ought to be rewritten in terms of the pioneering services which the Jews were forced to render by the particular circumstances of their history.[97]

Thus, Jews frequently stood at the forefront of new ventures and new opportunities. But, in addition, Baron departed from his secularized explanation to return to more traditional formulations: "the Jews have always cherished learning above all other values." The centuries-old emphasis on learning had penetrated Jewish consciousness: "These counsels sank so deep into the mind of the people that most Jewish women through the ages dreamed of their sons becoming distinguished rabbis and scholars. With the modern secularization of life, those ambitions were directed to the arts and sciences." Albeit discreetly, Baron's testimony had become, at least by his terms, personal. Consequently, I wonder if this remark also reflected a confession that his mother's influence had directed him away from his father's bank and estate and a commercial career.

Some explanation for the uncharacteristic nature of Baron's testimony can be found in a document from the Ben Gurion Archives. About two weeks prior to his testimony, Baron and Jeannette met with Prime Minister David Ben Gurion. Writing in his diary, Ben Gurion identified Baron by noting that eight volumes of his social history had already appeared and that six more are ready. Ben Gurion then added:

Concerned about his testimony. I told him that it is important to explain to our younger generation (and also to the rest of the world) how great was the qualitative loss in the destruction of the six million, and therefore, he must describe the spiritual character of the Judaism that was destroyed, illustrated by her great personalities: Einstein, Bialik, Dubnow, and others.

Ben Gurion was certainly actively involved in laying the framework for the prosecution in the Eichmann trial, which is well known. But this passage from Ben Gurion's diary also sheds light on some of the strains noted in Baron's testimony.[98]

The closing sections of his testimony brought Baron to the impact of Nazi rule.[99] The struggle against the Jews, Baron asserted, was opened with intellectual weapons despite the otherwise anti-intellectualism of Nazi ideology. He surveyed research programs established by the Nazis to investigate Jewish history and literature. Baron then reiterated his firm opposition to comparing the Nazi program to conditions during the Middle Ages with his recurring judgment: "Such assertions maligned the Middle Ages." Even the mob destruction of synagogues in 1938, inspired from above, was unheard of in medieval times; Baron explained that states generally avoided public outbreaks, including attacks on the Jews. If a state decided to cease its toleration of the Jews, it would expel them.

The gradual unfolding of anti-Jewish decrees during the 1930s succeeded in camouflaging from many the direction to which these enactments would eventually lead. The Nazis also concealed their campaign against organized religion in general. Both Hitler and Mussolini realized the difficulties faced by a state power in conflict with religion. Yet, while religious leaders were largely silent on the persecutions of the Jews, the Nazis pursued the objective of establishing a German national religion under their own control.

During the thirties, the Nazis implemented a program based on antisemitism to disrupt the unity of its neighbors. "By combining attacks on the Jews with attacks on Bolshevism through the myth of the Jewish responsibility for the

Communist revolution, the Nazi propagandists succeeded in undermining the unity of nations that were themselves to be victims of Nazi aggression." Especially in Eastern Europe, strong antisemitic organizations were active prior to the war.

Baron only briefly surveyed the introduction of the destruction process itself, emphasizing the attempts toward secrecy in implementing the program and the silence of the populations at large. In measuring the "effects of the catastrophe," Baron began with a discussion of spiritual resistance, as teachers and even institutions found ways to continue instruction secretly. "For the first time in many centuries, a Jewish generation was growing up without Jewish or general elementary schooling," while the secondary and college education of still others was "interrupted, often permanently." Only then did Baron turn to the task of measuring the extent of physical destruction.

As I have already indicated, his analysis confirmed the estimates that approximately six million Jews had been murdered by the Nazis.[100] But Baron also examined the question of how large the Jewish population would have been without the Holocaust, concluding that there would have been approximately twenty million instead of the twelve million by the time of the trial. Baron then added: "What is more, the Jewish communities in formerly Nazi-occupied Europe still are crippled, qualitatively even more than quantitatively. That great reservoir of Jewish population and of cultural and religious leadership has dried up."

In his closing remarks, Baron offered the interesting insight that if someone like Hitler had arisen instead of Bismarck in the 1871 Franco-German War, and if he had managed to penetrate the same lands later occupied by the Nazis—yet prior to the great Jewish migration to America and prior to the establishment of Israel—then "the genocide of the Jewish people would have been almost total."

Following his testimony for the prosecution, Defense Attorney Robert Servatius asked Baron as a professor of history to explain the causes of antisemitism "which has existed for so many hundreds of years, and of that war against the Jewish people." [101]

In response, Baron identified hatred of the Jewish religion as the most conspicuous explanation for historical antisemitism. But he also explained that in recent centuries a secularized formulation had emerged that he described as "the dislike of the unlike." Obviously sensing that the defense sought to establish a connection between Nazi crimes and the long history of hatred of the Jews, Baron emphasized that those crimes were unique. Referring for example to the Russian pogroms of 1881, Baron commented that those events were "trivial in comparison with what happened in the 1940s. What happened then has no precedent in Jewish history." Baron was determined to minimize the violent dimension of past periods: "Although there has been immemorial antisemitism . . . it is well to remember that there was practically no violence accompanied by bloodshed under the Persians or under the Greeks. There were minor outbreaks in the days of Philo of Alexandria. There were no pogroms under the Muslims." The extent of violent persecution under Muslim rule is actually a matter of dispute, but Baron obviously greatly underplayed the situation; Christian periods were glossed over in his response.

333

Servatius and Baron then proceeded to discuss the role of predetermination and free will in the shaping of history as the defense sought to suggest that the march of history represented broad forces "without being influenced by any particular person." Baron admitted that history was acted out independent of men's will. In fact, referring to his *Social and Religious History*, Baron commented that the work's theme was to demonstrate how greatly social and religious forces influence each other. Nevertheless, he concluded, individuals and groups are both "responsible for what they do and cannot plead that they are only carrying out what history demands of them."

After the defense had concluded its cross-examination, one of the three judges requested that Baron comment on the historicity of the Protocols of the Elders of Zion. Baron briefly reviewed the publishing history of that modern classic of antisemitic propaganda. He was then asked some additional questions on his demographic analysis, particularly to estimate how his estimate of twenty million Jews would have been distributed among the various communities around the world. Baron responded that although an answer was necessarily only hypothetical, he would estimate that about half would have been living in Europe, including the Soviet Union.

A Dutch correspondent covering the trial took offense at Baron's implication that the Nazi crimes were all the more grave because they sought to annihilate a cultured people.

Would the death of the Jews have been less of an evil if they were a people without a culture, such as the Gypsies who were also exterminated? Is Eichmann on trial as a destroyer of human beings or as an annihilator of culture? Is a murderer of human beings more guilty when a culture is also destroyed in the process? [102]

The correspondent, Harry Mulisch, put these questions to the prosecutor Gideon Hausner and concluded: "He thinks yes, I think no." Hannah Arendt, who cited these comments, obviously concurred with Mulisch. She considered the prosecution's case misguided in its emphasis on the destruction of a cultural elite and asked her own questions on the notion of privileged Jews with pointed cogency: "There are more than a few people, especially among the cultural elite, who still publicly regret the fact that Germany sent Einstein packing without realizing that it was a much greater crime to kill little Hans Cohn from around the corner, even though he was no genius." [103]

Being one of the opening witnesses at the Eichmann trial had made Baron into an even greater public celebrity. The American press not only reported on his testimony in detail, but the *New York Times* also published and circulated through its news service a lengthy biographical sketch. At the time, Baron was two years away from retirement in 1963 from Columbia. In later interviews, Baron indicated that retirement only meant he had more time to work harder. He occasionally lectured, and he continued to teach on a part-time basis at institutions such as the Jewish Theological Seminary, but he primarily pursued his writing. And whereas writing still meant simultaneous projects, his work was mainly on the second and revised edition of the *Social and Religious History*.

With fewer distractions, Baron and Jeannette focused more

and more on the magnum opus. Originally scheduled for publication in an expanded six volumes, the plan continued to expand. Eventually, the projected size of the project reached thirty volumes.[104]

At first, the work proceeded with some regularity, and eight volumes appeared by 1958. But in later years and with later volumes the pace of its progress decreased. Eventually, its significance also decreased because of the exponential growth of Jewish historical scholarship—for which Baron was partly responsible. His students and his students' students in America created an outpouring of high-quality research, as did the expanding circle of Israeli scholars, such that both quantity and quality necessitated increased specialization throughout the field.

After Jeannette's death in 1985, work on the project came to a standstill. Its writing had been so much a product of their joint efforts that Baron had virtually no working system to continue. Of course, he was also eighty-nine years old. In his concluding years, he was able to bring his reflective work *The Contemporary Relevance of History*[105] to press, and at the prodding of his family—including grandchildren and great-grandchildren, he began to compose his memoirs. These were unfinished when he died on 25 November 1989. The eventual publication of those memoirs should provide considerable additional material to his life story, especially concerning his early years.

Of the many written and oral reminiscences offered by students after his death, one anecdote directly relates to this study. Baron had fully cooperated with me and had mentioned to his visitors that a work on his life and writings was in progress. In fact, in a discussion with Moshe Davis, Baron related that an American scholar living in Israel was writing about his contributions to American culture. Davis mentioned Baron's satisfaction with the project in a piece written in Baron's memory. He also called me to ensure that I had seen the reference.

I would never have described my work on Baron in similar terms, so that his rendition provides a strong and clear indication of a closing version of how he himself wished to be remembered. Perhaps his own statement provides a certain correction to what I have written here, but I suggest it would be more accurate to claim that Baron provided the voice of historical Jewish consciousness to several generations of American Jews who were pursuing his own private dream more intensely and perhaps, more successfully. Baron himself remained far more a man of two worlds, a combination that could be summed up by the title of one of his earliest significant articles, a man of "Ghetto and Emancipation."

EPILOGUE: BEYOND
THE LACHRYMOSE
CONCEPTION

B ARON IS NOW thought of primarily in terms of the second and revised edition of the *Social and Religious History*. In many ways that is unfortunate because this work, which consumed him for the last forty years of his life, was not nearly as well received in professional circles as its earlier counterpart and fails to adequately express the basic principles of his approach to historiography. Conceived in the 1940s as a six-volume revision of the first edition, the plan expanded first to ten volumes, and then became open-ended.[1]

As the work expanded, reviewers became increasingly unhappy. The delicate balance reached in the first edition between a topical arrangement and a coherent presentation for the reader disintegrated as the new edition seemed to explode in size. With all the acclaim for awesome erudition, the reviewers wanted a history that could be read intelligibly. Not only was Maimonides scattered across multiple volumes and numerous entries, but as one reviewer observed, he had even been denied the pleasure of reading about the Golden Age in Spain as a single coherent unit.[2]

Both Cecil Roth and Ellis Rivkin objected adamantly to the massive burden of detailed information. The claim that no single scholar could compose an all-encompassing history of the Jews was now revived with increased vigor. Roth was adamant that no scholar could expertly provide such a detailed presentation. He listed errors from his own fields of specialization and indicated as well that Baron had at times suggested far-reaching conclusions based on incorrect assumptions. Rivkin criticized Baron's methods of categorization, arguing that facts were pried from their context in time and process and became "disengaged particles . . . available for whatever combinations are dictated."[3]

Baron's response to Roth that the forthcoming index would alleviate difficulties deriving from the topical arrangement no longer met the problems being raised. A reader might be able to combine scattered entries on a distinct topic or personality, but this tactic failed to provide a coherent presentation in the form of a narrative, with no clear presentation of the major themes at hand. Ultimately, not only events and personalities were lost to the reader; even the thrust of Baron's theories became obscured in the heavy setting now provided. Chapters and even sections were opened and closed with sweeping presentations, but their relation to the pages of detailed discussions was frequently obscure. This is all the more reason to conclude this study with a brief presentation of the basic principles of Baron's historical writing.

Baron's first usage of the term "lachrymose conception" came, as far as I know, in the closing lines of his 1928 essay "Ghetto and Emancipation." In the first edition of the SRH, he used the term only sporadically, and the subject did not arise with any great significance in most reviews or in his responses.[4] But in the second edition, the lachrymose conception terminology appeared with much greater frequency as Baron increasingly identified with the term as a mode of clear distinction between his historical conceptions and the earlier renditions of others. By then, Baron's antilachrymose stance had become his trademark.[5]

How Baron reached the conclusion that suffering was overemphasized in most Jewish histories is therefore an important but evasive question. When Baron moved to Vienna during the summer of 1914, he entered one of the most active centers of antisemitic thought at any time in history. In the Central European environment of the war and especially the postwar years, the Jewish communities of the region were immersed in an intense atmosphere of hostility. The setting must underscore the question: How within two or three years of his emigration from Vienna did Baron come to enunciate a basic principle that negated the centrality of suffering in Jewish history?

Two answers lie before us: Yitzhak Baer suggested in his 1938 review of the SRH that Baron, like other Jewish apologetes, had been influenced by the antisemitic argument that

Jews excessively bemoan their fate; Baron suggested virtually
the opposite explanation in his response to Baer, explaining
that he had been motivated by a combination of historical
principles and Jewish self-pride.[6]

Twenty years later in his 1963 "Newer Emphases in Jewish
History," Baron, again reflecting the double motif of historiographic and personal considerations, put it this way:

I too am a child of this age [that witnessed the Nazi period].
All my life I have been struggling against the hitherto dominant
"lachrymose conception of Jewish history"—a term which I have
been using for more than forty years—because I have felt that an
overemphasis on Jewish sufferings distorted the total picture of the
Jewish historic evolution and, at the same time, badly served a
generation which had become impatient with the nightmare of
endless persecutions and massacres.[7]

The problem of where Baron's approach derived from dissi-
pates at least partially when we realize that although Baron
formulated the abstract principle, he was not alone or even
the first to declare discontent with the emphasis on the role of
suffering and persecutions. Dubnow had written in a similar
vein in the 1925 introduction to his *World History*. Even
earlier, the more popular historiography being produced at
the turn of the century by Jewish historical societies focused
far more on accomplishments and contributions than on restrictions and persecutions.[8] The fact is that Graetz's style of
writing history, with its two heavy hands on scholarship and
suffering, was rejected especially—and in this sense Baer was
correct—by those who pursued and defended an expanded
Jewish role within the surrounding society. Baer called this a

symptom of apologetics; Baron called it an act of self-pride. I call it a postemancipation way of looking at the Jewish past.

A final word on Graetz himself. I argued in a previous chapter that singling Graetz out for this criticism was actually unfair, because even Graetz had tried to break out of the lachrymose mode precisely with his emphasis on rabbinic scholarship. Special notice might be taken of Graetz's lecture to Anglo-Jewry at the 1887 exhibition of Jewish history and religious objects. Graetz's proposals for the future directions of study strongly echo a mood of marked self-confidence. But pointedly, Graetz indicated that Anglo-Jewry could succeed in such undertakings, while German Jewry, in which Graetz was so disappointed, could not hope to do so.[9]

One of the important implications of Baron's position was his aversion to historical explanations rooted in antisemitism, including or perhaps especially in cases when the relevant significance of antisemitic causation had become widely accepted. Two such examples, almost simultaneous in their occurrence, were the rise of Zionism, and the beginnings of the mass migration of Eastern European Jewry to America in the later decades of the nineteenth century.

Baron argued that it was not the pogroms of 1881 and after that were the primary cause of the migration of Russian Jews. Rather, he maintained that it was the deteriorating economic conditions prompted by continued restrictions and rapid population growth, as well as technological advancement in international navigation and the resultant reduction in the costs of such movement. Noting that emigration figures began to climb already during the 1870s, Baron declared that "even without the Russian pogrom wave of 1881, emigration to America would have been inevitable"; in his view, the Polish famine of 1869 was the real turning point in provoking mass Jewish migration.

Of course, the validity of Baron's revision also required attention to the migration of other groups as well. In this way, Baron liberated the migration from a specifically Jewish context that was closely entwined with antisemitic causation. He was also able to display his deep respect for scientific advances and their relevance for historical developments. Baron emphasized that whereas the number of Jewish migrants increased in subsequent decades, the percentage of Jews within the Russian migration waned over time, again implying that the specifically Jewish element in the migration played only a limited role. Nevertheless, the rapid increase during the 1880s could not be ignored, and Baron admitted that "all these factors were accelerated by the pogrom wave of 1881, the restrictive May Laws of 1882, and later ordinances." [10]

In the second example, concerning the rise of Zionism, Baron was one of the first to question the tight conceptual bond between the emergence of Zionism and the growth of antisemitic movements and especially the Russian pogroms. In Baron's formulation, Zionism was "certainly not" a reaction against antisemitism, but rather emerged out of a realistic confrontation with grave economic and social problems. Its growth was stimulated by the developments of European nationalism. [11]

Both of these examples also demonstrate a conceptual difficulty in mitigating the antisemitic factor in explaining the course of Jewish history. Concerning the migration movement from Russia to the West, the question must still arise as to what prompted such considerable Jewish receptivity to the migration movement? In other words, didn't Baron's emphasis on broader economic suffering and technological and commercial advances do more to explain what enabled the movement to occur within the general population, rather than explain the considerable and still disproportionate Jewish receptivity to these developments? And concerning the rise of Zionism, how removed are such concepts as alienation and frustration from an explanatory catchword called "antisemitism"?

Still, alienation was not identical to pogroms, and a gradually developing movement emerging out of planned programs is not identical to political naivete and a shocked response to physical violence. In other words, one of the main implications of Baron's critique against the lachrymose conception was not so much that antisemitism played a limited role in Jewish history, but that the communities and their leaders throughout the centuries had not been woeful and passive players in determining their own historical course.[12]

Given these difficulties in reducing the role of antisemitism in describing and explaining Jewish history, it is not surprising that Baron was not always consistent regarding the place of tragedy and persecution in Jewish history. Suffering fills the pages of one well-known work in particular, *The Russian Jew Under Tsars and Soviets,* although the well-tuned Baron reader will still recognize the themes of a balanced social, economic, political, and religious presentation.

Of course, the most serious difficulty of all to the antilachrymose critique came with the realization of the dimension of the Holocaust tragedy. In fact, in a 1963 essay, "Newer Emphases in Jewish History," Baron lamented the decline of the lachrymose perspective. In a remarkable passage, which once again juxtaposes the lachrymose concept with social historical perspectives, Baron reversed his usual prescription: "Yet it is to be hoped that this newer emphasis on politics, economics and military affairs, . . . will not totally displace the understanding for the *Leidens- und Gelehrten-geschichte* which had so completely dominated Jewish historical writing of the nineteenth and early twentieth centuries."[13] The context for these remarks was a discussion of changing notions of heroism in the aftermath of the Holocaust and the rise of the State of Israel. Even more specifically, it might be relevant to note that the essay was prepared soon after Baron's testimony at the Eichmann trial.

But aside from any second thoughts, Baron's principal response to the post-Holocaust criticism was that the main thrust of the intended revision was to unlock hidden and undiscovered doors of Jewish history that had remained covered by thick veils of the orientation toward suffering. The significant observation was not to question whether persecutions had left their deep mark on the historical experience, but rather to establish that multiple dimensions of that experience had remained unexplored or unappreciated.

As a result, we have already seen that early on Baron appreciated the significance of American Jewish history, partly to help establish that community's position within world Jewry, but also as a laboratory for the study of Jewish history with considerably less emphasis on the lachrymose patterns. Even more important for the lachrymose critique was his revisionist perspective on the nature of the medieval period in Jewish history.

Beginning with his 1928 "Ghetto and Emancipation," a fundamental revision of the way the medieval period should be perceived played a central role in Baron's historical writing. The rise and spread of the Nazi regime made the reassessment all the more urgent in his mind, as he repeatedly chastened all comparisons between Nazi and medieval policies toward the Jews.

"The Jewish Factor in Medieval Civilization," published during the war years, provided his clearest statement of the legal, political, economic, social, and intellectual accomplishments of the period. Of these, it was the status of the Jews that required the most thorough reexamination. That concern eventually led Baron to a series of provocative essays that set out to explain the importance of church and throne to the protection of the Jews. Two essays that appeared in the early 1960s provided a kind of prelude to further expansion of the basic theories in the relevant volumes of the second edition. [14]

Fundamentally, Baron maintained that the concept of Jewish serfdom emerged within the rivalry for power between the church and the thrones of Europe, especially the Holy Roman Empire. The issue of Jewish serfdom became one specific battleground in the wider struggle. The thrust of Baron's thesis was that in contending sovereign control over the Jews each side also sought to defend and protect them. Baron emphasized that serfdom was not a term of humiliation,

346

but of protected status within the complicated structure of medieval society.

The idea that the church as well as the kings served an important historic role as protector of the Jews had come to Baron quite early on and was crucial to his revised presentation of the medieval period. Interestingly, Baron presented these ideas informally in an exchange of letters with Stephen Wise's wife on the occasion of a correspondence between herself and Carlton Hayes, the Catholic chairperson of Columbia's history department. Ironically, this exchange took place in December 1929, right at the time of Baron's appointment to Columbia. Mrs. Wise had questioned the position of the church toward the Jews, and Hayes had apparently responded in its defense. Baron was in total agreement with Hayes and firmly suggested that Mrs. Wise must arrange a dignified retreat. "My personal opinion is that the Catholic Church has contributed largely to the fact of the survival of the Jews throughout the middle ages. At the same time however, the Church tried to keep the Jews in a low social standing, a policy fully understandable in that period." [15]

As the chapter "The Wanderer" in the earlier *SRH* clearly shows, Baron was far from negating the extent of medieval persecution as demonstrated by pogroms and expulsions. But Baron sought to emphasize that there was more to Jewish history than suffering and tragedy and that daily life revealed a more positive perspective. He summed it up this way:

It would be a mistake, however, to believe that hatred was the constant keynote of Judeo-Christian relations, even in Germany or Italy. It is in the nature of historical records to transmit to posterity the memory of extraordinary events, rather than of the ordinary

347

flow of life. A community which lived in peace for decades may have given the medieval chronicler no motive to mention it, until a sudden outbreak of popular violence, lasting a few days, attracted widespread attention. Since modern historical treatment can no longer be satisfied with the enumeration of wars and diplomatic conflicts, the history of the Jewish people among the Gentiles, even in medieval Europe, must consist of much more than stories of sanguinary clashes or governmental expulsions.[16]

Baron particularly emphasized the extent of social relations between Jews and Christians, alluding to sexual contacts, intermarriage, and conversions as well. His attack against the lachrymose conception was neatly juxtaposed in Baron's own thinking with the need for Jewish social history.

This juxtaposition between the lachrymose critique and the need for a social history of the Jews was emphasized by Baron in his early historiographic writings. In his 1931 essay on Graetz, Baron maintained that "in general, he [Graetz] interpreted the history of the Jews in the Diaspora almost exclusively in terms of a 'history of sufferings and scholars' and hence paid little attention to economic and social history."[17] In 1939, Baron wrote of Dubnow's failure to write a true sociological history and, thereby, failing as well to avoid the trappings posed by a lachrymose history.[18] There was little elaboration, but the point of contrast had been made again: overemphasis on suffering prevented a true appreciation of the full Jewish historical experience. Thus, Graetz's formula that despite all the suffering, Jews had remained intellectually and spiritually creative was insufficient for Baron because it did not amply revise the historical portrait of the Jews' status within society at large.

Actually, the association of Baron with Jewish social history can easily be overstated. True, Baron quite consciously entitled his history *A Social and Religious History,* with due emphasis on the "social," contrary to alphabetical order. He also served as longtime editor of *Jewish Social Studies,* and historiographically, he emphasized the interaction of social and religious factors in Jewish history.

But it may be recalled that Baron had personally objected to the journal title, and he emphasized "social" in his own title to demonstrate that this work represented a departure from the intellectual orientation of his precursors. His historiographic position actually emphasized the reciprocal relations of the two forces, and he was as prone to discuss the social or economic teachings of religious sources as he was to demonstrate the converse social background of Jewish legal developments. Entire volumes of the second edition of the *SRH* are devoted to rabbinic literature. In short, the innovation in Baron's work lay in his extensive inclusion of social factors, but certainly not in his exclusion of the religious.

The notion that Jews actually possessed a social, economic, and political history was constructed on the basic assumption that the relevant historical materials could be collated across the vast space separating the scattered communities into a coherent entity that could still be defined as a specifically Jewish phenomenon. That there was, for example, such a notion as Jewish economic history even in modern society assumed a continued sociological entity somehow distinct from the collation of host societies in which Jews lived. Thus, the notion of a unified Jewish people even in the long Diaspora was emphasized not only by Zionist historians, but was virtually intrinsic to the discipline of Jewish history itself. Baron himself did not expand on this methodological question explicitly, but he did periodically address the factors that in his view provided that unity.[19]

These basic assumptions have occasionally been questioned over the years in different contexts. In one of the best-known examples in modern Jewish historiography, Gershom Scholem, in the opening pages of his *Sabbatai Sevi,* argued at length against the interpretation that associated the rise of Sabbatianism with the wave of anti-Jewish pogroms that swept over Poland in 1648–49; he simultaneously questioned the possible validity of a global social or economic interpretation to explain the widespread development of Sabbatianism, making the assumption that religious factors provided stronger unifying ties. However, in a different interpretation, obliquely suggested by Baron and later developed further by Gerson Cohen and Stephen Sharot, it would seem that Scholem exaggerated the globality of the Sabbatian movement, and that it was in fact more or less restricted to the Sephardi domain of world Jewry. If so, the possibilities of building a social interpretation become readily viable once again.[20]

A more far-reaching and penetrating critique, unfortunately clouded by personal polemics, was put forth by Jacob Neusner in an appendix to "Why Does Judaism Have an Economics?" There, Neusner questioned the entire enterprise of discussing Jewish economic history and extended the argument to Jewish intellectual history as well. Eventually, he concluded that all of Jewish history was "fictive."[21]

In a paradoxical way, the question of what Jewish history should be all about becomes more defined once the historian— as in the case of Baron—has demolished the ghetto walls that separate Jews from their environment. If the historian has already admitted that Jews must be studied within their broader social or intellectual context, then what separates them from the broader framework itself?

Baron did not seem especially troubled by that question because he readily accepted the fact that Jews were his subject matter. But the paradox remains. If Jews are viewed as ghettoized and separated from their immediate environments, then it seems acceptable to maintain that their history is a separate phenomenon, and that somehow—and this is the paradoxical part—those separate communities scattered around Europe, Northern Africa, and the Mediterranean find ways of linking up to each other. But if a historian maintains that Jews are both influenced by and influential on their immediate environments, the notion of linkage between the communities becomes suspect or unacceptable. Yet, for such a historian, if world history moves in broad contours, and if Jewish history is an integral part of that world historical process, then the history of the Jews within the broad framework will also move in those broad contours and demonstrate common developments that transcend national borders, while subject, presumably, to the same variations that occur within the various national settings.

The Jewish historian stands before two doors providing

diametrically opposite choices: to study the history of the Jews in segregated fashion and cross borders freely while ignoring environmental input, or to affirm the significance of the surrounding environment and become a comparative historian focusing on the Jews. Neusner was correct that one cannot posit a priori a global social history of the Jews. But, if Jews are one's subject, then surely one can engage freely in the enterprise of seeking out both common denominators and distinctive variations between the different national settings. In this regard, Baron's performance was uneven.

The recurring critique of Baron, especially with regard to the second edition, purported that the flood of details did not necessarily flush out a coherent, synthetic entity. Indeed, the construction of a paragraph, and perhaps even more the intermeshing of paragraphs, was often accomplished through adverbs and conjunctions lacking a logical connection. Nevertheless, one of Baron's great strengths, as I have suggested throughout this study, was his ability to synthesize broad historical trends and to scrutinize the constructive and destructive aspects of the changes taking place. In almost all cases, Baron achieved this level of comprehensive analysis better in the first edition than in the second and best of all in his essays. "Ghetto and Emancipation," "Plentitude of Apostolic Powers," "Democracy and Judaism"—regardless of specific criticisms that may have been put forth, are powerful presentations of broad, schematic themes.

Baron's call to view Jewish history as interacting with world history corrected what he called the isolationist approach, which seemed to ghettoize the Jewish historical experience.

Major developments would too often be explained as the result of internal causes, the outside world infiltrating the walls primarily through various forms of persecution.

Baron's perspective hardly reduced Jewish history to a passive object subject to stronger world winds. Rather, it envisioned interactive forces of mutual influences. The Jewish role in the spread of monotheism was one prominent example of Jewish contribution; his concessions to Sombart on the rise of capitalism provided another. Most important, he emphasized repeatedly that communal leaders and institutions were greatly responsible for continued Jewish survival. Nevertheless, in practice, the historical interaction was dominated by the outside environment.

As we have seen, Baron frequently raised these points in the context of his discussions of Dubnow's *World History,* and he returned to them again in his essay on "Newer Emphases in Jewish History." Baron seemed to be giving a signal in two important essays published in the early 1960s that he considered "the world dimensions of Jewish history" to represent one of the key characteristics of his own historical writing.[22]

It was Israeli historians who provided the most substantive discussions of Baron's historical thinking, and nothing separated Baron more from Israeli historians than his position on world dimensions. In his review of the *SRH,* Yitzhak Baer of the Hebrew University emphasized that his objections to Baron's historical approach derived from what Baer perceived as a disregard for internal factors. This was certainly Baron's understanding when he indicated an interest in responding to

Baer through an article in *Zion* on external and internal factors in Jewish history.[23] In an important 1950 essay on the emergence of communal organization, Baer argued extensively against Baron's theories regarding the evolution of the Jewish community and again maintained that internal factors had actually played the strongest role.

When Baron wrote of the oligarchic, nondemocratic character of the community, several scholars took exception. Louis Finkelstein, who headed the Jewish Theological Seminary, emphasized the democratic nature of the community in the second edition of his book on rabbinical synods and Baer launched an extensive critique on Baron's position. In a way, Jacob Katz's critique on the beginnings of the modern period in Jewish history reflects a similar dichotomy in perspective. Katz's argument that it is only in the late eighteenth century that one can detect new attitudes within the community itself differs widely from Baron's emphasis on earlier external developments—such as the rise of capitalism, the appearance of rationalism, and the peace of Westphalia of 1648.[24]

In fact, Baron went further than insisting on placing Jewish history within what he called world dimensions. He maintained as well that Jewish history must be treated as any other historical experience. This is what I called the normalization of Jewish history, and it is meant to imply that the contours of explanation applied to historical phenomena in general must be applied as far as possible to Jewish history as well.

Baron's treatment of the mass migration from Eastern Europe westward demonstrates some of the issues involved. By substituting economic deprivation and technological advances in place of antisemitic pogroms to explain the migratory movements, Baron not only reduced the significance of antisemitism as historical cause, but also the extent of uniqueness involved in this particularly important development. Thus, there was strong linkage between his attacks on lachrymosity and on isolationism, with antisemitism frequently filling an explanatory role that in other cases might have been filled by generalized and nonexclusive forms of explanation. Uniqueness didn't totally disappear from this conception. Indeed, as Baron himself indicated, the idea of uniqueness was basically a totally normal characteristic.

The notion of normalizing the Jewish historical experience was never subjected to the scrutiny that the lachrymose critique received. This was partly true because Baron didn't emphasize this aspect of his thinking to the same degree, and abstract references were far fewer than those against the lachrymose conception.

For whatever reason, this conception has been relatively ignored. But it represents, of course, the most encompassing and revolutionary dimension of Baron's historical thinking. By implication, the frequent reliance on antisemitism as explanatory mode as well as much of Jewish philosophical thinking becomes questionable with the challenge to a unique historical experience. Had the normalization tendency within Baron's thinking been more blatant, it would seem that it might have caused a historians' strife, especially between Israeli and Western scholars, on a Jewish *Besondersfrage*.

Eventually, such a dispute seems inevitable, and it would be appropriate for proper historical perspective to note Baron's role as a pioneer in the integration of Jewish history into its world dimensions. Indeed, Baron's position within one of the world's leading history departments stands in marked contrast both to the increasing ghettoization of Jewish studies in American universities and to the continued separation of history and Jewish history departments in most Israeli universities. Despite the tendency within any nation's universities toward emphasis on its own national history, matters have been exaggerated by the Israeli norm of treating world history and Jewish history as separate domains and differing disciplines.[25]

On the American scene, growing legitimization of ethnic studies in general and conflicts over faculty appointments and promotions are two of the important factors behind the current trends. Apologetic responses aside, the increased popularity of departments of Jewish Studies reflects by its very nature a decline in intellectual exchange between Judaica scholars and those specialists in different domains of content, but closest in discipline. Put differently, one of the central elements in Baron's legacy to Jewish studies has been significantly weakened by recent trends placing considerably less value on academic integration and deeming historical normalization as counterproductive toward the now more accentuated pursuit of ethnic identity.

Indeed, these trends find further expression in the diminishing value attributed to the study of Jewish social history itself, for social history posited as its basic axiom that Jewish social behavior could be explained in normative modes, and it adopted the jargon and methods of the broader disciplinary domain. The current trend toward uniqueness shuns away from seeking such common denominators.

.   .   .

It is probably safe to say that the shelf-life of Baron's *Social and Religious History* will not be as long as Graetz's *History of the Jews.* The enormous productivity of ensuing generations and the flood of Judaica publications outdated the later volumes of the series as soon as they appeared. The turbulent events of midcentury alone would seem to leave far behind any historical work conceived in an earlier period. But as Hannah Arendt wrote on his seventieth birthday, Baron should be long remembered: "For you became the first Professor of Jewish History in this country because you have been indeed the first to establish the history of your own people as an academic discipline." [26]

The historiographic keys to his legacy can be summed up not merely with the antilachrymose critique, but, as we have seen, with his emphasis on two other principles: the world dimension of Jewish history and the interrelationship of the social and religious elements in Jewish history. Both of these principles derived directly from the challenge of integrating Jewish history into the new academic environment of the university. When I once asked Baron for the sake of confirmation whether he was the first professor of Jewish history in an American university, he responded immediately: he was the first anywhere outside Israel. As far as I know, he was correct, but the remark also conveyed his global conceptions and his continuing search to find his own place as well as that of the Jews within that broad framework.

In building a place for Jewish history within the university world, Baron was a pioneer—a word that incidentally provoked in him the deepest admiration. It should certainly be used to describe him and his career as well.

But his legacy was also a personal one, and perhaps that partially explains why this study evolved more strongly in the biographical direction than originally intended. Even for those of us who missed Baron's tenure at Columbia by a generation or more, he symbolized a list of deeply significant characteristics: not only the academic legitimization of Jewish history, but the rigorous demands of a mentor that ensured the academic credibility of his students as well. Students writing a dissertation under his supervision needed knowledge of Hebrew as well as the languages of the environment in which they wished to specialize, knowledge of world history during the period of specialization, and a broad knowledge of all periods of Jewish history.

In today's setting, Israeli scholars often ask how one can specialize in Jewish studies without being fluent in Hebrew, while others ask in return how dissertations can be written without knowledge of Russian, Polish, or Spanish, depending on the period and community being studied. Baron students were not allowed to compromise on either score. It is a legacy to Jewish studies well worth perpetuating.

On a final point, the proliferation of Jewish studies in recent decades has left a marked paradox in Baron's legacy. For although the flood of publications speedily ran his *History* out of date, the abundance of material seems to virtually preclude any further single-handed attempts to master the total scope of Jewish history. It seems to be the one point on which all members of the profession agree; that is, Baron's *History* will be the last "History of the Jews" written by a single, responsible scholar. And yet that claim was already made almost sixty years ago in response to the appearance of the first edition of the *Social and Religious History*. If at that time Yitzhak Baer's endorsement rang true that the study of Jewish history also required works of scope that provided unified interpretations, it would seem to be just as true today. Jewish history—in all of its breadth, in all of its depth, in all of its recent drama and fundamental change—certainly requires that its contemporary interpreters be strongly rooted in the millennia of the Jewish historical experience and in the world history that surrounded it. In the end, that was the profound legacy of Salo Baron's life and thought.

NOTES

Notes to the Introduction

1. In addition to the first and second editions of the *Social and Religious History,* the best known of his volumes are *The Jewish Community,* 3 vols. (Philadelphia: Jewish Publication Society, 1942); *The Russian Jew Under Tsars and Soviets* (New York: Macmillan, 1964); *History and Jewish Historian: Essays and Addresses,* comp. Arthur Hertzberg and Leon A. Feldman (Philadelphia: Jewish Publication Society, 1964); *Ancient and Medieval Jewish History,* ed. Leon A. Feldman (New Brunswick: Rutgers University Press, 1972); *Steeled by Adversity: Essays and Addresses on American Jewish Life,* ed. Jeannette Meisel Baron (Philadelphia: Jewish Publication Society, 1971).

2. Graetz's *Geschichte der Juden* appeared in eleven volumes between 1853 and 1876; the six-volume American edition is *History of the Jews* (Philadelphia: Jewish Publication Society, 1891–98).

3. On the popularity of the American edition well into the twentieth century, see Solomon Grayzel, "Graetz's *History* in America," in *The Breslau Seminary,* ed. Guido Kisch (Tübingen: J.C.B. Mohr, 1963), 223–37; and Jonathan Sarna, *JPS: The Americanization of Jewish Culture, 1888–1988* (Philadelphia: Jewish Publication Society, 1989), 34–39. As late as 1957, the work was still selling some five hundred sets a year.

4. On Dubnow's historiography in general and especially on Graetz's influence, see Robert Seltzer, "From Graetz to Dubnow: The Impact of the East European Milieu on the Writing of Jewish History," in *Legacy of Jewish Migration,* ed. David Berger (New York: Brooklyn College Press, 1983), 49–60.

5. Simon Dubnow, *Weltgeschichte des Jüdischen Volkes,* 10 volumes (Berlin: Jüdischer Verlag, 1925–29).

6. Baron, *A Social and Religious History of the Jews,* 3 vols. (New York: Columbia University Press, 1937); 2nd ed., 18 vols. (New York: Columbia University Press, 1952– 83).

7. Talmon, *The Origins of Totalitarian Democracy* (London: Secker & Warburg, 1952); Hertzberg, *The French Enlightenment and the Jews* (New York: Columbia University Press, 1968).

8. The most complete statement of Baron's position on the shortcomings of emancipation appears in his 1960 essay "New Approaches to Jewish Emancipation," *Diogenes,* No. 29 (1960): 56–81.

9. See Hannah Arendt, *Eichmann in Jerusalem* (New York: Viking Press, 1963), and *The Jew as Pariah,* ed. Ron Feldman (New York: Grove Press, 1978).

10. Library of Congress, Manuscript Division, Hannah Arendt Collection, Box 7, General Correspondence, Ba-Bi, 1944–75; 23 May 1965.

11. Quoted in *Jew as Pariah,* 22.

12. "Newer Emphases in Jewish History," *Jewish Historians,* 102–3.

13. A recent issue of the *AJS Review* contains three fine papers with a number of important observations, but it reached me after I had completed this manuscript. See the articles by Louis H. Feldman, Robert Chazan, and Ismar Schorsch in *AJS Review* 17 (1993): 1–50.

Notes to Chapter 1

1. The Jewish population and its percentage of the general population grew as follows:

Year	Jews	% of General Population
1772	1200	34.0
1846	7914	—
1890	11677	42.4

1900	12586	39.7
1910	15108	41.2
1921	15608	44.2

On Tarnow, see *Encyclopedia of the Holocaust* (New York: Macmillan, 1990), 4: 1451–54; *Pinkas HaKehilot* [Encyclopedia of Jewish Communities]: *Poland* (Jerusalem: Yad Vashem, 1984), 3: 178–190.

2. *Under Two Civilizations: Tarnow, 1895–1914; Selected from the Memoirs of Salo Wittmayer Baron* (Stanford: Stanford University, 1990), n.p. Also, interview of Baron by Zvi Ankory, Diaspora Museum, July 1987. The following account of Baron's family and his youth in Tarnow is compiled from his own memoir; author's interviews with Baron, Shoshanna Eytan, and Zvi Ankory; and Baron's interview with Ankory.

3. Stanford, Box 6, Folder "Jeannette Outgoing to SB."

4. There are obviously some difficulties in taking these documents out of their chronological setting. In fact, these letters derive not only from a much later period, but a particularly stressful time as well. With Salo now living in America, there was considerable concern about who would run the family affairs. The problem was raised in Jeannette's letters and also by other testimony. During this same year, Baron tried to convince his sister Gisela that her oldest son would have to take over the business. This too proved to be a difficult conversation, because her son had other occupational plans and her children planned to live in Palestine. Interview with Shoshanna Eytan, April 1990.

Despite all of the difficulties involved with this evidence, the letters do provide a rare inside glimpse that certainly contributes to our picture.

5. *Under Two Civilizations,* n.p.

6. In light of later criticism, especially by Solomon Zeitlin, I asked Ankory how good Baron's Talmud education really was. He responded that his father had tutored Baron in Talmud, that Baron demonstrated that he had received the best possible training, and that it went beyond what he could have gotten at a yeshivah. For five months he studied only Talmud and then in the sixth month he had a crash course to prepare for his exams. When he later went on to Cracow to study, he was tested by a famous Talmudist that his father

363

wanted to teach him. Baron proved to be extremely well prepared. In fact, he passed his exams at the rabbinical school in Vienna with flying colors and quickly became an assistant there.

7. These articles are listed in "A Bibliography of the Printed Writings of Salo Wittmayer Baron," *Salo Wittmayer Baron Jubilee Volume,* 3 vols. (Jerusalem: American Academy for Jewish Research, 1974), 1: 1–37; see especially the years 1912–14.

8. "A Sad Phenomenon," *HaMitzpeh* 9, No. 43 (1912): 3 (Hebrew).

9. *HaMitzpeh* 10, No. 36 (1913): 4–5. On the movement for electoral reform, see Piotr Wandycz, "The Poles in the Habsburg Monarchy," in *Nationbuilding and the Politics of Nationalism: Essays on Austrian Galicia,* ed. Andrei Markovits and Frank Sysyn (Cambridge, Mass.: Harvard University Press, 1982), 89. This volume provides an excellent introduction to the complicated picture of nationalist movements in Galicia in general.

10. On the flight of Galician Jews to Vienna during this period, see Bruce F. Pauley, "Political Antisemitism in Interwar Vienna," in *Jews, Antisemitism and Culture in Vienna,* ed. Ivar Oxaal, Michael Pollak, and Gerhard Botz (London: Routledge & Kegan Paul, 1987), 153–54.

11. *Die Judenfrage auf dem Wiener Kongress* (Vienna and Berlin: R. Lowit, 1920); *Die politische Theorie Ferdinand Lassalles* (Leipzig: C. L. Hirschfeld, 1923).

12. See especially the discussion in *Judenfrage,* 134–45.

13. Ibid., 206.

14. For a full discussion on the history of JIR, see the chapter "Kelal Yisrael: The Jewish Institute of Religion," in Michael Meyer, "A Centennial History," in *Hebrew Union College-Jewish Institute of Religion at One Hundred Years,* ed. Samuel E. Karff (Cincinnati: Hebrew Union College Press, 1976), 137–69. The early history of JIR is also well described in Melvin I. Urofsky, *A Voice That Spoke for Justice: The Life and Times of Stephen S. Wise* (Albany: SUNY Press, 1982), 182–92. An earlier and useful study is that of Hyman J. Fliegel, "The Creation of the Jewish Institute of Religion," *American Jewish Historical Quarterly* 58 (1968): 260–70. Several important letters are in the collection *Stephen S. Wise: Servant of the People,* ed. Carl Voss (Philadelphia: Jewish Publication Society, 1969). Information on the early history of JIR was also obtained from the minutes of its faculty meetings

and the annual catalogues of the school, available to me at the JIR Library.

15. *Servant of the People,* 137–38.
16. Urofsky, *Life and Times,* 19.
17. Marlene R. Schiffman, "The Library of the Jewish Institute of Religion, 1922–1950," *Jewish Book Annual* 48 (1990–91): 183–96.
18. Contrary to Wise's letter of 18 April 1923, the question of Elbogen's joining the JIR faculty was apparently not yet closed by Elbogen, because the minutes indicate that Elbogen returned to JIR for the second semester of 1923–24 and that his final decision was still pending.
19. Wolfson's early difficulties at Harvard are not adequately treated in Leo Schwarz's volume *Wolfson of Harvard* (Philadelphia: Jewish Publication Society, 1978). Further references can be found in the American Jewish Archives, Henry Hurwitz Collection, Box 63, Folder 3.
20. *Jewish Institute of Religion Minutes of Meetings of the Faculty and Faculty Committees,* Vol. 1, 1 December 1926. Hereafter *Minute Book.* (Entries are by dates without pagination.)
21. Quoted in Meyer, "A Centennial History," 151.
22. Thus, for example, the suggestion of Richard Gottheil to seek English-speaking scholars; *Minute Book,* 1, 11 April 1923. On another occasion, Israel Abrahams, who had since returned to England, was asked to recommend possible candidates.
23. *Servant of the People,* 115.
24. In June 1922, Wise wrote to Chajes, "I want to talk to you about the possibility of getting some great scholars and teachers for the Jewish Institute of Religion, . . . which Hirsch of Chicago and I are together founding. I want your judgment as to the younger men." AJA, JIR Collection, Box 5, Folder 2 (Chayes). See also *Minute Book,* 1, especially the entry of 22 December 1927, at which Chajes's death was announced to the faculty. Also see 13 October 1926. On Wise's studies in Vienna, see Urofsky, *Life and Times,* 9–10.
25. Schwarz, *Wolfson of Harvard,* 91–92.
26. Columbia University, Central Files, Julian Mack to Butler, 20 December 1929.
27. *Minute Book,* 1, 11 September 1925.
28. Interview with the author, August 1987, and with Zvi Ankori, July 1987, deposited at the Museum of the Diaspora.

29. See also the discussion based on hearsay that Roth lost the position because of his personality in Martin A. Cohen, "History" [A Survey of Scholarly Contributions], in *Hebrew Union College,* 445–46.
30. Course listings taken from the annual catalogue for the years from 1925–26 to 1936–37, when Baron was last listed as a member of the faculty.
31. *Minute Book,* 2, 26 March 1931, 2.
32. AJA, JIR Collection, Box 3, Folder 1 (Baron, 1925–30), Kohut to Wise, 6 January 1926.
33. AJA, JIR Collection, Box 3, Folder 1 (Baron, 1925–30), Wise to Kohut, 1 December 1926 and 17 May 1927. The decision also required Chajes's approval to extend Baron's leave from Vienna. The situation in Vienna and elsewhere in central Europe is discussed later in this chapter.
34. *Minute Book,* 1, 5 July 1928: "The suggestion of the Alumni that a Director of the Department of Advanced Students be appointed was presented. Both Rabbi Lewis and Dr. Marcus thought that Dr. Baron was most fitted to occupy the post and recommended that he be invited to serve in this capacity."
35. Thus, Baron requested that this information be added to the biographical entry in the *Menorah Journal* with the publication of "Ghetto and Emancipation." AJA, Hurwitz Collection, Box 2, File 16, letter of 22 May 1928. For a later example, see the 1964 preface to *Jewish Historians,* xiv.
36. Stanford, Box 9, Folder 7, Curatorium Breslau to Baron, 3 April 1928.
37. Brann was succeeded by Israel Rabin, who specialized in Semitics and postbiblical literature. The position offered to Baron was later given to Hirsch Jacob Zimmels. Zimmels taught at Breslau from 1929 to 1933, then became communal rabbi in Vienna, and later moved to England, where he eventually became principal of Jews' College. Zimmels taught Talmud and Jewish history from the period of 1040 on. Lothar Rothschild, "Die Geschichte des Seminars von 1040 bis 1938," *The Breslau Seminary,* ed. Guido Kisch (Tübingen: J.C.B. Mohr, 1963), 152.
38. AJA, Hurwitz Collection, Box 2, File 16, Baron to Solow, 9 May 1928.
39. AJA, JIR Collection, Box 3, Folder 1 (Baron, 1925–30), Baron to

Wise, 20 April 1928; Wise to Kohut, 18 April 1928; biographical statement, May 1928.

40. AJA, JIR Collection, Box 3, Folder 1 (Baron, 1925–30), memo of 8 October 1928.

41. Stanford, Box 7, Unmarked Folder, Kohut to Wise, 5 April 1929. Also, Marx to Kohut, 4 April 1929.

42. *Minute Book,* 1, 4 January 1923.

43. *Minute Book,* 1, 22 December 1927, 2–3.

44. *Minute Book,* 2, 4 May 1931.

45. Stanford Special Collections, Baron Collection, Box 7, Folder 5, letter to Tepfer, 29 January 1929.

46. Contrast, Meyer, "A Centennial History," 153. Still, Meyer was obviously correct that JIR was too closely dependent on Wise's strong leadership.

47. The essay initially appeared in the *Menorah Journal* 14 (1928): 515–26. It was reprinted in the *Menorah Treasury: Harvest of Half a Century,* ed. Leo W. Schwarz (Philadelphia: Jewish Publication Society, 1964), 50–63. This was Baron's second publication in English; his first was an essay on the Renaissance Jew Azariah de' Rossi, published the previous year in a festschrift in honor of Israel Abrahams. See "A Bibliography of the Printed Writings of Salo Wittmayer Baron," 1:6, no. 27.

48. "Ghetto and Emancipation," 515–16.

49. Ibid., 516–19.

50. Ibid., 520–22.

51. Ibid., 523.

52. Baron credits this classic emancipation argument to the nineteenth-century Wissenschaft scholars. Actually, it was already in full use by eighteenth-century Enlightenment figures. See Arthur Hertzberg, *The French Enlightenment and the Jews* (New York: Columbia University Press, 1968). On its use in Germany, see Liberles, "From *Toleration* to *Verbesserung:* German and English Debates on the Jews in the Eighteenth Century," *Central European History* 22 (1989): 3–32.

53. "Ghetto and Emancipation," 522.

54. Ibid., 526.

55. Baron expressed these ideas in a number of places. See especially "Newer Approaches to Jewish Emancipation," *Diogenes* 29 (1960): 56–81. On a different track, but also concerning the problems posed

by the modern age, see "Modern Capitalism and Jewish Fate," first published in the *Menorah Journal* 30 (1942): 116–38, and reprinted in *Jewish Historians,* 43–64.

56. The *Menorah Journal* had been founded in 1915 as the organ of the American collegiate Menorah movement established in 1906 to spread Jewish culture within the campus communities and to secure for Jewish culture a respected position within American universities. The letter accompanying the manuscript is in American Jewish Archives, Henry Hurwitz/Menorah Association Collection, hereafter Hurwitz Collection, Box 2, File 16, Baron to the Editor, 9 February 1928.

On the Menorah movement, see Jenna Joselit, "Without Ghettoism: A History of the Intercollegiate Menorah Association, 1906–1930," *American Jewish Archives* 30 (1978): 133–54.

57. Hurwitz Collection, Box 2, File 16, Baron letters of 13 and 21 April, and Cohen's reply, 25 April 1928.

58. Hurwitz Collection, Box 2, File 16, Baron to Solow, 9 May 1928.

59. Hurwitz Collection, Box 2, File 16, Cohen to Baron, 11 May 1928.

60. Hurwitz Collection, Box 2, File 16, Baron to Cohen, 14 May 1928.

61. Hurwitz Collection, Box 2, File 16, 23 July 1928.

62. Hurwitz Collection, Box 2, File 16, Baron to Cohen, 13 December 1929.

63. On the availability of collections and individual books at reduced prices, see, for example, Marlene R. Schiffman, "The Library of the Jewish Institute of Religion, 1922–1950," *Jewish Book Annual* 48 (1990–91), especially 183–88.

64. Stanford, Baron Collection, especially Box 7 and Box 4, Folder 18.

65. AJA, JIR Collection, Box 3, Folder 1 (Baron, 1925–30), Baron to Wise, 23 July 1929, and Wise's response, 29 July 1929. On the last years of the Hochschule, see Richard Fuchs, "The 'Hochschule für die Wissenschaft des Judenthums' in the Period of Nazi Rule," *Leo Baeck Institute Yearbook* 12 (1967): 3–31.

66. Notably, however, the proportion of foreign students increased, and the point of origin changed as well. Earlier, foreign students had come from Hapsburg territories, but now students from Eastern Europe came to play a more dominant role. On the orthodox seminary, see Isi Jacob Eisner, "Reminiscences of the Berlin Rabbinical Seminary," *Leo Baeck Institute Yearbook 12 (1967):* 32–52; the fig-

ures are on 41. Hochschule numbers are in Fuchs, "Period of Nazi Rule," 7.

67. The financial plight in Vienna, involving the effects of the ongoing inflationary spiral and then the depression, caused a tremendous strain on the limited communal budget, by necessity increasing the role of social welfare and reducing allotments for cultural activities. See Harriet Freidenreich, *Jewish Politics in Vienna* (Bloomington: Indiana Univ. Press, 1991), 151–58.

68. AJA, JIR Collection, Box 5, Folder 2, Wise to Chajes, 22 June 1922; quotation is from letter of 1 January 1923. In later years, the thrust of Wise's and Baron's efforts to support the Viennese institutions was to provide continuing assistance for the leading scholars, especially Victor Aptowitzer, Samuel Krauss, and Adolf Schwarz, rabbinic scholar and former rector of the seminary. For more on these relief efforts, see chapter 7 in this volume.

The annual report of the Vienna seminary, issued in 1933 and covering the period from 1929, singled out Hebrew Union College and its president Julian Morgenstern, as well as the American Joint Distribution Committee for their support of the institution. "Bericht des Kuratoriums," in *Der Israelitisch-Theologischen Lehranstalt in Wien, Jahresbericht* (Vienna, 1933), vols. 37– 39, 152.

69. The question arose again in early 1927, and once again the consensus was against such a move.

70. On Chajes's conflicts with the more Orthodox wing of the Viennese community, see Freidenreich, *Jewish Politics in Vienna,* especially 133–34.

71. Eisner, "Reminiscences," 48–49. Christhard Hoffmann and Daniel R. Schwartz, "Early but Opposed—Supported but Late—Two Berlin Seminaries Which Attempted to Move Abroad," *Leo Baeck Institute Yearbook* 36 (1991): 267–305.

The Breslau seminary seems to have been less disrupted by the economic problems of the twenties. Rothschild, "Die Geschichte des Seminars von 1904 bis 1938," 150–53.

72. The Maimonides celebration comes from AJA, Nearprint Collection, Baron, Clippings. Baron provided a succinct summary of American Jewish scholarship in a letter to Joshua Trachtenberg, Stanford, Box 3, Folder 17, 15 June 1954. Two earlier scholars had passed away by this time: Henry Malter (1925) and Max Margolis (1932). Those

teaching at universities were Baron, Gottheil, Ralph Marcus, Husik, and Wolfson. Those born in America were Finkelstein, Jacob Marcus, and Ralph Marcus.

73. The story of the efforts of American and Israeli individuals and institutions alike to come to the aid of those who had stayed behind to lead their communities during the period of disintegration has not yet been properly told.

On an important aspect of this stage of the migration, see the moving and insightful article by Michael Meyer, "The Refugee Scholars Project of the Hebrew Union College," in *A Bicentennial Festschrift for Jacob Rader Marcus,* ed. Bertram Korn (New York: Ktav, 1976), 359–75.

74. Ibid., 362–63.

Notes to Chapter 2

1. Linda Miller was the widow of the late Nathan Miller, former head of the New York Stock Exchange firm Miller and Co. A beautiful and touching memoir was written soon after her death by Ruth Hurwitz, wife of the editor of the *Menorah Journal.* Linda Miller is described as an extremely intelligent and industrious woman, who concerned herself regularly with practical details of good deeds. Her *New York Times* obituary, posted in July 1936, is filed under Miller, Columbiana Collection of the Rare Book and Manuscript Library, located in Low Memorial Library.

The following discussion is based primarily on materials obtained from Columbia University's Central Files. Some of these documents were recently published in Michael Brenner, "An Unknown Project of a World Jewish History in Weimar Germany," *Modern Judaism* 13 (1993): 249–67.

2. Enelow had also been instrumental in arranging for the Littauer chair in Jewish studies occupied by Harry Wolfson at Harvard. On Enelow, see the biographic essay in *Selected Works of Hyman G. Enelow,* ed. Felix Levy, 4 vols. (Kingsport, Tenn.: Kingsport Press, 1935).

3. The initial correspondence between Butler and Enelow is missing from Columbia Central Files. I wish to particularly thank Ms. Vos for her repeated searches for this material. I was finally able to locate

this link in the story in the AJA's Enelow Collection, Box 3, Folder 7, letters of 12 March ; 4, 12, 13, n.d., 17, 18, 26, and 30 April.

At one point, Richard Gottheil claimed to carry a message from Butler to Enelow, indicating that the endowment would actually not be accepted by the university. Butler responded to Enelow's puzzlement that Gottheil had misunderstood Butler's intent.

Considering Gottheil's subsequent behavior, it is possible that Gottheil was actually attempting to sabotage the negotiations. He certainly sought to control their direction. This too was Lucius Littauer's interpretation when informed by Enelow that he had been told by Butler to disregard the Gottheil incident: "I can only hope that a better understanding of Gottheil's statement may mitigate my opinion of his despicable intention." AJA, Enelow Collection, Littauer Folder, letters of 23 and 26 April 1928.

Enelow had succeeded to the pulpit formerly occupied by Gottheil's father, and the two had known each other for years. But after the incident, Enelow no longer kept Gottheil informed of developments, provoking an angry reaction, Enelow Collection, Box 8, Folder 7, 30 May 1928. The relation between the two seemed to have improved when in 1931, Gottheil invited Enelow to deliver a national series of lectures on the history of Judaism. This extensive correspondence is in the same file.

4. Central Files, Miller File, Miller to Butler, 9 May 1928; Butler's response of 11 May; hereafter Miller File.
5. Miller File, Miller to Butler, 15 May 1928.
6. Miller File, Butler to Miller, 28 May 1928.
7. Miller File, Miller to Butler, 2 June 1928.
8. Miller File, Butler to Miller, 4 June 1928, and Miller's reply of 6 June.
9. Central Files, Butler to Woodbridge, 26 November 1928. "Jewish Studies at Columbia University", n.d., Columbiana Collection, Low Library.

In our interviews, Baron had told me that he knew of no conclusive evidence to indicate Enelow's personal interest in the position. Even the materials we have already cited strongly indicate otherwise, but in addition, there is an explicit exchange of letters between Enelow and Gottheil in 1932 in which Enelow blames Gottheil for not nominating him for the chair. AJA, Enelow Collection, Box 8, Folder 7, letters of 9 and 12 April 1932.

10. Central Files, Butler to Woodbridge, 7 June 1928.

11. Central Files, Confidential Memorandum apparently to Woodbridge, 20 June 1928.

12. Several responses from those appointed are in Central Files: Coffin letter, 22 June; Knox, 23 June 1928; Jackson, 26 June; Fife, 28 June; Gottheil, 9 July; MacIver, 9 July.

13. Central Files, Woodbridge to Butler, 21 November 1928, and Woodbridge File, 28 November.

14. Miller File, 22 November 1928.

15. Miller File, Miller to Butler, 25 November 1928.

16. Central Files, Butler to Woodbridge, 26 November 1928.

17. Miller File, Butler to Miller, 3 December 1928.

18. Miller File, Miller to Butler, 5 December 1928.

19. Miller File, Butler to Miller, 7 December 1928.

20. Stanford, Box 7, Folder 11, Kohut to Wise and to Baron with copy of letter to Wise, 3 October 1928.

21. Central Files, Woodbridge File, Woodbridge to Butler, 28 February 1929; hereafter, Woodbridge File.

  Earlier that month, Linda Miller had arranged for Lucius Littauer, a mutual acquaintance of both Butler and Miller, to inquire as to what progress was being made. Butler to Miller, 19 February 1929; Miller's reply, 20 February 1929.

22. Stanford, Box 7, Folder 11, Kohut to Ginzberg, 8 November 1928.

23. Woodbridge File, Woodbridge to Butler, 28 February 1929.

24. Woodbridge File, Butler to Woodbridge, 1 March 1929. Also, Miller File, Butler to Miller, 1 March 1929.

25. Miller File, Miller to Butler, 4 March 1929. This letter was also transcribed and sent to Woodbridge for the committee's consideration.

26. Woodbridge File, Hayden to Woodbridge, 22 March 1929, and Woodbridge to Butler, 25 March 1929.

27. Miller File, Butler to Miller, 1 April 1929.

28. Woodbridge File, Woodbridge to Butler, 11 April 1929.

29. Woodbridge File, Fackenthal to Woodbridge, 13 April 1929.

30. Woodbridge File, Woodbridge to Butler, 1 June 1929.

31. Woodbridge File, Butler to Woodbridge, 4 June 1929.

32. Central Files, Edman to Woodbridge, 11 July 1929.

33. Central Files, Butler to Elbogen, 20 July 1929.
34. Central Files, Butler to Elbogen, 12 September 1929.
35. Elbogen to Butler, 19 and 28 September 1929.
36. Miller File, Butler to Miller, 30 September 1929.
37. Formal communication of Elbogen's refusal is contained in the letter of 16 December informing Linda Miller of the Baron appointment.
38. Miller File, Miller to Butler, 3 October 1929.
39. Central Files, Equitable Trust Company of New York to Butler, 13 December 1929. It is certainly possible that the stock market crash of October 1929—only six weeks earlier—influenced the threat that the funds be returned, but there is no evidence to this effect in the documents, and the chronology also makes sense just in terms of the breakdown of the Elbogen negotiations.
40. Central Files, Butler to John J. Graeber, Equitable Trust Company, date of 14 December, changed by hand to 16 December 1929. The offer to Baron was dated 14 December.
41. It should be noted that the search committee had throughout followed the procedure of consulting leaders in related fields for the names of the best-qualified scholars to be approached. Nothing in the files indicates that the men mentioned in this report were "candidates" or necessarily interested in the position.
42. Baron was actually only thirty-four at the time. The error in math covered the fact that Baron was the youngest of the four nominees discussed.
43. In fact, Baron was known to the Columbia community. In his letter to Mrs. Miller informing her of Baron's appointment, Butler noted: "During the year 1927 he gave acceptable lectures at Columbia University on Jewish Civilization and thereby became known to many of our staff." Miller File, Butler to Miller, 16 December 1929.
44. Woodbridge File, Butler to Woodbridge, 13 December 1929.
45. Central Files, 19 and December 1929, and 2 January 1930. To place the salary in some perspective, comparison can be made with Baron's arrangement with JIR. For the year 1926–27, Baron was hired for $4,000 with the understanding that his future salary should he remain would be $5,000 for two years and then $6,000, "which is in accordance with the arrangements made for members of the Faculty." Extract of Minutes of Board of Trustees meeting of 14 April 1926; AJA, JIR Collection, Box 3, Folder 1 (Baron, 1925–30).

46. Miller File, Butler to Miller, 16 December 1929.
47. Miller File, Miller to Butler, 18 December 1929.
48. Miller File, Miller to Butler, 20 December 1929.
49. Miller File, Butler to Miller, 23 December 1929.
50. Central Files, Mack to Butler, 20 December 1929.
51. Miller File, Miller to Butler, 25 December 1929, and January 2, 1930.
52. Miller File, Butler to Miller, 31 December 1929.
53. Stanford Special Collections, Baron Collection, Box 9, Folder E, Elbogen to B, 10 April 1930.
54. Stanford, Box 4, Folder 11 (F); Finkelstein to Baron, 24 December 1929.
55. JIR actually issued a press release announcing the appointment and emphasizing Baron's connection with the institution. AJA, JIR Collection, Box 3, Folder 1.
56. Stanford, Box 4, Folder 18, Kohut to B, 23 December 1929.
57. Stanford, Box 4, Folder 18; there were a number of letters pertaining to the party, several concerned with the difficulties involved in arranging kosher catering.
58. *The American Israelite,* May 30, 1930.
59. This example, AJA, Henry Hurwitz Collection, Baron's letter of 10 January 1930.
60. These included Ismar Elbogen and Zevi Diesendruck. Baron later wrote to Elbogen that his hesitations had been dissipated when Butler agreed to Baron's continued instruction at JIR. Stanford, Box 5, Folder 11 (E), 21 January 1930. He explained to Diesendruck that the main reason for his indifference was that he thought the position primarily involved the teaching of undergraduates. He later realized, however, that the opposite was the case. Stanford, Box 5, Folder 10, B to Diesendruck, 27 February 1930.
61. Stanford Special Collections, Baron Collection, Box 9, Folder S, Schneider to Baron, 23 January 1929. Schneider wrote: "I wish to acknowledge receipt of the Journals you sent containing your articles and to thank you for letting us see them. I have read them with interest and I am showing them to several other men on the campus."
62. My interview, August 1987, and that of Zvi Ankori, July 1987. Also author's interview with Lloyd Gartner. Ginzberg's statement is in *My Brother's Keeper* (New Brunswick: Transaction Press, 1989), 35–36.

The primary description of Trilling's experiences is by Diana Trilling, "Lionel Trilling, A Jew at Columbia," *Commentary* 67 (March 1979): 40–46.

I am grateful to the current administration of the history department for searching in the attic of Columbia's Fayerweather Hall to find departmental records from this period. Unfortunately, this search was unsuccessful. The Carlton Hayes Collection in the Manuscript Division did not contain relevant material.

63. Central Files, Fackenthal to Baron, 24 December 1929, and Baron's reply, 27 December.
64. Central Files, Fackenthal to McBain, 3 January 1930.
65. Central Files, McBain to Fackenthal, 7 January 1930.
66. Central Files, Butler to Fackenthal, 9 January 1930.
67. Stanford, Box 4, Folder 14 (H), 13 and 14 January 1930.
68. Stanford, Box 5, Folder 17, letter of 16 January 1930.
69. Stanford, Box 4, Folder 14, Hayes to Baron, 31 January 1930.
70. Stanford, Box 5, Folder 13 (Fackenthal), 27 December 1929.
71. Stanford, Box 5, Folder 15, Baron to Gavin, 25 February 1930; also the letter to Diesendruck, where he speaks positively of the appointment to history. Stanford, Box 5, Folder 10, 27 February 1930.

Notes to Chapter 3

1. Miriam Yardeni, "Judaism and Jews as seen by the French Protestant Exiles in Holland (1685–1715)," *Studies in the History of the Jewish People and the Land of Israel* 1 (1970): 163–85 (Hebrew).
2. *Encyclopedia Judaica* (Jerusalem: Keter, 1971), 4:309.
3. Baron, "I. M. Jost the Historian," in *Jewish Historians,* 240–262; this discussion is on 254–55.
4. I. M. Jost, *Geschichte der Israeliten seit der Zeit der Makkabäer bis auf unsere Tage, nach den Quellen bearbeitet,* 9 vols. (Berlin, 1820–28).
5. Jost, *Neuere Geschichte der Israeliten von 1815 bis 1845,* 3 vols. (Berlin, 1846–47)
6. Baron, "I. M. Jost the Historian," 240–62. This essay is discussed at length in the next section. See also Reuven Michael, *I. M. Jost: Founder of the Modern Jewish Historiography* (Hebrew; Jerusalem: Magnes, 1983).
7. Ismar Schorsch, "From Wolfenbüttel to Wissenschaft: The Divergent

Paths of Isaak Marcus Jost and Leopold Zunz," *Leo Baeck Institute Yearbook* 22 (1977): 109–28; quotation is from 112–13.

8. On the other hand, Jost's three-part volume 10 is indispensable to the study of the early nineteenth century, especially in Germany, as Jost can be treated as a primary source written by a participant and yet sophisticated observer of developments. On Jost and Zunz, see Michael, *Jost,* 74; Schorsch, "Wolfenbüttel," 112.

9. Ben Zion Dinur, *Israel and the Diaspora* (Philadelphia: Jewish Publication Society, 1969), 17–22.

10. Michael, *Jost,* 8–9, 16ff. Schorsch, "Wolfenbüttel," 127–28.

11. For a lively sketch of Graetz's life, see Philip Bloch, "Memoir of Heinrich Graetz," in Graetz, *History of the Jews,* 6 vols. (Philadelphia: Jewish Publication Society, 1891–98), 6: 1– 86. In Hebrew, there is Reuven Michael's biographical chapter in *Heinrich Graetz. Essays. Memoirs. Letters* (Jerusalem: Mossad Bialik, 1969), 37–51.

12. On Hirsch, Robert Liberles, "Champion of Orthodoxy: The Emergence of Samson Raphael Hirsch as Religious Leader," *AJS Review* 6 (1981): 43–60. On Hirsch's relations with Graetz, some remarks are in Liberles, "Samson Raphael Hirsch on the Centennial of his Death," *Jewish Book Annual* 46 (1988): 195–205.

13. On the move, see the diary entry for 9 March 1853, Heinrich Graetz, *Tagebuch und Briefe,* ed. Reuven Michael (Tübingen: J.C.B. Mohr, 1977), 204.

14. On Frankel, see Rivkah Horwitz, *Zacharias Frankel and the Beginnings of Postive-Historical Judaism* (Hebrew; Jerusalem: Merkaz Shazar, 1984). On the conference initiative, see Liberles, *Religious Conflict in Social Context: The Resurgence of Orthodox Judaism in Frankfurt, 1838– 1877* (Westport, Conn.: Greenwood Press, 1985), 71, 76–77.

15. The notion that Graetz's appearance at Frankel's ill-fated conference is what secured their relationship is contradicted by Graetz's diary, which demonstrates previous contacts between them and that the essay "The Construction of Jewish History" had been accepted by Frankel prior to the conference episode. Graetz, *Tagebuch und Briefe,* 155, 157, and especially 162. The conference itself appears on 164.

16. The essay appears in English in Graetz, *The Structure of Jewish History and Other Essays,* trans. and ed. by Ismar Schorsch (New York: Ktav, 1975).

17. Graetz, *Structure of Jewish History,* 71, 123–24.

18. The basis for this suggestion can be found in ibid., 93–94.
19. Schorsch, "Ideology and History," Introduction to Graetz, *Structure of Jewish History*, 47–48. Less explicit is Bloch's "Memoir," 49.
20. See the references in Bloch, "Memoir," in Graetz, *History of the Jews*, 6: 41, 43–45.
21. In Graetz, *Structure of Jewish History*, 125.
22. Ibid., 94.
23. Ismar Elbogen, "Von Graetz bis Dubnow" in *Das Breslauer Seminar*, ed. Guido Kisch (Tübingen: J.C.B. Mohr, 1963), 205–21. On the decision around 1950 by the Jewish Publication Society not to update Graetz any further, see the essay by Solomon Grayzel in the same collection, "Graetz in America," with the relevant discussion on 237.
24. A concise biographical sketch by Koppel Pinson is in Dubnow, *Nationalism and History*, ed. Koppel Pinson (New York: Atheneum, 1970), 3–39. On Dubnow's early years, see Robert Seltzer, "Simon Dubnow: A Critical Biography of His Early Years," Columbia University Ph.D. dissertation (1970). Graetz's influence is also discussed in Seltzer, "From Graetz to Dubnow: The Impact of the East European Milieu on the Writing of Jewish History," in *The Legacy of Jewish Migration*, ed. David Berger (New York: Brooklyn College Press, 1983), 49–60. One volume of Dubnow's autobiography, covering the period through 1890, was translated into Hebrew, *Sefer HaHayim* (Tel Aviv: Devir, 1936).
25. References to the introduction are from "The Sociological View of Jewish History" reprinted in *Nationalism and History*, 336–53. Quotation is on 337.
26. Ibid., 349.
27. Ibid., 350–51.
28. Ibid., 336.
29. Ibid., 338–40.
30. Ibid., 338.
31. Ibid., 343–44.
32. Ibid., 345–51; quotation is on 346.
33. Baron, "Jost the Historian," 240–62.
34. Ibid., 261.
35. As he was by Baron in the *Social and Religious History*.
36. Baron, "Jost the Historian," 245–46.
37. Ibid., 254–55.

38. Ibid., 258.
39. See, for example, the use of the word with regard to American Jewry in various essays in the collection *Steeled by Adversity*.
40. "Azariah de' Rossi's Attitude to Life" (1927); "Azariah de' Rossi's Historical Method" (1928–29); "Azariah de' Rossi: A Biographical Sketch" (1929). The three essays were reprinted together in *Jewish Historians*, 167–239.
41. "De' Rossi's Attitude to Life," 198.
42. Baron, "Graetz and Ranke: A Methodological Study," *Jewish Historians*, 269–75, and "Heinrich Graetz: A Biographical Sketch," *Jewish Historians*, 263–69.
43. Thus, there have appeared in recent decades several studies on Graetz's intellectual involvement in the religious controversies of the day; the many accounts of Graetz's role in the controversy with Treitschke; and the renewed interest in his friendship with early Zionist thinker Moses Hess.
44. For example in the 1964 preface to *Jewish Historians*, xiv.
45. Baron, "Graetz and Ranke: A Methodological Study," *Jewish Historians*, 271–72.
46. Baron, "Graetz and Ranke," 273, and again in "Heinrich Graetz: A Biographical Sketch," 263–69; this reference is on 267.
47. Dubnow had referred to Graetz's approach as *Geistes-und Leidensgeschichte*. See the previous section.
48. Baron, "American Jewish History: Problems and Methods," reprinted in *Steeled by Adversity*, 32.
49. "Emphases in Jewish History," *Jewish Historians*, 76.
50. The same essay was presented and published in another forum, totally divorced from the Dubnow context. "World Dimensions of Jewish History," *Jewish Historians*, 23.
51. See, for example, the reference in Baron's 1939 essay "Emphases in Jewish History," 78.

    But Dubnow's political thinking *was* important to Baron. In fact, Dubnow's political views were of crucial significance in the development of Baron's positions as reflected especially in both the *Social and Religious History* and *The Jewish Community*. I discuss this thesis later.
52. *Literarische Wochenschrift* (Berlin, 1926), 72–73.
53. "World Dimensions of Jewish History," 23.

54. "Emphasis in Jewish History," 77.
55. Ibid., p. 78.
56. "Simon Dubnow's Historical Approach," *Bitzaron* 2 (1940): 212–15; quotation is on 213.
57. On Dubnow's relations and ideological exchanges with Ahad Ha'am, see Robert Seltzer, "Ahad Ha-Am and Dubnow: Friends and Adversaries," in *At the Crossroads, Essays on Ahad Ha-am,* ed. Jacques Kornberg (Albany: SUNY Press, 1983), 60–72.
58. Baron, *A Social and Religious History of the Jews* (New York: Columbia University Press, 1937), v; hereafter, abbreviated in the text and notes as *SRH*.
59. Interview of 10 May 1989.
60. Columbia University Rare Book and Manuscript Library, Herbert Schneider Collection, Box 1, Loorland to Schneider, 29 March 1934, with enclosures.
61. Stanford, Box 8, Folder 14. Edman sent an excerpt of the letter to Baron with a comment in the margin: "from letter from Viking Press. Sorry I. Edman." The document is undated, so that it could have pertained to publication of *The Jewish Community* with which Baron also had some difficulties, but more attempts were required to place the *SRH*. In April 1935, Baron proposed the work to another commercial publisher, whose response I did not find. Stanford, Box 8, Folder 10 (D), Baron to E. P. Dutton, 2 April 1935.
62. Columbia University Rare Book and Manuscript Library, Columbia University Press Collection (hereafter CU Press Collection), Box 13, "Baron, Social and Religious History, 1935"; Memorandum for the File, 8 May 1935. On the press in general, see Henry H. Wiggins, *Columbia University Press: 1893–1983* (New York: Columbia University Press, 1983).
63. CU Press Collection, Proffitt to Schneider, 6 June 1935.
64. CU Press Collection, Preliminary Editorial Report, 25 May 1935.
65. CU Press Collection, Memorandum for the File, 27 May 1935.
66. CU Press Collection, Geddes to Proffitt, 27 May 1935.
67. CU Press Collection, Proffitt to Baron, 28 May, and Proffitt to Schneider, 31 May 1935.
68. CU Press Collection, Proffitt to Schneider, 6 June 1935.
69. CU Press Collection, Proffitt to Schneider, 19 June 1935.
70. CU Press Collection, Geddes to Proffitt, 14 June 1935.

71. CU Press Collection, Memorandum from Proffitt to Ansley and Spur, 11 October 1935.

72. CU Press Collection, Proffitt to Baron, 2 December 1935, and Memorandum for the File, 6 December 1935.

73. CU Press Collection, Wiggins to Baron, 17 December, and Proffitt to Baron, 18 December 1935.

74. CU Press Collection, Box 13, "Baron, S.W. Social and Religious History of the Jews. 1936." Baron to Wiggins, 6 February 1936.

75. CU Press Collection, Read to Wiggins, 12 March 1936.

76. CU Press Collection, Baron to Proffitt, 23 March 1936.

77. CU Press Collection, Wiggins to Baron, 27 March 1936.

78. CU Press Collection, Wiggins to Read, 27 March 1936.

79. CU Press Collection, Proffitt to Read, 6 April 1936. Concerning the reference to critics' reports, no such reports were found within the relevant files.

80. CU Press Collection, Read to Wiggins, 4 May; Wiggins to Read, 6 and 11 May 1936.

81. CU Press Collection, Wiggins to Read, 6 May 1936.

82. CU Press Collection, Read to Wiggins, 12 May 1936.

83. CU Press Collection, Wiggins to Read, 25 May 1936.

84. CU Press Collection, "Office Memorandum Concerning Baron: Jews and Judaism," 5 June 1936.

85. CU Press Collection, Baron to Wiggins, 14 June 1936.

86. CU Press Collection, Read to Wiggins, 22 June 1936.

87. CU Press Collection, Wiggins to Read, 24 June 1936.

88. CU Press Collection, Read to Wiggins, 25 July 1936.

89. CU Press Collection, Wiggins to Read, 29 July 1936. Even at this late juncture, in early August 1936, Baron received some nine full pages of detailed comments, criticisms, suggestions, and corrections from Alexander Marx, based on the galleys. Indeed, Baron thanked Marx in the preface for reading the page proofs. As far as I can tell, Baron did not incorporate any of these changes into the final product. Nor was there any indication that he proposed to the press making any further changes in the text itself. Library of the Jewish Theological Seminary of American (JTS), Archive no. 80, Alexander Marx Collection, Box 18, Salo Baron File.

90. CU Press Collection, Box 13, 1935 file, Wiggins to Read, 26 December 1935.

91. CU Press Collection, 1936 file, Proffitt to Baron, 31 July 1936.
92. CU Press Collection, Baron to Proffitt, 3 August 1936.
93. CU Press Collection, Proffitt to Baron, 7 August 1936.
94. Carlton Hayes, *A Political and Cultural History of Modern Europe* (New York: Macmillan, 1936).
95. This primary association of Baron with social history was also probably due in part to his intensive involvement with the Conference on Jewish Social Studies and its journal, but note might be taken that he was almost as involved in the leadership of the American Academy for Jewish Research, which was usually identified with intellectual themes.
96. *SRH*, 1: 3–4. Later in his 1939 methodological essay "Emphases in Jewish History," Baron referred to his socioreligious approach, cautioning that the approach could not be generalized. In his latter-day musings on the historical discipline, Baron ventured into a more universal construction of the theme. *The Contemporary Relevance of History* (New York: Columbia University Press, 1986), 66–94.
97. *SRH*, 1: 26–31.
98. *The Jewish Community*, 1: 5–8; 3: 3–4.
99. Stanford, Box 7, Folder 5, Outgoing, 1928–29, Baron to Ginzberg, 29 January 1929. Still, in a reflective footnote and also in one of our interviews, Baron recalled that during the 1920s he had contemplated writing a book on "Jewish History in the Light of Numbers." The anecdote provides the earliest indication I have found that Baron was contemplating an encompassing work of Jewish history.

Of related interest, I think, is Baron's comment in the preface that he had consulted the most recent secondary literature: "Well over three-fourths of all the secondary literature mentioned in Volume III was published in 1930 or since then." *SRH*, 1: vii. Thus, much of his bibliographic research was completed starting in 1930.
100. *SRH*, 1: v.
101. Stanford, Box 8, Folder 10 (D), Baron to E. P. Dutton, 2 April 1935.
102. Stanford, Box 5, Folder 13 (Fackenthal). Letter Baron to Fackenthal, 27 December 1929. This letter was not mailed as explained in letter to Hayes, 16 January 1930.
103. Stanford, Box 5, Folder 15, 25 February 1930.

Notes to Chapter 4

1. Roth's review entitled, "A Great Historical Work," *Menorah Journal* 26 (1938): 248–50.
2. *Jewish Quarterly Review,* New Series 29 (1938–39): 45–50.
3. *Jewish Social Studies* 1 (1939): 125–27.
4. Dubnow's review appeared in *Die Zunkunft* 42 (1937): 765–68. I wish to express my gratitude to David Fishman and Paula Rubinick for their help in making the Yiddish review accessible to me.
5. The review appeared in *Revue Des Études Juives,* New Series 2 (1937): 141–43.
6. *Revue Des Études Juives,* New Series 4 (1938): 139–46.
7. Baer, *Kiryath Sefer* 15 (1938–39): 201–2. The longer review was in *Zion* 3 (1938): 277–99.
8. Baer, *Zion,* 278–80. The English summary repeated the paradox. "Baron picked out for himself, out of the first chapters of the history of Israel, that fixed program into which he fits the history of the captivity to this very day. But . . . the Jewish historian must discover, in the Biblical period, the *inner forces* ordained to continue and act under the various and changing conditions of the later periods. It is impossible to define and enclose the richness of historical life in rigid definitions" (emphasis in original). Obviously, the problem was not so much with "fixed programs" as with insufficient emphasis on "inner forces."
9. Ibid., 291.
10. Stanford, Box 11, Folder 7, Baer to Baron, Sukkot, 1938; and Box 20, Folder 10, Baron to Baer, 12 October 1938.
11. Gandz's review appeared in *Isis* 29 (1938): 148–50; Ephraim Fischoff in *American Sociological Review* 3 (1938): 419–20; Heichelheim in *Classical Weekly* 31 (1937–38): 154–55.
12. H. H. Hyvernat of the Catholic University of America, *Catholic Historical Review* 24 (1938–39): 80–81.
13. Both citations from *Book Review Digest* 33 (1937–38): 58.
14. Hyvernat's remarks are in *Catholic Historical Review* 24 (1938–39). Also on the theme of Jewish survival are the remarks by Princeton's E. A. Beller, *Annals of the American Academy of Political and Social Science* 194 (1937): 232–33.
15. Upon reprinting the article in 1964, Baron put it this way: "The

author used this occasion to explain certain fundamental views which are implied in and illustrated by the first edition of his *Social and Religious History of the Jews."* Baron, "Emphases in Jewish History," 65–89.

16. However, in 1985, at the age of ninety, Baron finished what would be his last published book, *The Contemporary Relevance of History: A Study in Approaches and Methods* (New York: Columbia University Press, 1986). Baron's daughter, Tobey Gitelle, told me the following anecdote, which I assume was concerned with the publication of this work. The story seems so characteristic that it warrants retelling. In the course of preparing this book, Baron spent part of the time in Israel and filed a claim for a deductible travel expense. An IRS auditor, however, expressed the opinion that someone of Baron's age, then in his late eighties, could not still work actively at research. Baron then reportedly appealed the decision and brought in a copy of the newly published work as evidence to the contrary.

17. Baron, "Emphases in Jewish History," 66–67.

18. Ibid., 68.

19. Ibid., 69. At this point in the essay and without comment, Baron actually changed his periodical divisions as outlined in the preface to the *SRH.* Compare *SRH,* 1: vi.

20. Baron, "Emphases in Jewish History," 68–69. Indeed, it may be recalled that the original title of the work was simply "Jews and Judaism."

21. Ibid., 70–72.

22. Ibid., 73–75, and 346 n.6.

23. Ibid., 77.

24. Ibid., 77–78.

25. Ibid., 79–81.

26. Ibid., 82–83.

27. Ibid., 81–82.

28. Stanford, Box 11, Folder 5, letter from Rabbi Morton Berman, 15 February 1938.

29. CU Press Collection, "Baron: Social and Religious History, 1935–44," Friedman to Baron, 24 January 1938; Baron to Proffitt, 28 January; Geddes to Proffitt, 24 February.

30. CU Press Collection, FWB to Geddes, 17 May 1939.

31. CU Press Collection, Proffitt to Baron, 26 May 1939; CU Press

Collection, "Baron: Essays on Maimonides," Baron to Proffitt, 30 June 1939.

32. CU Press Collection, "Baron: Essays on Maimonides," Geddes to Wiggins, 22 August 1939.

33. Stanford, Box 16, Folder 9. Baron responded with a proposal for *The Jewish Community* and was given a contract, but when the manuscript was submitted, the editors found it too lengthy and excessively scholarly. We return to this exchange later.

34. CU Press Collection, "Baron: Social and Religious History, 1935–44", Proffitt to Schneider, 8 June 1938, and Schneider's response, 10 June.

35. These figures come from *SRH* file, 1935–44: memo of 4 August 1938, and various office memos of May 1939.

36. CU Press Collection, "SRH, 1944–46," especially Baron to Scanlon, 23 March 1946, and her response, 26 March; FWB to Scanlon, 3 May 1946. Subsequent memos are concerned only with a revised edition.

As satisfied as Columbia was with the sales record of Baron's *SRH,* it paled alongside that of the Jewish Publication Society's American edition of Graetz's *History.* Solomon Grayzel, medieval Jewish historian and longtime editor at JPS, reported the accumulative sales of the Graetz work to have reached "into many tens of thousands though their price was not particularly low." Unfortunately, early sales records had been lost and Grayzel's report was somewhat impressionistic, but he did indicate with greater reliance that "the annual sale between 1947 and 1957 has averaged five hundred, which is excellent for a work of such difficulty and expense." One important difference between the two was that Graetz's *History* became a popular Judaica gift item, whereas Baron's work remained primarily a work for scholars. Solomon Grayzel, "Graetz's History in America," *Das Breslauer Seminar,* ed. Guido Kisch (Tübingen: J.C.B. Mohr, 1963), 223–37. Sales discussion is on p. 232 and in n. 3, and in Jonathan Sarna, *JPS: The Americanization of Jewish Culture, 1888–1988* (Philadelphia: Jewish Publication Society, 1989), 34–39.

Notes to Chapter 5

1. *Menorah Journal* 31 (1943): 197.
2. AJA, Hurwitz Collection, Box 2, File 16, Baron to Hurwitz, 18

October 1933. In an interview with the author, Baron recalled incorrectly adopting his middle-name right after getting married; he did meet Jeannette Meisel around that same time. He explained to me that Americans like middle-names and that the addition would help keep his mail straight; there were more Barons in New York than he had thought. He had greatly admired his grandfather and wanted to perpetuate his memory through his writings. Perhaps that last argument was connected to the fact that in 1933 Baron was finishing an early draft of his *History*.

3. Jewish Theological Seminary of America, Ratner Center for the Study of Conservative Judaism, Records of the Jewish Theological Seminary of America, R.G. 1A–2-54.

4. Interview with Tobey Gitelle. AJA, Jewish Institute of Religion Records, Box 3, Folder 1 (Baron, 1925–30), has a letter from Canaan, July 1934.

5. Stanford, Box 8, Folder 1 (A).

6. Interview with Shoshanna Tancer.

7. The date of 1941 is based on personal interviews, but several documents indicate the more permanent move to Canaan was in 1942. Thus, for example, a letter to Morris Cohen in August 1942 mentions the move, Stanford, Box 20, Folder 27.

    A wartime description of Columbia provides an account of the Navy's presence from April 1942 through 1944, based on an agreement signed in February 1941 between the Navy and Columbia providing for the use of Columbia's buildings and facilities "if and when it is declared necessary by the Secretary of the Navy as a war measure." The current navy population at the time of publication in 1944 was 2,600 midshipmen, 350 officers, and 450 enlisted personnel. Fon Boardman, Jr., *Columbia: An American University in Peace and War* (New York: Columbia University Press, 1944), 63–82.

8. AJA, Hurwitz Collection, Box 2, File 17, Baron to Hurwitz, 28 September 1944.

9. The *New York Times*, 26 May 1975, copy in Columbiana Collection, Baron File.

10. Shoshanna Tancer thought this procedure of Baron dictating and Jeannette typing the text began later on, perhaps around 1963, when after his retirement Baron no longer had secretarial help.

11. *SRH* (2nd ed.), 13: v-vi.

12. This interpretation was suggested to me by Lloyd Gartner.

    Actually, Baron did have assistance in preparing the first edition of the *SRH,* as indicated quite explicitly in the preface to the work. Herbert Bloom was particularly involved in checking materials, and Beryl Levy with preliminary editing. Stanford, Box 7, Folder 2, Bloom to Baron, 13 July 1932.

13. Interview with Lloyd Gartner.

14. Interview with Shoshanna Eytan.

15. Interview with Tobey Gitelle.

16. Interviews with Lloyd Gartner, Tobey Gitelle, Shoshanna Tancer, and with Baron, May 1988.

17. JTS Library, Marx Collection, Box 18, Salo Baron File, Baron to Marx, August 1935.

18. Marx Collection, Baron File, letters of 24 April and 19 June 1940.

19. Interviews with Baron, May 1988, and Tobey Gitelle.

20. Library of Congress, Manuscript Division, Hannah Arendt Collection, Box 7, General Correspondence, Ba-Bi, 1944–75; Baron to Arendt, 10 June 1955, Arendt to Baron, 23 May 1965.

21. The following discussion has been informed especially by H. Stuart Hughes, *The Sea Change: The Migration of Social Thought, 1930–1965* (New York: Harper & Row, 1975); also, Paul Lazarsfeld, "An Episode in the History of Social Research: A Memoir," in *The Intellectual Migration,* ed. Donald Fleming and Bernard Bailyn (Cambridge, Mass.: Harvard University Press, 1969), 270–337; Franz Neumann, "The Social Sciences," in Neumann et al., *The Cultural Migration* (New York: A. S. Barnes, 1953), 4–26.

22. Marlene R. Schiffman, "The Library of the Jewish Institute of Religion, 1922–1950," *Jewish Book Annual* 48 (1990–91): 183–96.

    AJA, Hurwitz Collection, references in letters of 1928, 1929, 1933; see letter of 23 July 1928 for discussion of reactions to the "Ghetto" essay.

23. Stanford, Box 5, Folder 9, 28 December 1929.

24. Marx Collection, Baron to Marx, 3 June 1937.

25. See "A Bibliography of the Printed Writings of Salo Wittmayer Baron."

26. AJA, Hurwitz Collection, Box 2, File 16, Cohen to Baron, 11 May 1928.

27. Hughes, *Sea Change,* 29.

28. Ibid., 27–29.
29. Ibid., 27–34.
30. For several similar observations, see Alan Mintz's review essay of Susanne Klingenstein, *Jews in the American Academy, 1900–1940: The Dynamics of Intellectual Assimilation.* The review appeared in *New Republic,* 9 March 1992, 41–44.
31. Marcia Graham Synnot, *The Half-Opened Door: Discrimination and Admission at Harvard, Yale, and Princeton, 1900–1970* (Westport, Conn.: Greenwood Press, 1979), 128–29.
32. The issue of Jewish trustees is well covered in Harold Wechsler's important study on selective admissions, *The Qualified Student: A History of Selective College Admission in America* (New York: Wiley, 1977), 136–41.
33. Eli Ginzberg, *My Brother's Keeper* (New Brunswick: Transaction Press, 1989), 34.
34. Wechsler, *Qualified Student,* 66–71. Harvard actually preceded Columbia in this regard, but greater significance has been attached to Columbia's decisions due to its New York setting. This point is discussed shortly.
35. Wechsler, *Qualified Student,* 135.
36. Ibid., 136.
37. Ginzberg, *My Brother's Keeper,* 34.
38. Synnot, *The Half-Opened Door,* 201.
39. Ginzberg, *My Brother's Keeper,* 38–39. These points are also discussed in Ginzberg, "Jew and Negro: Notes on the Mobility of Two Minority Groups in the U.S.," *Salo Wittmayer Baron Jubilee Volume* (Jerusalem: American Academy for Jewish Research, 1975), 1:491–92, and "Occupational Mobility: A Personal Perspective," in *Philosophy, History and Social Action,* ed. S. Hook et al. (Dordrecht: Kluwer Academic, 1988), 210–12.
40. R. Gordon Hoxie, *History of the Faculty of Political Science Columbia University* (New York: Columbia University Press, 1955), v.
41. John Burgess, *Reminiscences of an American Scholar* (New York: Columbia University Press, 1934), 150–51, 191–92. In accordance with Burgess's plan, establishment of the School of Political Science was followed by the Academy of Political Science, organized in 1881, and in 1886 by the Political Science Quarterly. Hoxie, *Political Science,* 41–43.

42. Hoxie, *Political Science,* 10–11.
43. This discussion is based on Richard Hofstadter, "The Department of History," which appears in Ibid., 207–49; quotation is on 207–8.
44. Quoted in ibid., 208.
45. Ibid., 235–36.
46. Arthur Joseph Hughes, *Carlton J. H. Hayes: Teacher and Historian,* Columbia University Ph.D. thesis (1970), 97–117. Quotations are on 101 and 104.
47. On Hayes's involvements in the Catholic Historical Association, see Hughes, *Teacher and Historian,* 165–70.
48. Interview, August 1987.
49. Actually, Baron's concern in that talk was with the disparity between written documentation and eyewitness observations. Baron, *The Contemporary Relevance of History* (New York: Columbia University Press, 1986), 107, n.20.
50. Interview, August 1987.
51. *A Community of Scholars: The University Seminars at Columbia,* ed. Frank Tannenbaum (New York: Praeger, 1965).
52. *Religion and Democracy, Papers from the University Seminar on Religion: Columbia University,* 1946–47, ed. Horace L. Friess. Reprinted from the *Review of Religion,* January 1948.
53. Stanford, Box 1, Folder 13 (E), 15 January 1953.
54. Stanford, Box 2, Folder 3, B to H, 17 November 1953.
55. Communication from Harold J. Jonas, Goshen, N.Y., 6 November 1989.
56. Interview with Lloyd Gartner, 6 December 1989.
57. Stanford, Box 19, 1937–44, Incoming, Folder 16, Trachtenberg. Specific reference is to letter of 10 November 1937.
58. Stanford, Box 6, Unmarked Folder, Beryl H. Levy to Baron, n.d.
59. Interview with Moshe Davis, April 1990.
60. There are a number of files of correspondence with Bloom in the Stanford collection.
61. Joseph L. Baron Collection, State Historical Society of Wisconsin, Letters of 13 May and 5 June 1947.
62. This discussion is based on interviews with Salo Baron, May 1989; Lloyd Gartner, December 1989; Tobey Gitelle, August 1989; Shoshanna Tancer, July 1990.
63. See the discussions in chapter 3 on Baron's criticisms of Dubnow and

NOTES TO CHAPTER 5

the significance of emphasizing both social and religious historical approaches.

64. Baron's interview with Ankory; Ankory's interview with the author.

65. Author's interview with Hertzberg, January 1992. Moshe Davis described Baron's attitude toward Zionism in similar terms.

66. On the whole, this must have referred to the years in which Baron lived in New York, but it is also clear from his correspondence that during the Canaan period, Baron devoted a great deal of his New York days to organizational work.

67. "Emphases in Jewish History," 65.

68. AJA, Henry Hurwitz Collection, Box 2, Folder 16, Hurwitz to Baron, for example, 10 January 1930; 7 October 1932; 23 November 1932, but also *passim.*

69. AJA, Henry Hurwitz Collection, Box 63, Folder 7, Hurwitz to Wolfson, 30 August 1944.

70. AJA, Henry Hurwitz Collection, Box 12, Folder 2, Hurwitz to Finkelstein, 24 September 1940 and 10 April 1941.

71. The Nearprint Files at the AJA contain useful press clippings reporting on Baron's lectures. I refer to some of these articles later. On the trip to South Africa, see *South African Jewish News,* 12 July 1946.

   A flyer from the JWB Lecture Bureau included some reactions to Baron's lectures: "Excellent—brilliant. The best of all so far." "Excellent. Better during the discussion. Lecture packed full of matter." "Considered as the finest lecture given in Baltimore during the past few years."

72. Material on the conference as discussed in this section derives primarily from the organization's files, to which I was given free access. The conference moved its offices several times over the years of its history. For that and other reasons, the files are neither complete nor systematically arranged. My references are to filing cabinet, drawer, and folder, but these citations will probably be meaningless to any future researcher. The Conference's files are now deposited as Jewish Social Studies Records (M670), Special Collections, Stanford University.

73. Morris Cohen, *A Dreamer's Journey* (Boston: Beacon Press, 1949), 160–61.

74. Cabinet 1, Drawer 1, "Studies and Essays," undated letter and brochure, probably from 1933.

75. The diversified activities of the conference warrant more attention,

especially with regard to the Nazi years and the postwar period. This brief discussion cannot fill that need, but a study of American Jewish responses to antisemitism abroad and at home during that period should certainly include the conference as well.

76. On Cohen's life, see his autobiography *A Dreamer's Journey* (Boston: Beacon Press, 1949), and Leonora Cohen Rosenfield, *Portrait of a Philosopher: Morris R. Cohen in Life and Letters,* 2nd ed. (New York: Harcourt, Brace and World, 1962). For an important study of Cohen's life and thought, see David Hollinger, *Morris R. Cohen and the Scientific Ideal* (Cambridge, Mass.: M.I.T. Press, 1975).

77. Rosenfield, *Portrait of a Philosopher,* 220.

78. Cohen, *A Dreamer's Journey,* 241.

79. Cabinet 2, Drawer 1, Remarks by Morris Cohen, 7 February 1937, 13–15.

80. "The Conference on Jewish Social Studies, Inc. (A Brief Sketch)," n.d., but written sometime after 1980. Also instructive is a list of topics for public lectures offered in 1937 by then Executive Secretary Melvin Fagen: "The Position of the Jews in the International Crisis," "The Economic and Social Problems of the Jews in the United States," and "Can it Happen Here? Anti-Semitism in America." Cabinet 2, Drawer 1, "1937 CJR," Fagen to Janet Weisman, 28 September 1937.

81. Cohen, *A Dreamer's Journey,* 245–47.

82. On the American Jewish Committee during this period, see Naomi Cohen, *Not Free to Desist* (Philadelphia: Jewish Publication Society, 1972), 193–226.

83. Cabinet 2, Drawer 1, "1936–37 (Cohen)"; Reuben Ottenberg, "Survey of the Situation of German Jewish Physicians," 2 December 1934.

84. Cabinet 1 Drawer 1, "Studies and Essays."

85. "The Conference. A Brief Sketch"

86. Oscar Janowski and Melvin Fagen, *International Aspects of German Racial Policies* (New York: Oxford University Press, 1937).
   For a brief discussion on the mission, see Cohen, *Not Free to Desist,* 182–83. Relevant correspondence in conference files is in Cabinet 2, Drawer 1, "1935 Corr." Also "A Brief Sketch."

87. Around the same time as the dinner presided over by Einstein, Cohen wrote a somewhat critical review of *The World as I See It,* a collection

of Einstein's essays. Cohen concluded the piece with the comment, "Einstein's faith has the stirring and driving quality of all truly spiritual leaders who are in the world but not of it. *It needs to be supplemented by a more realistic vision of the brute actualities of our existence*" (my emphasis). The review was first published in the *Menorah Journal* in the spring of 1936 and reprinted in Cohen, *The Faith of a Liberal* (New York: Henry Holt, 1946), 46–56.

88. Cabinet 2, Drawer 1, Remarks by Morris Cohen at conference held on 7 February 1937, 3–4.

89. The research was collected and analyzed in a volume published by the conference: Sophia Robison, *Jewish Population Studies* (New York: Conference on Jewish Relations, 1943).

90. I found one direct indication of this influence in a 1938 letter that discussed a joint study with Pi Lambda Phi Fraternity on Jewish college students. The research was intended to provide a "'Middletown' type of study for minority groups." Robert Lynd was appointed chairperson of the committee involved. Conference Files, Cabinet 2, Drawer 1, Harry N. Rosenfield to Joseph Cohen with similar letter to others, 6 May 1938.

91. Cabinet 2, Drawer 1, "1938–CJR"

92. Cabinet 2, Drawer 2, "CJR, 1942–45", Minutes of meeting of 14 June 1943 with representatives of American Jewish Committee. Also letters in that file from October 1944 requesting support for conference's new projects.

93. That title appears in the Conference *Minutes,* 12. Baron's conditions are stated in a letter to Cohen of 12 January 1937. Stanford, Box 8, Morris R. Cohen File. Baron wrote to Cohen in this letter: "I am not anxious to serve as the editor of a journal, but only of one of the type and quality which I have often discussed with you."

94. Stanford, Box 7, Folder 11, copy of letter, Kohut to Wise, 25 April 1928. Also, Stanford, Box 7, 1929–33 Incoming/Outgoing, Folder 1, Kohut to Baron, 2 May 1928. Other relevant letters are in the Kohut files in Boxes 4 and 5. Harry Wolfson and Ralph Marcus apparently opposed the proposal.

95. Materials related to the forming of the journal come from Cabinet 2, Drawer 1, "1938 CJR." The JTA bulletin is included in the file.

96. *Loc. cit.,* Baron to Cohen, 17 July 1937.

97. *Loc. cit.,* Pinson to Baron, Tarnow, Poland, 9 July 1937.

98. *Loc. cit.,* Baron to Pinson, 30 July 1937.
99. *Loc. cit.,* Pinson to Baron, 10 August 1937.
100. *Loc. cit.,* Baron to Pinson, 26 August 1937.
101. Cohen, *A Dreamer's Journey,* 161; Rosenfield, *Portrait of a Philosopher,* 101ff.
102. Cabinet 2, Drawer 1, "Conference on Jewish Relations, 1937–38," letter of 15 March 1938 to the board of directors.
103. Minutes, 37.
104. Ibid., 25, 29.
105. Cabinet 2, Drawer 2, "1942 Hostesses," American Jewish Committee announcement of the panel discussion and pamphlet on their institute on postwar problems.
106. *Loc. cit.,* The American Jewish Committee, *Research Institute on Peace and Post-War Problems, Preliminary Announcement* (1941). On cooperation between the two organizations, see also the minutes of a joint meeting held on 14 June 1943, Cabinet 2, Drawer 2, "CJR, 1942–45."
107. This assumption is supported by Cohen in his memoirs, *A Dreamer's Journey,* 252.
108. Cabinet 2, Drawer 2, "1943 Operations."
109. Cabinet 2, Drawer 2, "1942–44 CJR."
110. Cabinet 2, Drawer 2, "CJR, 1942–45" and "JTCC, 1941, 42–43."
111. This last activity was undertaken jointly with the research institute. Cabinet 2, Drawer 1, "CJR, 1938–1944."
112. There are a few references to Jewish Cultural Reconstruction (JCR) in the conference files. The following discussion is based primarily on my interview with Baron, July 1988 and Ankory's interview, July 1987. Some papers from the fifties and sixties pertaining to JCR are in the Library of Congress, Hannah Arendt Collection. An extensive project to document the work of JCR has been undertaken by the Skirball Museum of the Hebrew Union College in Los Angeles.
113. Ankory interview, July 1987.
114. Conference Files, Cabinet 2, Drawer 1, "CJR 1938–39," letter from Rabbi William Rosenau of Baltimore; Littauer to Baron, 31 March 1942; Stanford, Box 16, Folder 14.

Notes to Chapter 6

1. *SRH*, 1:12. All references in this chapter are to the 1937 edition.
2. Baron, "An Historical Critique of the Jewish Community," *Jewish Social Service Quarterly* (September 1935): 44–49.
3. Baron may possibly have been responding to Louis Finkelstein's analysis of Rabbi Gershom's legal innovations when describing this widespread belief. In a subsequent printing, Finkelstein was more explicit when he referred to the "democratic self-government" of the Jewish community. Finkelstein, *Jewish Self-Government in the Middle Ages*, 2nd ed. (New York: Philipp Feldheim, 1964), xv, 15, 33–34, 49–55. Later, Baron was criticized by Yitzhak Baer for describing the community as nondemocratic. Baer, "Origins of the Organization of the Jewish Community of the Middle Ages," *Zion* 15:1–41 (Hebrew). On Baer's critique of Baron, see more in the epilogue later.
4. Baron, "Freedom and Constraint in the Jewish Community: An Historic Episode," in *Essays and Studies in Memory of Linda R. Miller*, ed. Israel Davidson (New York: Jewish Theological Seminary, 1938), 9–23; quotation is on 9.
5. Baron, "Democracy and Judaism," *Hadassah News Letter* (January 1938): 66–67.
6. JTS Library, Alexander Marx Collection, Baron to Marx, 19 July 1938.
7. *Loc. cit.*, Baron to Marx, 24 April 1940.
8. Stanford, Box 16, Folder 9. Correspondence with Alfred Knopf Inc., 10 February 1937, 30 March 1937, 6 February 1940.
9. JTS Library, Marx Collection, Baron to Marx, 19 June 1940, and Marx's response of 24 June.
10. Baron, *The Jewish Community*, 1: 5–8; 3: 3–4.
11. Ibid., 1: 28–29.
12. "Emphases in Jewish History," 85.
13. Baron, *The Jewish Community*, 1: viii.
14. Ibid., 1: 41.
15. Ibid., 1: 62–63.
16. Ibid., 1: 59.
17. Ibid., 1: 111.
18. Ibid., 1: 116.
19. Ibid., 3: 21, n. 1.

20. Ibid., 1: 206.
21. Ibid., 1: 284.
22. Ibid., 1: 216–26.
23. Ibid., 1: 227.
24. Ibid., 1: 266.
25. Ibid., 2: 123–24.
26. Ibid., 2: 208, 246
27. Ibid., 2: 180–81.
28. Ibid., 2: 361–62.
29. Stanford, Box 18, Folder 23, R. L. Schuyler to Baron, 3 April 1943.
30. Stanford, Box 11, Folder 20, letter from Abraham J. Brachman from Ft. Worth, Texas, 19 July 1943, and Baron's answer, Box 20, Folder 21, 17 August 1943.
31. *American Historical Review* 50 (1944): 103–4.
32. *Journal of Near Eastern Studies* 3 (1944): 106–7; also with some variations in *Church History* 12 (1943): 217–19.
33. *Church History* 12 (1943): 219.
34. *Catholic Historical Review* 30 (1944): 319–20.
35. *Menorah Journal* 31 (1943): 196–99.
36. *American Journal of Sociology* 49 (1943–44): 95–96.
37. Baron to Roth, 5 October 1943. Cecil Roth Collection, Leeds University Library, MS 266. My gratitude to David Katz for calling this letter to my attention.
38. Robert S. Lynd and Helen Merrell Lynd, *Middletown* (New York: Harcourt Brace and World, 1929), and *Middletown in Transition* (New York: Harcourt Brace and World, 1937); W. Lloyd Warner, *Yankee City* (New Haven: Yale University Press, 1941–59).
39. Baron, *The Jewish Community,* 1: vii; 3: 3. The Simpson work was a Columbia Ph.D. thesis written under the supervision of Robert McIver, defended in 1934 and published in 1937; George Simpson, *Conflict and Community: A Study in Sociological Theory* (New York: T. S. Simpson, 1937).
40. Baron, *The Jewish Community,* 1: 29–30.
41. Ibid., 1: 25.
42. *New York Times,* 18 May 1952, in AJA, Nearprint Files, Baron, Clippings.

Notes to Chapter 7

1. Thus Cecil Roth wrote that Baron had assumed "that the historian of today has inherited some shred of the mantle of the prophet of ages past." *Menorah Journal* 26 (1938): 249. Also, Ismar Elbogen described the epilogue as "a messianic hymn," and explained that it was beyond his task as an historian to take a stand on it. *Jewish Social Studies* 1 (1939): 127.

2. "Reflections on the Future of the Jews of Europe," *Contemporary Jewish Record* 3 (1940): 355–69; quotation is on 356.

3. AJA, Nearprint Files, Baron, Clippings. Even earlier, Baron sought to find support for European scholars. AJA, David Lefkowitz Collection, Box 1, Folder 2, letters from 5 November 1930 and 3 April 1931. At the time Lefkowitz was president of the Central Conference of American Rabbis.

4. CJR, Cabinet 2, Drawer 2, "CJR, 1942–45," Minutes of 14 June 1943. As noted earlier, conference leaders also proposed Alaska as a potential haven for those fleeing the Nazis.

5. Interview, May 1988. I took advantage of the opportunity to raise the question of Sombart's antisemitism and reported Nazi sympathies. Baron responded that he thought that what people say about his becoming a Nazi was not true. "He was a little bit of an opportunist." "Sombart was not an antisemite in the normal sense," and *Jews and Capitalism* was definitely not an antisemitic book.

   Elbogen's letter and Arendt's opening letter to Baron are in Stanford, Box 10, Folder 14, Arendt to Baron, 28 October 1941, and Box 13, Folder 5, letter from Elbogen, 23 October 1941. Johnson's correspondence is in Stanford, Box 15, Folder 11, "Johnson, Alvin (New School)."

6. JTS Library, Alexander Marx Collection, Box 18, Salo Baron File, 19 July 1938 and August 1939.

7. Although I did not succeed in locating the fuller documentation, an index to State Department records in the National Archives indicates Baron's name as sponsor for at least four cases during the years 1940–41. National Archives, State Department Records, Card Catalogue.

8. The requests from the two Barons are in Stanford, Box 11, Folder 1, Ba-Be, 24 October 1938. Baron's reply is in Box 20, Folder 8 (B), letter of 17 November 1938. Box 8, Folder: Emergency Committee

for Displaced German Scholars, contains about five letters, all of which relate only to Guido Kisch. Stanford, Box 10, Folder 17: Rabbi Julius Augapfel. These letters are from September to November 1938. Other letters are in Box 20, Folder 1, and other locations.

9. AJA, Hurwitz Collection, Box 2, File 17, 13 September 1941. Stanford, Box 10, Folder 9, letters from American Jewish Joint Distribution Committee, 2 and 10 September 1942, indicate that in May 1941, Baron had made a deposit to the Transmigration Bureau of the Joint for passage of his cousins Emil and Rivla Rosenkranz from Prague. References to Rosenblatt are in Box 20, Folder 1. Baron's remarks are from 12 May 1943.

10. Interviews with Shoshanna Eytan, February 1991, and Zvi Ankory, May 1991.

11. Stanford, Box 20, Folder 13, Baron to his father, 3 January 1940. In this letter, Baron requests direct information and explains that until now, he has only heard through others.

12. Cohn's letters are in Stanford, Box 12, Folder 4 (Cohn); Baron's, Box 20, Folder 28.

13. Correspondence with the State Department is in Stanford, Box 12, Folder Baron, Elias and Minna, and in Box 21, Folder 3.

14. This account is based on the entries in *Encyclopedia of the Holocaust* 4: 1451–1454; *Pinkas HaKehilot: Poland*, 3: 178–190.

15. What happened to the Barons themselves has been related to me by Eytan and Ankory and compiled by them from several different sources.

16. "Germany's Ghetto, Past and Present," *Independent Journal of Columbia University* 3, No. 3 (15 November 1935).

17. *SRH*, Epilogue, 2: 418–31.

18. "Reflections on the Future of the Jews of Europe," *Contemporary Jewish Record* 3 (1940): 355–69.

19. "The Future of European Jewry," *Jewish Forum* (October 1940): 164–65, 171.

20. "American and Jewish Destiny: A Semimillennial Experience," in *Steeled by Adversity*, 16–25; quotation is on 16.

21. *The Effect of the War on Jewish Community Life* (New York: Harry L. Glucksman Memorial Lecture, 1942), 13. The reference was to *Bibliography of Jewish Social Studies, 1938–39* (New York: Conference on Jewish Relations, 1941).

22. AJA, Nearprint Clippings File, *New York Post,* 18 November 1940.
23. AJA, Nearprint, Biographies, Baron.
24. JTS Library, Marx Collection, Box 18, Baron to Marx, 16 September 1940.
25. David S. Wyman, *The Abandonment of the Jews: America and the Holocaust, 1941–1945* (New York: Pantheon Books, 1984), especially 25 and 66, on the conviction that winning the war was the most effective, possibly the only hope of saving Europeans Jews. The discussion on the Zionists is on 157–77. There Wyman concluded that by 1943 the Zionists found themselves in the position of choosing between applying limited resources to the more plausible achievement of Zionist goals or the nearly hopeless task of rescue, as demonstrated by the utter failure of the Bermuda Conference of April 1943. "As limited as Zionist resources were, it seemed reasonable to concentrate them on the possible rather than on what appeared to be a nearly hopeless cause" (176–77).
26. The bibliography of his writings virtually leaps from entry 91 at the beginning of 1939 to 188 by the end of 1945. See "A Bibliography of the Printed Writings of Salo Wittmayer Baron."
27. Actually Hurwitz had requested permission to print a chapter from the forthcoming work on the Jewish community. Baron suggested instead that he "place at your disposal an original article which would retain its value for a number of years." AJA, Hurwitz Collection, Box 2, File 17, 13 September 1941. The article was published in the *Menorah Journal* 30 (1942): 116–38, and reprinted in *Jewish Historians,* 43–64. Citations here are to the latter.
28. "Modern Capitalism," 43–48. For Sombart's thesis, see *The Jews and Modern Capitalism* (Glencoe, Ill.: Free Press, 1951).
29. "Modern Capitalism," 48–52.
30. Ibid., 52–54.
31. Ibid., 56.
32. Ibid., 56–62.
33. Ibid., 62–64.
34. Baron's major essays on the medieval period are collected in *Ancient and Medieval Jewish History,* ed. Leon A. Feldman (New Brunswick, N.J.: Rutgers University Press, 1972).
35. "Yehudah Halevi: An Answer to a Historical Challenge," in *Ancient and Medieval Jewish History,* 128–48.

36. Ibid, 133–34.
37. Ibid., 148.
38. "Saadia's Communal Activities," in *Jewish Historians*, 95–127.
39. "Rashi and the Community of Troyes," in *Jewish Historians*, 268–83; quotation is on 275.
40. *The Jewish Community*, 1: 150, 155; 2: 243–44. Other references include 1: 346; 2: 50–51, 205–7.
41. And yet, at least the written version contains no reference at all to Pearl Harbor, although the lecture was delivered only three weeks after the event. The essay is in *Ancient and Medieval Jewish History*, 239–67.
42. "Jewish Factor," 258–59; Baron had expressed similar ideas in his 1935 essay "Germany's Ghetto, Past and Present," mentioned earlier.
43. *Ancient and Medieval Jewish History*, 513–14, n. 54.
44. "The Economic Views of Maimonides," in *Ancient and Medieval Jewish History*, 232.
45. Examples include a dictum against Jews becoming a public charge, Maimonides' insistence that sufficient time be devoted to the study of Torah, and discussions on the requirements for a just price in merchandise.

    Yet, note should be taken of Baron's remark in a footnote to "The Jewish Factor," that "a clearer knowledge of the social teachings of rabbinic Judaism in their historical development seems to be one of the urgent tasks for contemporary scholarship" (509, n. 38).
46. AJA, Hurwitz Collection, Baron letter of 13 September 1941. Baron requested two cents a word for an estimated seven to ten thousand words. Hurwitz response, 3 October.
47. *Loc. cit.*, letters of 16 and 19 January 1942.
48. References in this discussion are to AJA, Hurwitz Collection, letters of 8 October, 7 and 10 November 1941; 16, 19, 20, 23 January, and 10 April 1942. Most of these letters are actually several pages long.
49. *Cyrus Adler: Selected Letters*, ed. Ira Robinson, 2 vols. (Philadelphia: Jewish Publication Society, 1985), 2: 360–61.
50. Stanford, Box 5, Folder 38 (Y-Z), Baron to Zeitlin, 21 February 1928.
51. An earlier discussion was in a review essay entitled "Maimonides," *JQR* 27 (1937–38): 276–77, and the review now under discussion,

"The Main Institutions of Jewish Law," *JQR* 32 (1941–42), with the section on Baron, 107–14.

52. *JQR* 32 (1941–42): 321–25.
53. Ibid., 326–36.
54. Ibid., 336. Zeitlin repeated the accusation on a different issue in *JQR* 34 (1943–44): 378–79.
55. *JQR* 34 (1943–44): 371–84.
56. Ibid., 384.
57. Baron, "An Historical Critique of the Jewish Community," *Jewish Social Service Quarterly* (September 1935): 44–49.
58. *SRH*, 2 (1937 ed.): for example, 365, 432.
59. Ibid., 364–462.
60. Ibid., 461, his emphasis.
61. Ibid., 433.
62. Baron, "Democracy and Judaism," 66–67.
63. *The Jewish Community*, 1: 25.
64. *Effect of the War on Jewish Community Life.*
65. *Cultural Problems of American Jewry* (New York: Jewish Welfare Board, 1939).
66. *Effect of the War*, 7.
67. Ibid., 12–13.
68. "At the Turning Point," *Menorah Journal* 33 (1945): 1–10.
69. AJA, Hurwitz Collection, Box 2, Folder 17, Hurwitz to Baron, 18 January 1945.
70. Rabbi Irving F. Reichert, Congregation Emanu-El, 15 August 1945; AJA, Nearprint, Baron, Clippings.
71. AJA, Nearprint, Baron, Clippings.
72. *New York Times*, 2 December 1946, AJA, Nearprint, Baron, Clippings.
73. *New York Times*, 6 May 1946, AJA, Nearprint, Baron, Clippings.
74. *South African Jewish News*, 12 July 1946; AJA, Nearprint, Baron, Clippings.
75. Arnold Eisen, *The Chosen People in America: A Study in Jewish Religious Ideology* (Bloomington: Indiana University Press, 1983), 147.
76. JTSA Records, R.G. 1A-2–54, 7 January 1943.
77. Baron explained in an interview that Jeannette's modesty was the reason other publications did not bear a joint byline. Interview with Zvi Ankory, July 1987, Diaspora Museum.

78. "American Jewish History: Problems and Methods," in *Steeled by Adversity,* 32.

79. Baron, "A Documentary History of the Jews," in *Steeled by Adversity,* 74–79; quote is on 76.

80. Both essays are in *Steeled by Adversity;* the emancipation essay on 80–105; "Palestinian Messengers in America, 1849–79," 158–266.

81. Baron, "American Jewish History: Problems and Methods," in *Steeled by Adversity,* 26–73, 32.

82. Ibid., 9.

83. Minutes of the Executive Council of the American Jewish Historical Society from 15 February 1953 to 13 February 1955. I am grateful to the late Nathan Kaganoff, librarian of the society, for his extensive efforts to locate this material for me.

84. Arthur Goren places the tercentenary celebration in broader context in "A 'Golden Decade' for American Jews, 1945– 1955," *Studies in Contemporary Jewry* 8 (1992): 3–20. My appreciation to Goren for an advanced copy of his manuscript.

85. See the Goren essay for an illuminating discussion of the celebration and the resulting criticism.

86. *The Writing of American Jewish History,* ed. Moshe Davis and Isidore Meyer (New York: American Jewish Historical Society, 1957); Baron's remarks are on 137–40; Dinur's are on 196–209.

87. Material pertaining to this period are in CJS Files, Cabinet 1, Drawers 1 and 2. The historians' conference was organized by Moshe Davis; the social science meetings by Werner Cahnman.

88. Stanford Special Collections, Box 54 — Canaan contains the following documentation: Pinchas Rosen to Benjamin Eliav, 26 December 1960; Eliav to Baron, 7 February 1961; Hausner to Baron, 20 March 1961.

89. Interviews with Baron, May 1988; and Shoshanna Eytan, April 1990.

90. Author's interview with Hertzberg, January 1992.

91. "European Jewry Before and After Hitler" appeared in the *American Jewish Year Book,* vol. 63 (New York and Philadelphia: American Jewish Committee/Jewish Publication Society, 1962). Subsequent references are from *The Castastrophe of European Jewry* (Jerusalem: Yad Vashem, 1976), 175–239.

92. *European Jewry,* 177.

93. The demographic and economic discussions are in ibid., 177–187.

94. Ibid., 187–93.
95. Ibid., 193–203.
96. Ibid., 203–16.
97. Ibid., 215.
98. Ben Gurion's Diary, entry of 10 April 1961, Ben Gurion Archive, S'de Boqer. I wish to express my special gratitude to Zacki Shalom for calling this passage to my attention.
99. *European Jewry,* 216–27.
100. Ibid., 227–33.
101. This exchange is reprinted in ibid., 233–39.
102. Hannah Arendt, *Eichmann in Jerusalem* (New York: Viking Press, 1963), 96–97.
103. Ibid., 131–34.
104. In 1947, Baron wrote Louis Finkelstein that he was "under contract with my publisher to submit during the next academic year a completely revised ms. of my Social and Religious History." JTSA Records, R.G. 1D-56–42–1947, 8 July 1947. As noted earlier, in 1961 he related to David Ben Gurion that the work would extend to twenty volumes. I recall a reference to a projected thirty volumes the one year I studied with Baron in 1968–69. Also, *New York Times,* 26 May 1975, interview on Baron's eightieth birthday.
105. *The Contemporary Relevance of History* (New York: Columbia University Press, 1986).

Notes to the Epilogue

1. The following references will give a sense of the gradual change in conception. In July 1947, Baron wrote to Louis Finkelstein that he was under contract with his publisher to submit a completely revised manuscript of the *SRH* during the next academic year. But in November 1950, Baron wrote to Finkelstein: "I am far from sure that I could assume the task in view of my numerous other commitments and particularly my obligation to complete the revision of my Social and Religious History in the next three or four years." When the first two volumes appeared in 1952, Baron's former student Abraham Duker indicated that the work was then being planned for six volumes, yet he also predicted that it would reach nine or ten. In 1961, Baron informed David Ben Gurion that the finished work

would comprise some twenty volumes and that he would require fifteen more years to complete it. The letters to Finkelstein are in Jewish Theological Seminary Records, R.G. 1D-56–42–1947 and R.G. 1F-82–30–1950. Duker's remarks are in *JWB Circle,* April 1952. Ben Gurion's Diary, entry of 10 April 1961, Ben Gurion Archive, S'de Boqer.

There are several possible explanations for the continual expansion of the work. Unfortunately, they are all speculative. It is clear that Baron sought to be considered as successor to Graetz and Dubnow. As such, the recurring critique that the first edition represented a series of essays and required considerable expansion to become a *History of the Jews* may have been a driving influence. Baron alluded to such a formulation in his 1938 response to Zeitlin. On a far more prosaic level, Baron once half-jokingly explained in one of our sessions that the work was ordered primarily by libraries with standing orders and that there was interest in increasing the number of volumes in order to increase the income.

2. Ellis Rivkin, "The Writing of Jewish History," *The Reconstructionist* (June 1962).

3. Roth's reviews appeared in *Jewish Social Studies* (*JSS*), which edited by Baron himself, resulted in several awkward situations. *JSS* 20: 102–3; 21: 246–47; Baron's communication and Roth's response in 22: 125–26; and a brief notice of the index volume in 25: 92.

4. It seems rather striking that Baron's first real defense of the concept came in his 1942 essay on the "Jewish Factor in Medieval Civilization," thus supporting my contention that his wartime fascination with the medieval period was directly related to the Nazi phenomenon and specifically to distinguishing between the two.

5. Thus, in one case, Baron ridiculed the use of the lachrymose idea to explain the disappearance of Talmudic manuscripts. In a far more positive vein, he explained how it had been harnessed to foster the ideal of continued Jewish survival despite the suffering in Jewish history. Some references in the second edition include: 4: 146–47; 6: 194; 9:71; 11: 4ff., 282.

6. *Ancient and Medieval Jewish History,* 513–14. In response to Baer, Baron wrote that "I am still unable to locate any antisemitic forerunners; and, to the best of my knowledge, I was the first to coin the term 'lachrymose conception,' when my scholarly conscience (perhaps

also, subconsciously, pride in the Jewish heritage) made me impatient with the eternal self-pity characteristic of Jewish historiography."

7. *Jewish Historians,* 96. The statement that speaking generally Baron had been using the term for over forty years would seem to indicate that he had opposed the lachrymose conception from the beginning of his career.

8. I have dealt with this theme in my forthcoming, "Post- Emancipation Historiography and the Jewish Historical Societies of America and England," *Studies in Contemporary Jewry* 10 (1995).

9. "Historical Parallels in Jewish History," in *Structure of Jewish History,* 259–74.

10. Baron discussed the Russian migration movements in the first edition of *SRH,* 2: 264–66; and *The Russian Jew Under Tsars and Soviets,* 84–89; quotation is on 86–87.

11. On Zionism, see *SRH,* 2: 307–10. The description in *The Russian Jew,* 172–81, does not deal with these interpretative questions.

12. Perhaps the best-known example in twentieth-century historiography of seeking to sever the course of Jewish history from antisemitic causation factors can be found in the work of Gershom Scholem concerning the rise of the Sabbatian messianic movement in the seventeenth century. Scholem argued at length and convincingly against the popular and well-established historical linkage between the pogroms in Poland in 1648–49 and Sabbatianism. But in the course of his work, Scholem came to place tremendous significance on the Spanish expulsion of 1492 and its influence on the nature of Lurianic Kabbalah, which in turn provided the stimulus for Sabbatian messianism. As Scholem's thinking developed, the expulsion became for him a moment of powerful impact in the course of Jewish history.

The contradiction in Scholem's work can be answered in part on at least two grounds. First, Scholem had not expounded a theoretical position against the role of tragedy or suffering as historical causation. Rather, he seemed to view the Chelminiki pogroms as more of a local affair and the Spanish expulsion of global Jewish significance. Second, Scholem did not maintain that the expulsion had actually caused the messianic movement, but rather that it had ignited a process of religious change that in turn provided the causal effect. Still, a close examination of Scholem's objections to the Chelminiki connection with the rise of Sabbatianism will still raise some of the same questions if applied to a possible causal linkage with Spanish expuslion. See especially Scholem, *Sabbatai Sevi* (Princeton: Princeton University Press, 1973), 1–3.

13. Newer Emphases in Jewish History," 100.
14. The two essays—" 'Plenitude of Apostolic Powers' and Medieval 'Jewish Serfdom' " and "Medieval Nationalism and Jewish Serfdom"—appeared in 1960 and 1962, respectively, and are reprinted in *Ancient and Medieval Jewish History*, 284–307, 308–22.
15. Stanford, Box 5, Folder 35, Baron to Mrs. Wise, 28 December 1929.
16. *SRH*, 1st ed., 2: 40
17. Baron, *Jewish Historians*, 267.
18. Ibid., 78
19. See, for example, *SRH*, 2: 106.
20. Scholem, *Sabbatai Sevi*, 1–8. For a summary of the literature and for one response to Scholem on this point, see Stephen Sharot, *Messianism, Mysticism, and Magic* (Chapel Hill: University of North Carolina Press, 1982).
21. Jacob Neusner, *Why Does Judaism Have an Economics?* The Inaugural Saul Reinfeld Lecture in Judaic Studies (New London: Connecticut College, 1988). The last reference is to 27–28.
22. His 1962 "World Dimensions of Jewish History" and 1963 "Newer Emphases in Jewish History" were both reprinted in *Jewish Historians*.
23. Stanford, Box 20, Folder 10, Baron to Baer, 12 October 1938.
24. Louis Finkelstein, *Jewish Self-Government in the Middle Ages,* 2nd ed. (New York: Philipp Feldheim, 1964), xv, 15, 33–34, 49–55. Baer, "Origins," 1–41.

Katz's views are best expressed in *Out of the Ghetto* (Cambridge, Mass.: Harvard University Press, 1973), especially chapter 3, a restatement of his earlier *Tradition and Crisis.* This work, which asserts that the major transition toward modernity took place only after 1770, is primarily an argument again Baron's periodization of the modern period, but fails to mention that fact, occasionally targeting works by Shmuel Ettinger and Ezriel Shohet instead. Katz reduces the question to whether or not the changes that were admittedly taking place during earlier times were enacted consciously.

There were also Israeli historians who were in some ways quite close to Baron's historical outlook, especially Yehezkel Kaufmann. Ismar Schorsch has developed this suggestion in "The Last Jewish

Generalist," *AJS Review* 8 (1993): 39–50. I expect to further discuss Baron in the context of Israeli historians in a forthcoming essay in Hebrew.

25. The history department at Ben Gurion University, of which at the time of writing I am the chair, is the sole exception to this practice in Israel.

26. Library of Congress, Manuscript Division, Hannah Arendt Collection, Box 7, General Correspondence, Ba-Bi, 1944–75, 23 May 1965.

BIBLIOGRAPHY OF
PRIMARY SOURCES

A bibliography of Baron's published works is available in *Salo Wittmayer Baron Jubilee Volume,* 3 vols. (Jerusalem: American Academy for Jewish Research, 1974), 1: 1–37.

Archival and Library Collections

American Jewish Archives, Cincinnati
    Salo Baron Nearprint File
    Hyman Enelow Collection
    Henry Hurwitz/Menorah Association Collection
    JIR Collection
American Jewish Historical Society, Waltham, Mass.
    Minutes of Annual Meetings and Executive Council
Columbia University Central Files
    Mrs. Nathan J. Miller File
    F.J.E. Woodbridge File
Columbia University Rare Book and Manuscript Library
    Nicholas Butler Collection
    Carlton Hayes Collection
    Columbia University Press Collection

Horace Friess Collection
Herbert W. Schneider Collection
Columbia University Library, Columbiana Room
Salo Baron File
Conference on Jewish Social Studies—office records (these files are now deposited as "Jewish Social Studies Records" [M670], Special Collections, Stanford University)
Jewish Institute of Religion, New York City
Minutes of Meetings of the Faculty and Faculty Committees
Jewish Theological Seminary of America, New York City
Rare Book Room
American Academy for Jewish Research Collection
Louis Ginzberg Collection
Alexander Marx Collection
Ratner Center for the Study of Conservative Judaism, Records of the Jewish Theological Seminary of America
Library of Congress, Washington, D.C., Manuscript Division
Hannah Arendt Collection
Stanford University Library, Special Collections
Salo Baron Collection
U.S. National Archives, State Department Records
State Historical Society of Wisconsin, Archives Division
Joseph Baron Collection

Interviews by Other Institutions

American Jewish Committee, William E. Wiener Oral History Libary, interview with Salo Baron, by Chaim Potok, 1987
Museum of the Diaspora, Tel Aviv, interview with Salo Baron, by Zvi Ankory, July 1987

Author-conducted Interviews

Zvi Ankory, May 1991
Salo Baron, August 1987; May 1988; 26 July 1988; 8 August 1988; 10 May 1989
Moshe Davis, April 1990
Shoshanna Eytan, April 1990; 19 February 1991

BIBLIOGRAPHY OF PRIMARY SOURCES

Louis Feldman, September 1992
Lloyd Gartner, 6 December 1989
Tobey Gitelle, August 1989
Arthur Hertzberg, January 1992
Shoshanna Tancer, July 1990

INDEX

Stern, Selma, 56

Suffering. *See* Lachrymose conception of Jewish history

Sulzberger, Arthur H., 198

Supercommunities, 253

Sussman, Gisela (née Baron; Baron's sister), 19, 21, 193, 214, 270–71, 274

Synchronistic approach to Jewish history, 105–6

Synnot, Marcia, 200

Talmon, Jacob, 8

Tancer, Shoshanna (née Baron), 19, 182, 184, 189, 213, 385 n.10

Tarnow, Poland
  Baron's early years in, 16–24
  Baron's parents in, 19–20, 192, 193
  Jewish population in, 16, 362 n.1
  during Nazi years, 270–74

Tartakower, Arieh, 268

Täubler, Eugene, 56

Tchernowitz, Chaim, 56

Temple Emanuel, New York City, 59, 61–62, 313

Titles, Baron's concern with
  Dubnow's *World History of the Jewish People* and, 120, 140
  "Ghetto and Emancipation" and, 48, 50
  "The Jewish Factor in Medieval Civilization" and, 294
  journal of Conference on Jewish Relations and, 229–31, 234
  meaning of, and *A Social and Religious History of the Jews,* 140–47
  original, for *A Social and Religious History of the Jews,* 126, 138–39

Torczyner, Harry, 53

Trilling, Lionel, 88, 197

Umansky (Baron's teacher), 23

United Nations, 238

Universities, American
  attitudes toward Jewish scholars and, 197–201
  legitimacy of Jewish historiography in, 3, 259, 357–58
  See also entries for specific institutions

University of Wisconsin, 210–11

Vienna, Austria
  Baron's early years in, 24–27
  Jewish scholars from, 52–54, 269, 369 n.67, 369 n.68

Volksgemeinde, 144, 249

Voluntarism, 263–64, 306–7, 308–9

Warner, Aaron, 206

Warner, W. Lloyd, 230

Weber, Max, 107, 162

Wechsler, Harold, 199–200

Weizmann, Chiam, 328

Westerman, William, 205

Wiener, Max, 56

Wiggins, Henry, 132, 133–34, 135–36, 138, 174

Wise, Mrs. Stephen, 347

Wise, Stephen, 47, 52, 68, 86, 192
  history of Jewish Institute of Religion and, 27–39

Wissenschaft des Judenthums, 44–45, 52–53

Wittmayer, Hirsch (Baron's grandfather), 21, 179–80, 385 n.2

Wittmayer, Minna. *See* Baron, Minna

Wohlgemuth, Joseph, 55

Wolfson, Harry, 1, 29, 55, 56, 78, 86, 219
  Littauer chair and, 31, 38, 370 n.2

Woodbridge, F. J. E., 62, 64, 65, 69–74, 77, 81, 86

World War II
  attitudes in academia toward Jews and, 200–201